"*The Children's Inquiry* is a detailed account of societal failure during the pandemic. That failure is already being forgotten or its history is being deliberately rewritten. That failure by the state, the civil service, political parties, the health service, schools, the teacher unions and many individual teachers, was a failure to protect, care for and educate our children. We must never forget. By reading this book you can refresh your memory and join the authors in a detailed discussion of how we can ensure such neglect is never repeated. We can have this discussion because one good thing that came out of the pandemic was UsForThem, founded by the authors. It is a new form of spontaneous nation-wide organisation that will help us defend our children now and in the future."

*Dennis Hayes, Emeritus Professor of Education,
the University of Derby*

"During Covid, the state and society put adults first but let children down badly. As teenage contributors say, they were treated 'like criminals' and the environment they faced was 'horrible, tense, smothering'. Yet the first draft of the terms of reference of the official inquiry failed to mention the word 'children' once.
This book combines expert witnesses, vivid personal testimony from parents and children and the commentary of Cole and Kingsley, who campaigned for children's rights throughout the pandemic. It's an important compendium of the collateral damage that was inflicted upon children. At times it is a painful read, but it's necessary and galvanising. It thoroughly dissects the impact of the Covid response on children, but it asks much deeper questions. As a society, can we say we truly cared about children? And is now the time to imagine a better vision for childhood? Brave, urgent and fierce, this book is a vital counterpoint to the official inquiry."

Laura Dodsworth, author of A State of Fear

"This book, with its evidence-based 'forensic' analysis of the catastrophic failure of politicians to protect the best interests of children during the Covid pandemic, should induce outrage in every British reader; it must be required reading for every parent and professional and especially for politicians and policy makers. It is but the latest coruscating analysis of the betrayal of our children and childhood. Key questions arising are: will it influence any change and improvement in children's status and outcomes? And what will every individual reader do about it?"

Sir Al Aynsley-Green, former Children's Commissioner for England

"If you are a parent, this is the most important book you will ever read. The chilling way in which our children were used and abused by those in authority is spelt out here. UsForThem came together to be the voices of our silenced children. Our children are not 'super spreaders', nor are they 'vectors of disease', they are our future: we the adults are there to protect them. This book lays out all the facts and it is our duty as parents to hold to account those who allowed this to happen and most importantly never let this happen again."

Tonia Buxton, television presenter, restaurateur and author

"*The Children's Inquiry* sets out in meticulous detail the many harms our national response to Covid-19 inflicted upon children. In their impassioned account, Cole and Kingsley make a powerful case for rethinking both government policy and social attitudes to better prioritise childhood. This valuable contribution to public debate demands to be taken seriously and read widely."

Joanna Williams, Head of Education and Culture at Policy Exchange and author

THE
CHILDREN'S
INQUIRY

HOW THE STATE AND SOCIETY FAILED THE YOUNG DURING THE COVID-19 PANDEMIC

Liz Cole & Molly Kingsley

The Children's Inquiry: How the state and society failed the young during the Covid-19 pandemic

First published by Pinter & Martin 2022

ISBN 978-1-78066-780-5
Also available as ebook and audio book

British Library Cataloguing-in-Publication Data
A catalogue record for this book is available from the British Library.

Index: Helen Bilton

Set in Dante

Printed and bound in the UK by Clays

Pinter & Martin Ltd
6 Effra Parade
London SW2 1PS

pinterandmartin.com

Contents

For our children

About the authors

Liz Cole and Molly Kingsley are parents, writers and co-founders of UsForThem. Together with others in the UsForThem team they've led multiple national political, media and letter writing campaigns advocating for children to be prioritised during the pandemic. They write frequently for national print and online media including the *Daily Mail*, *Express*, *Telegraph* and *The Critic*, and are regular commentators on issues impacting children.

Foreword

This is a hard book to read. Not because of the writing, which is excellent, but because of the content. The anger I feel about children being sacrificed at the altar of Covid is something I think I will take to my grave. I do not write these words lightly. It takes immense strength to speak out about the harms of the measures used to attempt to stop the spread of Covid. I applaud the authors for their courage and tenacity in speaking out, and for doing something about it. In setting up UsForThem and in writing this book, they have demonstrated extraordinary leadership and advocacy for children and young people where academia, the government and third sector organisations failed. Cole and Kingsley have done this in the face of trolling and abuse on a scale which is hard to take in, even two years after the pandemic began.

Early in the book the authors pose a question: whether we really need research to tell us that taking away essential supports and services for children would be a catastrophe. As a researcher working with sensitive topics and vulnerable groups part of me agrees with this sentiment. Indeed, trying to get policymakers to listen to the potential harms in the absence of data in the first lockdown was deeply frustrating to me and many other academic and clinical colleagues. However, the picture emerging from data that has been gathered is just as we predicted. The measures imposed by adults at the expense of children have been disastrous. As demonstrated in this important book, the harms have been enormous, globally. We need to name these harms and account for them. *The Children's Inquiry* does this comprehensively.

I won't reiterate all the harms, as they were diverse, and

are eloquently discussed here. Instead, I reflect on the fact that we collectively allowed restrictions to continue for as long as they did. And still, despite all the harms we now witness, those in power refuse to rule out such restrictions as tools of public health in the future. It is hard to take in what we have allowed to happen to children in this crisis. We adults should hang our heads in shame.

I led the open letter from psychologists quoted in this brilliant book. When the Government announced that children would not return to school before the summer of 2020 I was incensed and horrified. The letter, written to the Government in June 2020, was signed by many leading child psychology experts. There was a coalescing of concern from psychologists and paediatricians (who also wrote an open letter), but the intervention of parents on the ground through UsForThem was crucial. Parents needed a voice and, through UsForThem, they got one.

The title of this book could not be more apt. Written at the time of the setting-up of the UK Government Covid Inquiry (which in draft format did not mention children except in the context of impacts on education), *The Children's Inquiry* is a sorely needed counterpoint. A vital document historically and in terms of advocacy for children. One can only hope that those reading this will take on board the many lessons and insights that are articulated here.

The stories of the lived experience of parents and their children in this book are heart-rending. If you care about children and young people they will resonate, and they will upset you. But we need to be upset. Will the children of the Covid generation ever forgive adults for what they did? My prediction is that they will be incredulous and angry at our selfish folly.

On the ground, the damage done to children and young people through lockdowns, school closures and mandated NPIs is now being openly discussed in clinical and academic meetings. It has been a catalyst for some experts to change the direction of research to focus on children and young people to try to make amends for the mistakes made and the damage done.

At the time of writing some experts are still attempting to deny or minimise the enormity of the harm done to children and adolescents. As *The Children's Inquiry* highlights beautifully across a range of issues, cherry-picking data to support your argument is not how science works. So much damage has been done to our young – the evidence is incontrovertible. It has taken brave parents like the authors to highlight it and call out the many mistakes that have been made by so-called experts.

I urge everyone, but especially those professionals who work with or for children, to read this book. Perhaps all teachers and MPs could be given a copy? We must never let the vile 'inversion of nature' of the past two years happen to children again.

Professor Ellen Townsend
Self-Harm Research Group
University of Nottingham
May 2022

Introduction
Through the Faultlines

'We need him [Chris Whitty] *to say: And it was worth it. Because that's really what's being said: we knew it would harm kids but we did it anyway. Because these consequences are not a surprise. Children's harm was viewed as necessary collateral damage.'*[1]

Claire McGuiggan, educational psychologist

They say it takes a village to raise a child, but in March 2020, that village slammed shut its gates. Children's services – from care, support and therapies for vulnerable children and those with special needs, to antenatal and maternity care, to children's health and social care – were heavily restricted or withdrawn in their entirety. Schools and universities closed or taught only remotely. At times institutions effectively incarcerated students in halls of residence during periods of isolation. A series of 'non-pharmaceutical interventions', or NPIs, were imposed on children, designed to stop the spread of Covid. However, these NPIs were frequently not assessed for their often significant downsides for child interaction, socialisation, and welfare.

The impact on children has been devastating, resulting in a cohort which is unhealthier, unhappier and behind educationally relative to pre-2020, and leaving children's services – many already at crisis point even before the pandemic – overwhelmed.

In February 2021, Anne Longfield CBE, then Children's Commissioner for England, said it was 'impossible to overstate how damaging the last year has been for many children – particularly those who were already disadvantaged',[2] but in truth a great many children – if not indeed the cohort as a whole – were, to a greater or lesser extent, made vulnerable by a policy response that deprioritised their health, welfare and education.

That this has been done against the backdrop of a virus which blessedly does not seriously harm the vast majority of children has led to the charge – with which we agree – that throughout the pandemic, children have been treated as a mere means, with their health, welfare and bodily integrity itself 'othered' for the protection of adults.[3]

As early as summer 2020, studies began documenting the effect of lockdown and school closures on children and young people's wellbeing, safety, education, and physical and mental health. They have not stopped since. The magnitude of the harm, spanning cradle to career, is so vast that repeatedly hearing the statistics at times becomes desensitising. But we cannot afford to become desensitised when each data point represents a young life and when the full extent of the harm is still unfolding.

As examples of the most extreme suffering make their way into mainstream consciousness, it's hard not to give in to frustration and anger: about safeguarding failures leading to surges in child abuse and domestic violence;[4] about the 1.5 million children in the UK now at risk of not being able to speak or understand language at an age-appropriate level;[5] about the millions of lost learning days;[6] and about the mental health tsunami directly affecting one in six children. Many of these outcomes were intuitively predictable at the most basic human level. Did we ever really need research papers to tell us that stripping away critical support systems for our children would end in catastrophe?

In the spring of 2020, before a single word of any report had been penned, many child health professionals, psychologists, and parents warned of the serious adverse consequences of school closures. As early as April 2020, paediatric researchers Alasdair Munro and Saul Faust laid down an essential marker with their *BMJ* Viewpoint, 'Children are Not COVID-19 Superspreaders, Time to go back to school',[7] recommending that, 'Governments worldwide should allow all children back to school regardless of comorbidities.' As this book strives to demonstrate, they have since been proved right, but at the time they were largely ignored, and schools continued to be closed to the vast majority of pupils for months afterwards. Meanwhile, the damage was stacking up.

Schools are more than educational settings; they are wellbeing hubs and, for the most vulnerable, a sanctuary. We feared from the outset that loss of schooling would lead irrevocably to a safeguarding catastrophe, and so it proved. Despite the assurances that schools would welcome vulnerable children during the first lockdown, 94% did not attend. This absence was no mere blip; it was a trend, and we now know that close to 100,000 children never returned fully to school after closures.[8] Childhood is marked by transitions and rites of passage, leading us from one stage to the next – historically these steps, from home or pre-school to school, or from primary school to secondary, have been carefully managed to try to ensure that every child gets his or her best start. Figures tell us that 46% of children who entered the reception year in 2020[9] were not 'school ready' compared to 35% in 2019, and concerning data is starting to emerge about the implications of the last two years for the development of our youngest children.[10]

In obeying the instruction to 'stay at home', parents were effectively required to collude in policies that many felt were harmful to their own children's development. At various points during the pandemic, full lockdowns, school closures, and rules including strict social distancing and a ban on meetings of more than two persons outdoors,[11] meant that children without a sibling could go for months without playing with a single other child. Play is the acknowledged bedrock of infant and childhood development. From early on, we knew that outdoor transmission of the virus was minimal, but playgrounds were taped off, music and sports clubs were forced to close, and thus children were denied the essential nourishment of fun and friendship.

Teenagers, suffering a pre-pandemic wave of prior mental health issues, experienced an exacerbation of existing problems and an explosion of entirely new crises. Emergency referrals for crisis care increased by 62% compared to 2020, and in 2021 a staggering one million referrals of children were made for specialist mental health services.[12] Waiting lists for mental health referrals are now so long that significant numbers of young people will not get treatment before they have entrenched mental health issues that could have been avoided, and the Royal College of Paediatrics and Child Health has warned that the greatest challenge facing children and young people in 2040 will be poor mental health.[13]

With such a weight of testimony, it is hard not to concur with UNICEF's brutal indictment that 'across virtually every key measure of childhood, progress has gone backwards'.[14]

However, there are still many questions. When a whole cohort of children is affected, what will be the long-term outcomes and how will that impact on their relationships? How has the cumulative stress affected children's long-term physical and mental health prospects? Perhaps most concerningly, to what extent will the loss of social interaction impact on childhood development itself?

As with so much of the pandemic response, with data continuing to be presented every day, what we already know is matched by what we don't know, but an Ofsted report from April 2022[15] reads:

'Many providers reported that there are still delays in babies' and children's speech and language development.

For example, some have noticed that children have limited vocabulary or lack the confidence to speak. Also, some babies have struggled to respond to basic facial expressions, which may be due to reduced contact and interaction with others during the pandemic... Some providers continue to notice delays in babies' physical development.'

Nor does development halt in early childhood. Another vital, and often overlooked, 'window of opportunity' occurs in adolescence. Teens are not fully formed adults, and during this period, change continues to occur in 'the area of the brain involved in high level cognitive functions such as decision-making, planning, social interaction and self-awareness.'[16]

In the first few months of the pandemic, we received an email from a clinical psychologist who was deeply concerned about the regime of interventions as applied to children. She wrote of her disbelief at the plans, saying, 'You cannot enforce social distancing in a fundamentally social species without serious negative consequences.'

Her words were prophetic and the reality is that we simply do not know yet how being deprived of the building blocks of experience will translate into negative consequences experienced by this cohort of young people – although we fear the accumulating data on children and adolescent mental health is starting to speak for itself.

For decades to come, academic groups will be reporting on the aftershocks. But none of them should ever have needed to report on the damage caused – our body politic could and should have stopped it from happening in the first place. That was always our aim.

We stumbled our way into events in May 2020.

It was a chilly May day, about six weeks into the pandemic and at the start of a process which would see two years of interventions rolled out to all members of society in a bid to stop the spread of Covid. One of the most controversial of those interventions was school closures. On that May day, schools had already been closed to most students for some six weeks. The government had just announced that certain primary year groups, and nurseries, would reopen, and had published guidance outlining the 'protective' measures under which they might do so. A new oxymoron was taking root: 'social distancing', as it was euphemistically called. Reading the guidance, it was clear that when primary schools did reopen – there was no prospect of secondary schools reopening – it would be on this basis.

Other countries were grappling with similar issues, and a dystopian photo was flying around the internet: very young children penned into two by two-metre squares, sitting on the floor of a French nursery playground while a masked supervisor looked on. It was a portrait of a deeply troubling future coming our way, in which play, friendship, socialising – childhood – was to be curtailed.

That scene looked instinctively wrong then, as it does now.

One of us scribbled a heartfelt blog post. With a fortuitous retweet by a journalist, Allison Pearson, suddenly there we were in Allison's Twitter feed, three parents, with children of different ages, but all sharing the same, viscerally uneasy reaction. A few DMs later, we had agreed we couldn't stay silent and there, deep in the discussion on Twitter, UsForThem was born.

By that point, it had already become clear that, thankfully, Covid did not harm the vast majority of children. As we now know, the survival rate among children and adolescents appears to be around 99.995%,[17] mortality figures which – for children – are similar to seasonal flu,[18] a virus for which we've never closed schools nor introduced other control measures. Neither could we find any verified evidence that the measures proposed would slow the spread of Covid-19, nor any evidence that schools were significant drivers of community transmission, just as Munro and Faust had suggested.

Against that, our instinct as parents suggested what we now know from the weight of evidence: certain of the so-called 'protective measures' were nothing of the sort when viewed through a child welfare lens. In fact, we believed they were likely harmful at a population level, with harms potentially significant enough to negate any potential incremental benefits. We were most concerned that these costs and trade-offs were not even considered worthy of discussion, despite the potential consequences for children.

One of the criticisms that has been levelled against us since May 2020 is that we claim to speak for all children and parents. Of course, we do not. We also recognise that while the vast majority of children are little affected by Covid-19, there are some who have experienced long-term effects – as is the case for other respiratory viruses – although thankfully this is rare and for most children Covid is a short-lived illness,[19] if indeed it is symptomatic at all.[20] We are also conscious that a very small number of children, with severely compromised immune systems, are sadly more vulnerable to worse outcomes from all infections, including coronavirus.[21] There were no simple answers, but applying blanket interventions without recourse to the harms or quantification of benefits should not, in our opinion, have been the starting point.

Our first campaign was called #NotOK and was launched with a letter to Gavin Williamson MP, then Secretary of State for Education, asking uncomfortable but necessary questions about the balance of risk versus benefit and the likely impact of the measures on children. In the weeks to come, our letter was joined by others from psychologists and paediatricians raising similar points. 'The recent decision of the government to delay returning children and adolescents to school is a national disaster', said a letter signed by more than 100 psychologists. 'It is crucial that social distancing measures are minimised, or removed as far as possible, to enable in-person play'.[22] Article 3 of The UN Convention on the Rights of the Child (UNCRC) provides that 'In all actions concerning children, whether undertaken by public or private social welfare institutions, courts of law, administrative authorities or legislative bodies, the best interests of the child shall be a primary consideration', and many of the voices speaking out – ourselves included – asked how the pandemic response heeded this foundational pillar of international children's law.

Over the following weeks and months, our band of three became a band of a few thousand, then tens of thousands, scattered across the UK and beyond. During two years of the pandemic to 2022 we've heard the testimonies of thousands of parents, children, grandparents, educators, doctors and psychologists. There's been a tendency throughout the pandemic to discount this type of anecdotal evidence – we suspect in an effort to minimise the effects. We resist such attempts. We believe that alongside the studies and academic papers there must be room for the lived, eyewitness accounts of those who have been detrimentally impacted by a pandemic response which failed to include their interests.

As we piece together the ripple effects of the pandemic on children's lives, we should let the evidence we've seen speak for itself. The examples which follow are just a small sample.

My child needs lifelong support from the NHS...

'Cara was 13 when the pandemic struck, on track to achieve top grades in her GCSEs, with aspirations to become a vet. During the second round of school closures, she developed a severe tics disorder which her consultant paediatrician confirmed likely developed due to the stress of lockdown. She can no longer eat or sleep and is covered in bruises from hitting herself. She shouts, she swears; she hits, she throws things, she drops to her knees, her legs kick out, her arms fly out, she head-butts things and smacks herself in the face. My child will require lifelong support from the NHS.'

Everyone in my family is now under strain...

'I'm the father of two children, one severely disabled with complex physical and mental needs. Lockdown "blew apart" her routines, closing off all the activities she used to rely on. This had a devastating impact on my daughter and our whole family; dealing with such huge disruptions to her daily routine has made my child more violent and much harder to deal with. This puts everyone in my family under strain.'

The damage to my daughter is unquantifiable...

'My daughter goes to a speech and language special-needs school for children who have severe communication difficulties. Even on a good day, the children struggle to express themselves, read the room and get by in a world that relies so heavily on language. It's a total nightmare when you add masks into the equation. I exempted my daughter, but it's been crushing for her to have so many of her friends wearing masks. I don't believe it's even possible to quantify the damage that has been done to my daughter this year.'

My daughter blamed herself...

'My children were 8 and 6 when the first closure happened. My eldest was always a happy, energetic girl who bounced through the days. When closures hit, she cried every night, didn't sleep, couldn't wake in the mornings. She wrote songs about death and how maybe it was her fault that this was happening.'

My son missed his physical outlets and became jaded...

'With all the online lessons, my teenagers started to sound like jaded old businesspeople, with phrases like "death by powerpoint". My daughter was growing tired of nearly a year's worth of online piano lessons, and as a result, stopped learning piano entirely after that term. My son, a black belt,

missed a whole year of in-person karate lessons, which was a shame as this was such a good outlet for him.'

My high-achieving son has lost all motivation....

'Prizes/trophies had to be collected beforehand and kept secret, and we were meant to watch the recording. Despite winning three prizes, including one for Best Academic Achievement and for being Head Boy, my son had no interest in the event and has not even bothered to watch the online version. He didn't ask to see his awards and certificates. They appear to have little meaning for him. But prizes and awards normally mean a LOT to him and have been a huge motivator in the past. I know that had the event been live, he would have attended, as would I, and he would have been proud to walk on stage in front of his peers and collect those prizes.'

Sometimes, we are sent letters from children themselves.

A poem received from a child shortly after the requirement for pupils to wear masks in secondary schools was first introduced reads:

'And now I wear a mask
So I cannot be seen
You cannot hear my quiet voice
You cannot hear me scream

Control me now when I am scared
And shut me in all day
Take away what made me me
It's a heavy price I pay.'

A scribble in the top right corner of a teenager's homework reads:

'I may not have gotten very far on this, but that's because I

can't ask you for help (since I don't wear a mask) and we can't talk. It's okay though. I understand.'

April Mackay, a teenager who blogs about her experiences, writes:

'As I've described so many times, school was like a prison or a punishment. It was full of teachers... treating us like criminals who'd done something wrong when the only crime we'd committed was being able to spread disease, going crazy if we spoke to someone in another year we'd missed since March, took off our masks, went in the wrong 'area', hugged anyone or had too much fun. For a couple of weeks, they made my year group sit in classrooms at break, facing the wall and not being allowed even to turn our heads because we had the most cases. ...The school had a horrible, tense, smothering atmosphere and felt like a place you went to be punished. By Christmas, we'd had all we could take with lockdown and school being hell. Almost everyone's mental health was in bits. So a second lockdown wasn't a relief – it was the thing that broke us. It was three months of emptiness.'[23]

And on masks, she explains:

'I barely ever get to speak to anyone because no one wants to talk when they've got a thing over their mouth, and they're tired, and their head feels like it's going to explode... I feel like I've just been hurled off a cliff. It's not the masks I'm worried about – I'm exempt anyway – it's the other stuff. People seem to think that being exempt protects you from all these aspects, but it doesn't. It doesn't protect you from everyone being depressed and silent. It doesn't protect you from your friends breaking. Being exempt makes you lonely because you feel fine, but everyone else feels too tired and sad and ill to talk.'[24]

We've received countless examples over the last year of children made to eat lunch outside, sometimes in winter and sometimes in the rain; children not allowed to go to the loo during lessons even when bursting and asked to shiver through class with open windows to the extent that their parents wrote in to tell us their hands had gone blue – hands raw from overuse of hand sanitiser.

That school had ceased to be a nurturing, perhaps even safe, environment for children, is a sentiment we heard expressed often. 'I am growing increasingly concerned about my child's welfare in school', one parent writes. 'I am beginning to feel that no one in the school cares a damn about the children', says another.

Sentiments like this are uncomfortable, laying – as they do – serious charges of a failure to have proper regard to child welfare and even safeguarding. It is tempting to argue that the failings were purely systemic – a failure of Government and its guidance that created an impossible tension between the needs of the pupil population versus the requirement to implement heavily restrictive, even damaging, Covid interventions. There is some truth in this, and we do not for one second doubt that school leaders were placed in an impossible and unenviable position. Nor do we doubt that most in the teaching profession are highly motivated by the welfare of children, nor that many genuinely feared for the welfare of pupils in their care. Indeed, we've had the honour of speaking to many in the course of researching this book.

However, neither should we gloss over the fact that, at times, schools and universities became places of harm for children and young people. As we will see in the next chapter, sometimes these instances were extreme. It is in part the work of this book to explore how as a society we reached a point where so many good people, including in some cases people charged with protecting children, failed to recognise harm and prevent it from happening.

* * *

We began writing this book on World Children's Day, 20 November 2021. It was no occasion for celebration. Around this date, we learned that in Uganda, schools had been closed for more than 77 weeks as weeds grew in children's neglected classrooms. In New York, as the mayor of the city revelled freely at a mass event, speech-delayed toddlers in the city's kindergartens were forced to wear masks all day. A reader question to the *New York Times* asked if it was 'safe' to celebrate indoors if children – as yet only partially vaccinated – formed part of the dinner party with fully vaccinated adults, and boosted older guests. Yes, the response came, from an engineering professor, but only if they 'wear masks, eat quickly, and stay away from older adults when eating'.[25] In the UK, despite assurances that schools would be last to close and first to open, classes around the country were once again thrust back into remote schooling. While adults planned their holiday festivities, with the stroke of a pen, council officials cancelled children's nativities, fairs, and festivals for the second time.

The inequity is real and intensifying. Children are lesser, and childism is rife. Somehow the growing disparity between adults' and children's lives is rarely highlighted within public discourse. There is a palpable sense of denial about the impact that adult decisions have had on children and a couple of familiar narratives are now circulating which attempt to minimise these harms. One, particularly relevant at the time of writing due to the Russian invasion of Ukraine, is 'it's not war' – so the kids should 'toughen up' and count their blessings. Another is that it is the virus, rather than our response to it, that has upended children's lives.

Neither argument holds water for long.

Covid was not a war and the trauma that children endure during war is incomparable to any other living horror. However, to minimise the impact of the pandemic response on children because it was not sustained in war demeans the real and, in some cases, not only life-changing but also fatal injuries that children have suffered. Disruption to healthcare services during the pandemic is thought to have caused some 228,000[26] additional child deaths in South Asia alone; in England, within weeks of the first lockdown, Great Ormond Street Hospital reported a 1,493% rise in cases of abusive head trauma. The case of Logan Mwangi, a five-year-old boy 'hidden from the outside world' while isolating with Covid, only to be murdered by his mother, stepfather and a teenager before his body was dumped 'like fly-tipped rubbish' in a river,[27] is a shocking but sadly not unique example of a child killed in circumstances where routine safeguards had been disrupted during the pandemic.

The argument that these outcomes for children's physical health, mental health and education were inevitable consequences of a natural catastrophe is shown to be a fallacy by the handful of Western nations which took an alternative path and ring-fenced children's lives as far as possible to protect them from the harms of the pandemic response itself. Examples include Sweden, where schools stayed open for children up to age 16 (the Swedish Government commenting that 'The Public Health Agency of Sweden made the assessment that closing all schools in Sweden would not be a meaningful measure, based on an analysis of the situation in Sweden and possible consequences for the entire society');[28] or Hungary, which prioritised continuity of education over restrictions by point-blank refusing to allow schools to mandate masks and social distancing,[29] and banning whole classes from switching to remote learning above 6th grade.[30]

As we shall see, in many cases the toll our public health interventions took on children was not only predictable, but predicted, yet even from policymakers we've seen only the most meagre of acknowledgments of the gravity of the harms which flowed from their decisions. Sir Chris Whitty, the Chief Medical Officer for England, on the second anniversary of school closures, acknowledged that children could see their lives cut short because of a 'significant' worsening in obesity since the first lockdown, and that they may face 'substantial' long-term damage as a consequence of aspects of public health that have 'gone backwards' in the last two years.[31] Current Secretary of State for Education, Nadhim Zahawi MP, has said school closures were a mistake.[32]

Both acknowledgments ring hollow.

As Chief Medical Officer, Whitty was uniquely positioned to influence and shape key decisions. In the words of journalist Allison Pearson, 'he was at the wheel'.[33] And as educational psychologist Claire McGuiggan points out in the context of Whitty's acknowledgement above, these consequences can have surprised no one: they were inevitable outcomes of a policy response which shut down children's education, health services and outlets for sport, play and physical exercise for months on end.

What purpose, then, does Whitty's retrospective statement, without, it would appear, even an apology, serve in the context of damage already done? Similarly, Nadhim Zahawi MP's apology, though presumably well intentioned, was not supported by any action to prevent school closures from happening again.[34] On the contrary, the desire to 'move on' appears strong: Michael Gove – who as Minister for the Cabinet Office at the time on occasion chaired pandemic COBRA meetings – politico-splained on social media that, 'They [Johnson and Sunak] made the right calls on the big issues... Lessons have been learnt and now our focus must be on the huge global challenges we all face.'[35]

More widely, there has been scant public acknowledgement that the ethos underlying the wider pandemic response – the *de facto* deprioritisation of children's health, welfare and education – was in any way regrettable, unethical or to be avoided in the future.

In part, our purpose in writing this book is to provoke thought and discussion about whether we did, in fact, get the 'big calls' right – especially in terms of how they affected young people.

To those who might say, 'surely that is the purpose of the official public inquiry' – we agree. But we have to be realistic. While we very much hope that the official Covid public inquiry will look with a genuinely independent lens at these issues, the first draft of the terms of reference of that inquiry failed to mention the word 'children' once. Although the updated terms did correct this, such an inauspicious start does not bode well.

Perhaps the root of this ongoing failure to face the harm that adults have caused to children lies in the principle of cognitive dissonance. After all, the story we have told ourselves as a society is that we prioritise children, we care for them. Adults reassure themselves that 'we had no choice', and that the actions and measures were somehow intended to protect children. As social psychologists Carol Tavris and Elliot Aronson say in their book *Mistakes Were Made but Not by Me: Why We Justify Foolish Beliefs, Bad Decisions, and Hurtful Acts*:[36] 'In the horrifying calculus of self-deception, the greater the pain we inflict on others, the greater the need to justify it to maintain our feelings of decency and self-worth.'

Against this backdrop of self-deception, adult society digs in further, pushing away the uncomfortable truth that there may have been another way.

So, this is a story of failure: the failure of policymakers and adult society to protect children from a fear-led disaster of their creation, and the failure to face the truth.

Admiral James Stockdale, a United States Navy vice admiral and prisoner during the Vietnam War, became known for his lesson in prioritising faith and discipline over blind optimism. He wrote, 'You must never confuse faith that you will prevail in the end – which you can never afford to lose – with the discipline to confront the most brutal facts of your current reality, whatever they might be.'[37]

Taking inspiration from Stockdale, we must face the brutal facts of our current reality, not only about the pandemic response's impact on children, but also about how adults collectively let them down. Only through painful and honest appraisal can we hope to rebuild and recover our children's lives.

Chapter 1
Inversion of Nature

A photo circulating on social media in summer 2021 shows a scene which would have been unimaginable in 2019.[38] In it, a row of small children – aged four or five perhaps – line up holding hands. They are all masked. Behind them stands a row of adults, one of whom is the Governor of New York. None of the adults are masked, and their smiles beam out at the camera. It is an archetypal example of the inversion at the heart of our global pandemic response.

Over the last two years the youngest members of society have often borne the heaviest burden of Covid restrictions, even though the risk from Covid-19 increases dramatically with age. This has created a deep and seemingly perverse inequity between adults' and children's lives, spanning contexts and borders. Indeed, it has become so ubiquitous that it risks becoming normalised.

The BBC's *Great British Sewing Bee* is a popular reality show that features amateur sewers competing in various challenges. In May 2021, during its 'Children's Week', it jarred to see primary school-age child models standing masked beside the unmasked adult contestants, despite under-11s having always been exempt from routine mask-wearing in England. The BBC claimed that the decision was made to 'protect the sewers'.[39]

In November 2021, in Belfast, Northern Ireland, Minister Nichola Mallon visited students at Edmund Rice College. The college's social media account[40] described the visit as a 'lovely morning', yet the contrast between the unmasked minister and the rows of masked children was stark and unsettling. In a photo taken during Prime Minister Boris Johnson's visit to North Wales in the spring of 2021,[41] he is shown standing, grinning, and gesturing an enthusiastic 'thumbs up', next to a group of primary-aged children. It's impossible to say if they are smiling because they are, again, masked.

Secondary school children in England spent months forced to wear masks in their classrooms – up to seven hours a day, potentially more with time spent on school transport taken into account – at a time when neither the vast majority of adults nor policymakers themselves were prepared to do that. On the very same day, 28 November 2021, when masks were – amid great controversy – reintroduced to communal areas in English schools, Secretary of State for Education Nadhim Zahawi was photographed[42] unmasked at a Teachers Award ceremony. In January 2022 he visited a local Conservative party association meeting of mostly elderly and middle-aged grassroots members while the school mask policy was in place. A snap taken at the event shows a smiling, unmasked, group crowded into a room.[43] On the same day, schoolchildren in the region were required to wear masks for the entirety of their school day.

In some US states, in May 2022, children as young as two are required to wear masks all day in kindergarten. There are reports[44] that even those taking part in vital speech therapy are masked. Certain districts decided to require heavy-duty KN95 masks for students, which are notoriously uncomfortable to wear.[45]

As Jessica Hockett, [46] a Chicago parent, points out, 'There is no other group of adults in the United States, or globally that has to wear a mask for as long as kids do without getting paid. Some people, for example, doctors or healthcare workers, may say, well, I wear a mask all day at my job. And I think, but doctor, you're getting paid $200,000 a year.'

* * *

These uncomfortable portraits are simply the tip of an iceberg. There is now an overwhelming body of evidence about the collateral damage caused by lockdown. Yet, even before this evidence emerged, it was obvious that many Covid measures were incompatible with the conditions needed for children to flourish. It is shocking, now, to see the landscape of spring 2020: playgrounds cordoned off with police tape at a time when most children had no other avenue for exercise; those that remained open were adorned with banners carrying warning signs. Swings were taped up or padlocked: one sign draped over a toddlers' swing in a London park read 'For your health, and the health of others, DO NOT USE THIS PLAY EQUIPMENT.' Behind closed doors most children worked alone, often alongside stressed parents juggling work and the care of other siblings, while those lucky enough to be in school and nursery were subject to strict social distancing regimes.

The very fact that for large chunks of the pandemic schools have been closed in itself reflects a public health response that put children's lives on hold to protect the adult population. However, even when schools were fully open it was almost invariably against a backdrop of 'Covid-safetyism', which has spawned a myriad of child welfare issues, some serious.

An emphasis on improved ventilation might sound sensible, but it led schools to insist on open window policies throughout the pandemic. As a result, children shivering their way through the school day has been a consistent theme of the pandemic's winters.[47,48]

As one parent wrote to us in February 2021:

'Today I sent [my daughter] *in with a thermometer, it ranged between 10 and 14 degrees in her classroom. She's being sent in with a hot water bottle, blanket, hot soup, hand warmers and a flask of tea. How is that acceptable!?!'*

One special needs assistant in a Dublin primary school, Linda O'Sullivan, claimed the classroom temperature had dropped to 14°C, saying 'It's absolutely freezing. It's colder inside the classroom than it is outside', adding of the pupils themselves, 'And you can see it in them, they're uncomfortable. The odd time we've had children with teeth chattering. It's cruel.' On the same day, a similar story was reported in Scotland under the headline 'Pupils freeze in bitterly cold classrooms',[49] reporting that the temperature in that case had fallen to a meagre 11°C. Under health and safety law in Scotland air temperature would be expected to be at least 16°C.[50]

At various points over the last two years children were required to eat lunch outside, regardless of weather conditions, in the name of Covid safety.[51] 'The kids have to stand outside eating their lunch – like cattle', one parent writes; another reports that 'they refused to give her a cup (Covid reasons of course) and told her she had to drink out of her hands instead.' According to one report in December 2021,[52] children were made to eat lunch outside including on soaking wet benches. Children have been denied sufficient water in the hot summer months, some to the point of near fainting,[53] and parents alerted us multiple times to pupils being denied access to toilet facilities.

An email we received in November 2021 sums up the exasperation felt by many parents:

'Today my child was sent home for the third time. Whilst she was waiting to be collected a teacher actually instructed her to stay away from her parents and to wear a mask at home. Being told to stay away from her parents. I am furious. My children's secondary school is almost going out of their way to scare the children even more than they already have been. They have been refused access to the toilet during lesson time and on more than one occasion been told they have to train their bladders. ...It's a secondary school with a lot of children trying to access the toilets at break time. Even in

year bubbles that's a possible 300+ children trying to access the toilets in a 15/20-minute window. It's complete madness. It's cruel... My youngest who is usually a very happy little boy is a nervous, anxious wreck, my eldest has a referral to a mental health specialist and my daughter has become very disengaged with school. She informs me her year group have to stand under a tent at break times which has a small path but then the rest is mud. Her clothes and bag are a mess at the end of most days and yet they are unable to change their clothes or shoes or have coats in the classrooms. What is happening to our children is just heartbreaking.'

There has often been a cruel hypocrisy in our treatment of children. In summer 2021, as tens of thousands of adults gathered in packed stadiums to watch Wimbledon, Euro 2021 and the British Grand Prix, the media was flooded with reports of sporting events for children being pared back, 'virtualised', or abandoned altogether. The same happened in December 2021[54] when children's Christmas nativities were cancelled while adults enjoyed a largely restriction-free Christmas. The majority of remaining Covid measures were dropped in the UK for adults on 26 January 2022; yet in the week that followed the press was awash with reports of children's curtailed lives: Girl Guides requiring primary school-aged children to mask;[55] schools and even nurseries recommending or requiring daily testing; and graduation ceremonies switching to Zoom.[56]

Children have been subrogated to adults even before they've been born. In 2020 the BBC reported that a mother had been made to endure labour in a mask: 'I feared I would vomit,' she said.[57] This case was not unique. A survey of nearly 1,000 new mothers in December 2020 showed that one in five had been asked to wear a mask during birth[58] – a stunning finding that reflects a society that has prioritised a perceived need to protect against a virus to the almost absolute exclusion of all other harms. Often the situation has looked, and felt, deeply unethical: California, in autumn 2021, became the first US state to mandate the Covid-19 vaccine for children aged 5 upwards as a condition of access to education.[59]

At its most extreme, this upending of society's natural responsibility to care for our young has endangered children's lives.

In autumn 2020, UK university students finally returned to their campuses after months of isolation during lockdown. Even pre-pandemic, mental health issues were spiralling into a full-blown crisis for this age group. Barely out of childhood, this extremely vulnerable cohort deserves our protection and care. Yet, with a single-minded fixation on 'protective' measures, the institutions' leadership too often discarded any compassion for these vulnerable teenagers in favour of decisions that can only be described as inhumane.

In November 2020, with the second lockdown underway, University of Manchester students awoke one morning to find metal barriers constructed around their halls of residence.[60] The reported objective was to prevent student households from mixing. Horrified by the lack of prior warning, students protested by tearing down the barricades. The university backed down, but for a nervous 18-year-old away from home for the first time, the effective imprisonment must have been terrifying, and the mental health consequences could have been fatal. Indeed, there had already been one tragic suicide on the campus earlier that term – that of Finn Kitson, just 19 and a mere three weeks into his degree, who took his own life 12 days into a 14-day isolation period after one of his flatmates contracted Covid.[61] Then, at the nearby University of York, during the same period, health and safety guidance decreed that in the event of a fire, self-isolating students should wait behind to allow 'non-self-isolating' colleagues to exit first.[62] This ludicrous diktat not only displayed a profound lack of risk balancing, but also a dereliction of a fundamental duty of care and an ignorance of basic safety standards.

The following year, in winter 2021, a little boy in Cumbria developed a mild cough and cold symptoms at school. Under the school's isolation guidelines, he was kept away from others in a 'separate space' until a parent could collect him. In this case, the 'separate space' was an outdoor shed-like building doubling as a classroom. By the time his mother could make her way by public transport to pick him up, the four-year-old was shivering with cold and his hands were raw. In fact, he had developed hypothermia. When reports of the incident hit the press, the school's headteacher insisted that 'The priority for everyone in Wigton Infant School has always been the wellbeing of the children.'[63]

In January 2022, in a particularly shocking example, officers in Texas arrested a teacher for suspected child endangerment after her son was discovered in the boot of her car at a drive-through PCR testing site. The mother allegedly told officials that she had transported her child in this way so she wouldn't be exposed to his infection.[64]

These distressing cases testify to something deeply dysfunctional in our societal response to Covid. We have normalised the mistreatment of children, collectively justifying it against the backdrop of the pandemic state of exception.

Jennifer Sey, a parent and open schools campaigner from the US, powerfully highlights this contextual blindness through the lens of her traumatic experiences as a child gymnast. She told us, 'It's as if within a particular context, we're able to collectively dismiss everything we know to be true. If I were to describe to you – without you knowing I was an elite athlete on the national team – what I endured, being denied food, being forced to train on broken bones, being called horrible names and belittled... and having that brushed under the rug on a regular basis, you would say, that's clearly abusive. But in the context of elite athletics, it was considered acceptable. And so, it's as if in the context of a pandemic, it's okay to be totally dismissive of kids regardless of what the facts are.'

And the facts should tell us that this treatment of children should be unacceptable in any civilised society, no matter what respectability it is given by the cloak of 'public health'.

Much has been made throughout the pandemic response of the need for public health to act in the interests of an ill-defined concept of a 'greater good'. Yet it's striking that a now reengineered concept of 'public health' has barely acknowledged children as part of the 'public'. In its name, we have not only marginalised our young people's wellbeing, but often actively put them in harm's way.

A pre-pandemic 2019 Public Health England strategy document lays out its vision and goals for the next five years.[65] The document notes that 'Giving children the best start in life is vital for a healthy thriving society. The foundations of good physical and mental health, healthy relationships and educational achievement are laid in preconception through to pregnancy and the early years of life, which is when many inequalities in health often begin.' In crisis, we chose to cast aside these principles and priorities and inverted our public health paradigm by requiring the young to sacrifice their own health and wellbeing to safeguard that of adults. In doing so, we have shattered our implicit social contract.

Sunetra Gupta, Professor of Theoretical Epidemiology at Oxford University, believes that this societal breach is evidence of a more general 'rise of individualism.' She says, 'Surely, all of us over the age of 50 should have said, "Do what you like to us, let's protect younger people"... And of course, you should protect grandma, but there are ways... to ensure we protect the elderly. But the focus of the elderly themselves is to protect the children. Everyone protects the children. That's the fundamental reason to be alive – to celebrate life. If you don't do that, what's the point?'

Far from celebrating life, we have stunted it.

We leave this chapter with an illustration from the natural world.

In the brutal landscape of the Arctic Circle, reindeer do whatever it takes to protect their young. When the herd is threatened, the animals stampede in a cyclonic formation, making it impossible for predators to target an individual. A swirling wall of adult deer on the perimeter shields the fawns at the heart of the circle from harm.

How is it that the UK and most Western democracies have failed this basic tenet of nature, systematically and deliberately placing our young on the outside of our societal herd and demanding that they shoulder a burden that should never have been theirs to carry?

Chapter 2
'Public Health'

As laypeople and parents, we perhaps naively had certain expectations of public health.

At the most basic level, we expected the emergency public health response to Covid-19 to consider the entirety of the public. This public included children and young people as a vulnerable cohort worthy of protection. We also expected a holistic approach that considered all wellbeing, mitigating not only the disease itself, but its risk factors, and interventions targeted to those who needed them. We expected a balanced approach to the evidence – incorporating consideration of harms, as well as benefits, of any intervention. In line with this, we hoped for transparent communication founded on this evidence, underpinned by trust and honesty.

These hopes and expectations were not met.

It is a matter of public record[66] that in many cases, policymakers introduced measures with scant quantification of benefit or consideration of harms. It is no wonder that the efficacy of a great many (if not all) of these measures is now being called into question. As Robert Dingwall, Professor of Sociology at Nottingham Trent University, has said:

> 'At times, however, policy-makers did not put Covid-19 into context. Nor did they ask what responses would be possible, effective and proportionate. Indeed, we must recognise that too many interventions were ineffective, poorly evaluated and damaged important institutions.'[67]

In the light of this lack of a holistic evaluation of responses, all too often measures were merely performative: more about signalling safety than having an impact on suppression of the virus itself. For example, who really thought Perspex screens in shops would stop the spread of an airborne virus? In fact, this intervention may have actually been counterproductive.[68]

The disproportionate focus on visible and theatrical measures, often centring on mitigations for children, seemed to be rarely matched by a willingness to address glaring substantive issues such as sufficient financial and practical support during isolation when sick with Covid-19. A study by King's College London, published as a pre-print in September 2020, found that an astonishingly low 18% of respondents were self-isolating when symptomatic with Covid symptoms. The study authors noted that, 'Our results suggest that financial constraints and caring responsibilities impeded adherence to self-isolation, intending to share details of close contacts, and quarantining of contacts', and that as well as reimbursing potential financial losses, policies should 'facilitate practical considerations, such as shopping for groceries and medicines during self-isolation.'[69]

We suspect that greater focus on areas such as these, rather than on safety theatre, may have yielded better results.

From the outset there were doubts about the evidence base for certain decisions. As early as June 2020, Dr Margaret McCartney, a GP who writes about evidence-based medicine, called for rigorous evaluation of NPIs, noting that:

'It is as though non-drug interventions are not considered capable of doing harm, or regarded as either too hard to investigate, or too obviously beneficial to bother with trials. I think this is an error.'[70]

McCartney also noted that in contrast to drug trials, which are typically used in small cohorts, such non-pharmaceutical interventions apply to whole populations. Given that these populations also include millions of children, we might assume that there would, if anything, be a greater imperative to gather high-quality data to inform decisions.

Policymakers appear to have disregarded calls from public health professionals to establish evidence. We know that interventions have harms as well as benefits, and just because we can do something doesn't mean we should. Particularly in the context of a paediatric population, certain measures, as well as being ill-founded in science, seemed cruel and thoughtless. For example, the 'rule of 6', which in England included children, unfairly penalised larger families.[71]

Throughout the pandemic response, the harms of interventions have often been minimised in favour of amplifying the benefits, however marginal. It's an acceptable argument to suggest that we should have captured incremental advantages to suppress transmission, but it's far less acceptable to dismiss the resultant harms completely, especially when applying restrictions and measures to an entire population of children.

A phrase we have heard throughout the crisis is 'the precautionary principle'. In the context of the pandemic response, the precautionary principle has come to mean taking action and applying an intervention on the basis that if it could have a beneficial effect on the course of the pandemic, then it would be worthwhile. The decision to apply universal community masking reflected this idea. Proponent Professor Trisha Greenhalgh wrote in the *BMJ* urging policymakers to 'apply the precautionary principle now and encourage people to wear face masks on the grounds that we have little to lose and potentially something to gain from this measure?'.[72]

However, as Robert Dingwall tells us, this is a distortion of the precautionary principle, which is highly sensitive to the potential harms of interventions. 'I first came across it in the mid-nineties in discussions about genetically modified crops, but it goes back a bit earlier than that in conventions about biosafety and biodiversity. And its standard meaning in the health and safety world and more generally among professionals outside medicine is that you do not introduce innovations until you are quite clear that the benefits will exceed the harms and that you have looked very hard for the harms.'

Children have been on the sharp end of many Covid-19 measures. School closures are the interventions most likely to cast the longest shadow over children's lives. Even early in the pandemic, the potential harms of school closures were known, as we discuss in more detail in Chapter 4. Similarly, cloth masks, which we explore in Chapter 3, became a talisman of the pandemic, despite patchy evidence of benefit and intuitive harms for children: a conclusion eventually confirmed – we would argue at least a year too late – by the Department for Education's own evidence.[73]

Asymptomatic testing of children is another measure that has been promoted as an unchallengeable public good, but which in fact raises myriad issues both in terms of evidence of effectiveness, and the lack of evaluation of harms. In the UK, children were subjected to regular lateral flow rapid testing – even when exhibiting no symptoms – both in school and at home for the best part of a year. Sold as a way to keep children in school, in our view, the programme all too often seemed to do the opposite.

Without a firm and transparent evidence base from the outset, it proved incredibly difficult to establish an off-ramp for this particular intervention. Despite the suggestion in October 2021 from Dr Camilla Kingdon, President of the Royal College of Paediatrics and Child Health (RCPCH) that asymptomatic testing of children should be discontinued,[74] it was only dropped from all education settings in England in April 2022.[75]

In fact, the programme had rung alarm bells from the

very first day back in November 2020, when the government announced the deployment of the army to help roll out mass testing of children at schools in Liverpool as part of a so-called 'pilot'.[76]

It was an extraordinary sight to see images of military trucks rolling up outside school gates, with personnel in army uniforms. Parents who contacted us told us that it was distressing for them and for their children. One mother, in a frantic email, said, 'the army being around the school ground is very intimidating for the kids' and that she didn't 'feel safe' sending her child into school.

We cannot know the rationale for the Department for Health and Social Care choosing to involve the military in this programme. Still, it seems baffling that no decision-maker considered the impact on already anxious teenagers of seeing soldiers arrive at the school gates. We must also surely consider the possibility that – like the Nightingale hospitals – the choice was as much for PR optics and a show of strength in the 'war' against the virus as for efficiency.[77]

This heavy-handed wrapper was the thin end of the wedge of the project, which was a reengineering of the bombastically named 'Operation Moonshot'. This government mass-testing scheme proposed expanding testing to 10 million tests a day by early 2021 using rapid lateral flow tests to complement the PCR testing programme. The Moonshot scheme had attracted controversy, and a *BMJ* editorial slammed it as scientifically unsound.[78] Importantly, the authors noted that the proposals failed to account for harms, including the risk of false positives that could cause 'unnecessary but legally enforced isolation of both cases and contacts', with potentially damaging consequences for the UK economy and civil liberties. At any rate, had the Liverpool programme been a true pilot, it should have followed due research process.

Medical investigation, treatment, and research in children must follow well-established principles, including informed consent, for good reason. In times of crisis, we rely more than ever on transparency, governance and even greater commitment to the good practices that were designed to protect the vulnerable. In our view, this project failed to observe these tenets.

Professor Allyson Pollock, a co-author of the earlier *BMJ* editorial about Operation Moonshot, raised red flags in a letter to Liverpool MPs citing a range of concerns, including the lack of transparent research design and the diversion of funding from testing symptomatic people.[79]

For many of the directly affected parents, the rushed nature of the rollout to schools was distressing. One school issued an alarming letter asserting that there was no time to implement proper informed consent procedures. The letter said, 'under normal circumstances parental permission is sought for the testing of children, however under these very challenging and unprecedented circumstances that is not possible, therefore we would ask that if you wish to exclude your child from this test please do so in writing to me first thing on Monday morning.' It also added that in the case of a positive result the school would 'secure' the individual concerned.[80]

After a public outcry about the lack of due process, the school withdrew the messaging. A spokesperson for the council said that they hadn't had sight of the school's letter before it was sent out. It's hard to disagree with Dr Mike Gill, who wrote later in the *BMJ*[81] that 'In the case of schools, the programme has been culpably rushed'. In the same article he said that 'Evidence that this pilot will reduce transmission is not yet established. This makes it even more critical that it is carefully planned; the different components, including testing centres, contact tracing, laboratories, and primary care contributions, are quality assured; its total resource requirements identified and costed; and the pilot evaluated for cost effectiveness.'

It is a scandal that this never happened.

Perhaps even more irregular was the exclusion of experts

from the National Screening Committee – a body that 'advises ministers and the NHS in the 4 UK countries about all aspects of population screening' – from the programme.[82] Professor Ellen Townsend describes the decision as 'mind-blowing', adding that 'people who've dedicated their lives, they've written the medical textbooks on this field and they have not been involved.'

As we have seen, from September 2020, and throughout the spring and summer terms of 2021, the requirement that healthy children isolate when coming into contact with a positive case led to huge numbers being absent from school – a requirement which was only scrapped on 19 July 2021 after most schools had broken up. [83] Before that, a 'bubble policy' frequently led to up to 30 healthy children being isolated from school for every positive case. Bafflingly, a Freedom of Information (FOI) request[84] submitted in December 2020 by the authors revealed that no data was being captured at the time on the numbers of these children – who were themselves healthy – who eventually went on to test positive for Covid. Yet, until summer 2021, the policy wreaked havoc. One parent's Year 10 son was isolated as a 'close contact' and missed his mock exams, then returned to school only to experience isolation once again. We have heard of children subject to as many as five isolation periods despite never testing positive themselves. In one single week in June 2021 there were over one million children at home:[85] roughly 10 percent of the school population.

Dr Ellie Cannon, a GP and broadcaster, tells us of her horror at the cruelty of this policy, not only as a medical professional, but as a parent, saying that 'from a parental point of view, it felt like we were constantly on a knife edge.' She also highlights the lack of demonstrable effectiveness, noting that 'we'd never proven that this isolation was necessary.'

In October 2020, along with a colleague, Dr Sunil Bhopal, Ellie had written in the *BMJ*,[86] urging greater care over these policies because of the obvious harms: 'Given that children are hugely affected by lockdown and social distancing restrictions, greater care must be taken over exclusions,' noting that evidence of effectiveness must also be provided. 'We now have many weeks of data from schools in the UK's four nations. These should help us understand whether excluded children go on to develop Covid-19. If found that keeping children out of school in this way does not help fight the pandemic, this damaging practice should be halted.'

The policy continued for a further nine months after this intervention. As Ellie sadly told us, 'There was no appetite to be interested.'

The effects of pandemic restrictions on the paediatric population

The costs of many of the last two years of public health interventions were foreseeable in many cases.

One of the most troubling legacies of the pandemic may prove to be the significant drop in vaccination rates in other essential programmes, leading to a recurrence of potentially deadly childhood diseases such as measles.[*][87] This was expressly warned against by the Government's advisory panel of vaccine experts, the Joint Committee on Vaccination and Immunisation (JCVI) when it originally failed to recommend the mass roll-out of the Covid-19 vaccine to children. The committee said:

'Although relative benefits have not been formally compared, in JCVI's view, most non-COVID-19 childhood immunisations are likely to offer more benefits to children and young people than a COVID-19 immunisation programme. On top of existing routine programmes, a

---

[*] Over the last 20 years vaccination has dramatically reduced the number of deaths from measles. Worldwide, since 1990 (when measles killed 872,000 people), it is estimated that over 1 in 5 of all child deaths averted have been due to measles vaccination.

COVID-19 programme for children and young people is likely to be disruptive to education and will require more resource. The scale of additional resources required will be considerable.'[88]

These concerns were directly raised in a House of Commons Education Select Committee hearing with Whitty and Professor Jonathan Van-Tam, Deputy Chief Medical Officer for England, and were dismissed.[89]

This is a shame, as the warning proved prescient.

Commenting on the significant drop in vaccination rates in other essential programmes, Professor Helen Bedford, Professor of Children's Health at the UCL Great Ormond Street Institute of Child Health, said 'There has been so much focus on Covid over the past two years, but we mustn't forget about measles, which has not gone away.'[90]

Even when schools closed for the first time in March 2020 it is arguable that much of the damage that would ensue was so inevitable, that it was, in effect, 'known'. However, by the time of the second round of school closures in England harms were both known and documented, with ample lived and reported evidence from the first set of closures. It was further known that those harms went far beyond education and presented a clear, present and serious danger to some – perhaps many – pupils.

In April 2022, Matt Hancock, the former Secretary of State for Health, appeared in an interview to discuss the pandemic response with broadcaster Dan Wootton on GB News. Reflecting on events, Dan asked, 'Given that the impacts of school closures on children were predicted and actually predictable... did you just decide that children should be collateral damage?'[91] Unsurprisingly, Hancock issued a politician's denial, but it's a question which surely must be probed further given the facts.

SAGE had acknowledged in April 2020 that 94% of vulnerable children were not in school during the first lockdown and as such 'the risk to vulnerable children's welfare has increased significantly as a result of school closures';[92] in June 2020 the UCL Institute of Education had found that 'children locked down at home in the UK spent an average of only 2.5 hours each day doing schoolwork,' and that 'one fifth of pupils... did no schoolwork at home, or less than one hour a day'.[93] In September 2020, the then Children's Commissioner found that before the pandemic there were '2.1 million children in England living in households affected by any of the so-called "toxic trio" of family issues: domestic abuse, parental drug and/or alcohol dependency, and severe parental mental health issues'.[94] Another report from the former Children's Commissioner, published in January 2021, revealed that 1 in 6 children aged 5 to 19 had a probable mental health condition in 2020 (up from 1 in 9 in 2017).[95] On 19 January 2021 the Education Select Committee heard expert testimony from Professor Russell Viner in which he told the committee of the 'considerable mental health harms' of school closures for children and young people.[96]

Yet schools remained closed for several weeks after Viner shared this evidence.

As we have seen over and over, our myopic public health response brought with it a myriad of other health harms. But it was curious, in fact, that health ever came to be thought of in such narrow terms.

The World Health Organization describes health as 'a state of complete physical, mental and social wellbeing and not merely the absence of disease or infirmity'. Similarly, it defines 'public health' as activities that 'provide conditions under which people can maintain to be healthy, improve their health and wellbeing, or prevent the deterioration of their health'. Importantly, it notes that 'Public health focuses on the entire spectrum of health and wellbeing, not only the eradication of particular diseases.'[97]

We began this chapter with our own assumptions as laypeople about the nature of any 'public health' emergency response. But what were public health's own pre-pandemic principles for promoting and protecting young people's health?

A Public Health England document published in 2019[98] helpfully describes the parameters of 'what good looks like for public health for children and young people', and the programmes required to accomplish it. In the first 1001 days of a child's life, it explains, 'All women and infants should receive high-quality care in line with the antenatal and newborn screening programme'. Preschoolers should be 'able to socialise with other children' and 'have their full range of vaccinations and immunisations before they start school'. Primary school children need to be equipped with resilience-building and readied for the transition to secondary school. Secondary school-aged children need resilience strategies to support them through times of stress, including the 'adverse impact' of technology and social media. For young adults, the document urges that 'All areas should have plans to minimise the risk of suicide in this age group'.

By these self-stated performance indicators, public health, in its single-track response to Covid, has dismally failed children. Severe disruption in maternity care has resulted in 'women feeling their antenatal and postnatal care to be inadequate'.[99] For months it was illegal for pre-school children to socialise with other children; routine and essential immunisation programmes have been badly affected. MMR uptake is now at a 10-year low.[100] Far from being ready to transition to secondary school, primary school children were deprived of in-person transition days. Secondary school children have endured severe mental health impacts and were actively encouraged to spend more time on screens and social media during school closures despite the known harms. Young adults at university were locked away in halls of residence and deprived of support during their vulnerable first months away from home. An already burgeoning obesity problem – with some 37% of UK adults forecast to be obese by

2033 and the number of children who are obese by the time they start school up by 45% during 2021[101] – was exacerbated by a pandemic response which considered it appropriate to indiscriminately ban those at least risk from the disease from partaking in sport or going to playgrounds for months on end.

We knew that children were less directly affected by the disease from early on – the difference in risk stratification between younger and older cohorts was clear. While older adults directly benefited from public health efforts designed to suppress the virus, children stood to lose the most from pandemic measures – most notably from school closures.

Indeed, under the guise of public health, children have consistently borne a far heavier share of the restrictions designed to suppress the virus in a wholesale 'intergenerational transfer of harms'.

As a cohort, children will emerge from the pandemic with diminished health outcomes under each of the metrics acknowledged by Public Health England: mental health, obesity, readiness for school. We contend that these poorer outcomes link directly to the measures taken to handle the infectious disease outbreak: school closures, self-isolation, lockdown, and social distancing.

Of course, Public Health England no longer exists, having been axed by the former Secretary of State for Health Matt Hancock and replaced with the Orwellian-sounding 'UK Health Security Agency'.[102] The cynical among us might ask why. Was the decision to disband the institution a genuine operational decision, an attempt to deflect criticism, or to provide an expedient scapegoat for pandemic failings? The question gives pause for thought and we hope the public inquiry will consider it. In relation to the Department for Health's failure to protect care homes, the defunct PHE has already come under fire in April 2022, with ministers asserting that the failure ('to tell ministers what they knew about asymptomatic transmission')[103] was PHE's – an assertion which has been vigorously challenged.[104]

Some may maintain that restrictions applied to children were a necessary evil. We say that a public health paradigm which strives to protect adults without weighing up the costs to children is the very antithesis of 'public health'.

Chapter 3
Help Me!

In April 2021 a video of a mother in the US state of Georgia went viral on social media.[105] In it, the mother stands in front of the board of her children's school and in a speech laden with emotion so strong that even now it's almost impossible not to be affected, says:

> 'Every month I come here, and I hear the same thing. "Social-emotional health". If you truly mean that you [glaring towards the school board] would end the mask mandate tonight. Tonight.
>
> Every one of us knows that young children are not affected by this virus and that's a blessing. But what have we done with this blessing? We have shoved it to one side, and we have said we don't care – we are still going to require you, little children, to wear masks on your faces every day… We are still going to force you to carry a burden that was never yours to carry. Shame on Us.
>
> It is April 15, 2021, and it is time. TAKE THESE MASKS OFF MY CHILD.
>
> Defend our children.'

The fire running through the mother's veins is obvious, and there is something almost evolutionary about her anger. She feels the mask mandate on her seven-year-old as a physical wound and her need as a parent to protect her cub is primal.

* * *

From the start, the mask mandate* for children has sparked great controversy. For many, the image of a child in a mask intuitively looks very wrong: 'stop covering children's mouths and noses – where they *BREATHE*' screams the American mother, a reaction that is shared by other parents we spoke to. 'It almost feels like a violation, like an attack on them. Like someone putting a hand over their mouths,' says one. Another says, 'I can't explain, but deep in my bones I just know that it's wrong'. 'Imagine', pointed out one parent, 'if it had been the other way around and children had before 2020 insisted on wearing masks in the classroom for 7 hours a day with limited breaks. Would we have let them?'

However strong that visceral reaction is, though, we recognise the necessity of pausing and considering whether the mask mandate was reasonable, or whether actually this measure – although it went against a great many parents' instincts – was justified on public health grounds.

Non-pharmaceutical interventions have costs as well as benefits, and as we have discussed in Chapter 2 ('Public Health') in very broad terms a measure will be justified when the evidence of benefit outweighs the costs.

The question of how far face coverings work to reduce infection – the 'benefit' side of the equation – became one of the most divisive topics of the pandemic. The evidence for community use in general is mixed. Claims made about the effectiveness of masks to reduce transmission tend to be based not on 'gold standard' randomised controlled trials, but on lower-quality studies;[106] and the evidence for the use of masks in schools is thinner still. In December 2021, a month before the announcement of the reintroduction of the mask mandate in lessons in England, Department for Education Minister for Children and Families, Will Quince, appeared

---

* In theory the requirement for children to wear masks in, variously, communal areas and classrooms was only 'guidance'. However, as we discuss in Chapter 13, 'Rogue State', it appears that the intention was for it to be treated as mandatory, and in practice it was treated as rule of law.

to acknowledge this, stating 'at the moment there is very limited evidence as to the efficacy of masks in educational settings'.[107]

This was subsequently confirmed following the reintroduction of the mandate for secondary school pupils in England by evidence eventually produced, under pressure, by the DfE, which was roundly criticised by experts and media, including – notably – some of those traditionally supportive of Covid interventions.[108]

That a measure is of limited effectiveness might not matter if it were a net-neutral intervention, but masks have never been that for children. There has in fact, from the outset, been ample evidence of potential harm, especially when masks are worn for long periods of time, reinforcing the deep unease felt by many parents. Back in January 2021 – before masks were mandated in England's secondary school classrooms – DfE guidance had acknowledged that face coverings in the classroom 'may inhibit teaching and learning'. England's Deputy Chief Medical Officer, Professor Jonathan Van-Tam, as recently as November 2021, had said face masks 'could be quite inhibitory to the natural expressions of learning in children involving speech and facial expression. I think it's difficult for children in schools with face masks'.[109] At one point Boris Johnson had even remarked that masks in lessons would be 'nonsensical – you can't teach with face coverings; you can't expect people to learn with face coverings'.[110] When it finally arrived, DfE's evidence package, though failing to provide convincing evidence as to benefit, laid out clear evidence of negative educational and communication outcomes.

Indeed, significant evidence of concerns associated with prolonged mask-wearing has been available throughout. Issues raised by peer-reviewed studies on adults[111] include potential physical issues: papers detail eye problems,[112] skin problems,[113] headaches,[114] and respiratory[115] problems associated with long-term mask-wearing. There is no reason to think similar concerns wouldn't apply to children, and one comprehensive study from April 2021, which analysed proven psychological and physical side effects from wearing masks, concluded that 'further research is particularly desirable in the gynecological (fetal and embryonic) and pediatric fields, as children are a vulnerable group that would face the longest and, thus, most profound consequences of a potentially risky mask use.'[116]

How, then, was a measure which crossed a clear line for many parents, was lacking a strong evidence base for effectiveness and which raised so many flags of potential harm to so many children, able to be pushed through under the guise of public health?

A narrow version of 'public health'

On 23 November 2020, masks were made compulsory for Welsh children in communal areas. On learning of the news, Debbie Thomas, head of policy at the National Deaf Children's Society Cymru, said:

> *'face masks and coverings in communal areas could have serious consequences for Wales' 2,500 deaf children, almost all of whom rely on lip-reading and facial expressions to communicate... Public health is the priority, but schools and colleges must move quickly to introduce reasonable adjustments to help deaf young people during this difficult time.'[117]*

This is a telling comment.

Masks have crushing implications for deaf children – their reliance on facial cues means the mask mandate, whether or not the child themselves is exempt, has a catastrophic impact on their ability to access learning and social interactions, and yet here is the spokesperson for those children accepting that their needs come second to 'public health' – a concept which here seems intended to exclude the harms caused to deaf children from masks. We do not judge Debbie Thomas for this statement – she is merely echoing the prevailing climate of the times – yet it is not immediately clear why these harms are considered any less eligible public health considerations. This epitomises a public health paradigm that, throughout 2020 and into 2021, considered one aspect of health to the exclusion of all others.

However, as we have discussed at length, it is a prerequisite of a good public health response that the harms associated with an intervention are evaluated and considered – how else, in fact, can the benefits of an intervention be balanced against the evidential justification for the measure? This is especially so in the context of a virus that does not seriously affect children, where the benefits are even more marginal. The WHO had recognised this, recommending in August 2020 that if national authorities decided to introduce masks for children, monitoring and evaluation of the harms of the measure should be set up at the outset and continue on an ongoing basis.

It appears this was never done. Instead, after the mask mandate was originally introduced to English classrooms, it appears that the only assessment of harm was a series of surveys with 'stakeholders': schools, trusts, pupils and parents, but weighted heavily towards the first two categories.

When the mandate was reintroduced a second time – in January 2022 – the impact on communication and education was mentioned in the Evidence Summary later produced,[118] which was again based largely on the same survey data from the previous April.* The sum total of consideration of the wider impact was the one line 'wearing face coverings

---

* A survey conducted by the Department for Education in April 2021 found that almost all secondary leaders and teachers (94%) thought that wearing face coverings has made communication between teachers and students more difficult.

may have physical side effects'. There was still no formal consideration of what these might be.

Since schools reopened in September 2020, after the first lockdown, England's secondary-school children have been masked for around 29 weeks (18 in communal areas, 11 in classrooms) of the 57 weeks they have been in school (up to the end of January 2022), which across the cohort equates, very roughly, to a total of 2,348,000,000 mask hours (720,000,000 in communal areas, 162,800,000 in classrooms). It's a sobering reflection to think that these 2,348,000,000 hours of impeded communication, socialisation and education have not ever been thought worthy at policy level of a serious evaluation of harm.

Much has been made of the 'precautionary principle' and we discussed the distortion of it in Chapter 2 ('Public Health'). In reality, if applying the precautionary principle as intended, it was the duty of the proponents of this intervention to demonstrate the absence of harm, rather than opponents' responsibility to prove that harm exists.

It's revealing, and consistent with other public health decisions, that the language used by ministers in rolling out the mandate has consistently downplayed the drawbacks of masks for children. Public Health England was unable, in 2021, to call them 'harms', instead labelling them, euphemistically, 'disbenefits'.[119] Nadhim Zahawi, in reintroducing the mandate in 2022, noted that 'all these interventions are imperfect' and not 'ideal'.[120]

The denial has become increasingly absurd as time has gone by. 'It's only a piece of cloth', is a rebuke we have heard often, but children's experiences tell a different story.

In their own words

One of the most important and intuitively predictable effects of mask-wearing in schools is on communication and social interaction for all children. It's a grim irony that, prior to Covid, our educational approaches had moved away from 1950s-style lecturing from the front of the classroom. Instead, teaching involved group work, dialogue, and interaction. In the context of 'only Covid matters', it was apparently acceptable to brush all of this positive educational development away – replacing it with rows of masked, silent children listening to the pronouncements of an unmasked teacher speaking from a yellow square at the front of the class.

This pervasive effect, with its enduring consequences, is perhaps the one that matters most. The primary function of a school, after all, is learning. Unimpeded communication is not just a 'nice to have' – it is essential. Not least in the context of two years of disruption and social isolation with all that implies for mental health and wellbeing.

One teacher told us that with masks in place children were 'a bit more quiet and a bit less happy.' It is a bleak comment.

A child who wrote to us echoed this impression, describing a 'subdued, flat' atmosphere, with fewer pupils putting up their hands to ask questions, especially in language lessons.

April Mackay, who has spoken passionately about the impact of restrictions on children sums up the bleakness and strain she has experienced: 'It's the fact everyone is so silent. It's the way everyone is so depressed and anxious… It's the feeling of constant loneliness because no one talks and no one's reachable and no one's doing anything to stop it and no one cares if you feel like this because the restrictions are "worth it"'.

Parents told us of a range of other ill-effects for their mask-wearing teenagers. One described their asthmatic child returning home 'wheezy'; another mentioned their son's headache and numb feeling around the mouth. Several parents reported an exacerbation of their teenagers' acne – which has an intuitive knock-on effect on wider wellbeing and self-consciousness. There are also other more severe, hidden issues which are rarely acknowledged but important, such as a PTSD reaction to face coverings after a traumatic early childhood experience.

Mask discrimination

There are also significant impacts not for the wearers themselves, but for children who are effectively excluded from communication by their peers' masking. It's extraordinary that despite the discriminatory effect, so little attention was paid to this aspect.

As well as deaf children, many other SEN children have similar reliance on facial cues.

Developmental Language Disorder affects approximately two children in every class and persists to adolescence and beyond, requiring strategies and interventions to reduce the impact of communication difficulties and ensure children's access to communication and education.[121]

Speech and language therapist Sandy Chappell told us, 'If you go on to any website about developmental language disorder there'll be a section, what can I do to help my child or a child in my class? And one of the points will be, make sure they can see your face because they need all the cues they can get. That's one of the basic things we tell parents to do. Don't talk to them when you've got your back turned because they'll struggle. Make sure you are face to face. That's the only way you can be sure they're paying attention; they're listening and they're using visuals to help them understand what you are saying.'

The impact of universal mask-wearing on this cohort of children appears to have been almost entirely overlooked.

Children who are exempt from wearing face coverings may have hidden disabilities. In a pre-Covid school, these children's difficulties might have passed unnoticed, allowing them to integrate with their peers. In our new world – which flirted with and perhaps even normalised stigmatisation in the name of Covid – children with mask exemptions were often forced to wear a lanyard or other symbol, signalling their disability to the rest of their cohort. Parents told us about their mask-exempt children being subject to active discrimination in school: separated at the back of the classroom at the furthest point from the teacher, or asked to use a different entrance to their mask-wearing friends.

It demeans all these children and their experiences to say, 'it's just a piece of cloth'.

When children adapt

What about potential longer-term consequences?

Of the concerns we had at the outset – in the context of all the pandemic restrictions on children – ours was never that children wouldn't adapt. It was that they *would*. Already, distressing social media reports are emerging about teenagers, often girls, who are clinging to their masks as comfort blankets, a way to hide themselves away from a hostile and stressful world.

One parent, who spent time teaching in China, said of mask-wearing habits there, 'It was always the quietest children who wore them – teenage boys covering up acne, girls using them to avoid being too visible in classrooms. It made me sad long before I was a parent'.

Yuzo Kikumoto, the author of a book discussing this phenomenon, agrees. He explained to *Japan Today* in 2012 that some Japanese students 'have an abnormal fear of showing who they really are to their peers.'[122] In the light of the spiralling mental health issues among young people, this is a deeply concerning outcome.

'Kids don't mind'

It's important to acknowledge that not every parent, or

every child, had the same visceral and negative response to mask-wearing. As the visual symbol of the crisis, masks have become a focus of polarisation in the wider community as well as for children. For some, they have been a symbol of protection and reassurance amid the confusion and fear, while for others they have provoked anxiety and a sense of exclusion.

It has often been reported by media outlets that children say they don't mind, and feel more comfortable wearing a mask in schools, a sentiment which has been reiterated by the national leaders imposing these mandates. For example, Governor Kathy Hochul of New York compared universal masking to wearing shoes: 'My daughter had a meltdown about having to put sneakers on to go to kindergarten. She got used to wearing sneakers in school. They adapt better than adults do.'[123] Here, Nick Gibb MP, then Schools Minister, told an Education Select Committee hearing in April 2021 '[students] seem to not mind wearing them'.[124]

This may be true, but we have to examine why children and their parents say this.

For one, children have been egregiously imposed upon throughout the crisis. They were isolated for months, locked out of their schools and friendships, and enthusiastically sold masks as the 'price to pay' for restored access to their education and their lives.

We would argue that based on the evidence, this transaction was always false – a cynical attempt to manipulate young people. They have been presented with an inaccurate and often exaggerated picture of the benefits, without mention of the negative effects.

· Mask-wearing has also been heavily promoted as the 'virtuous' option for adults and children alike. The desire for social conformity has been an exceptionally powerful force and children have been told that their needs and interests should be routinely subrogated to those of their elders.

Most disturbingly, they have been told that they themselves

are something to be feared: that their very act of breathing is a danger to others. It's no surprise that one mother told us that her children 'think they are going to kill someone if they don't wear a mask.'

Punitive mask measures

How much has this irrational but pervasive fear of children as 'vectors' contributed to the ever-increasing cycle of restrictions and continued masking? At times, the way in which mask burdens have been applied to ever-younger children – as in the US, or enforced in schools and youth settings in the UK – has felt punitive in nature.

In January 2022, a school district in Pennsylvania USA was forced to apologise after an image emerged on social media of a teacher taping a mask to a child's face.[125] Similar incidents were documented in October 2021 in Colorado where children were 'taped' after receiving two warnings about their mask falling down below their nose. A parent quoted at the time described this as a 'punishment' and a 'restraint.'[126]

In a statement, one of the schools involved in the taping incidents said 'no malice was intended'. But regardless of the intention, the impact on children is the same. As Jennifer Sey commented in a social media post, referring to her time as an elite athlete, 'I don't care that my coaches meant well. They withheld food from kids, degraded and belittled us, forced us to train with serious injuries. It doesn't matter that they were simply adhering to the standards of the day... Good intentions mean nothing.'[127]

She is right. The fact that some adults have become so numbed to the extreme nature of the restrictions they are enforcing on children is deeply disturbing.

The WHO defines child maltreatment – in other words, abuse – as 'all forms of physical and emotional ill-treatment, sexual abuse, neglect, and exploitation that results in actual or potential harm to the child's health, development or dignity.'[128]

It is our view that society's masking of children in circumstances where there is little evidence base for the measure, plenty of evidence of harm, and often when adults have not been subject to the same strictures, comes uncomfortably close to meeting this definition. That is a disturbing realisation, and one we appreciate not everyone will agree with, but we should reflect on it seriously.

No society sets out to mistreat its children, and the American mother is right to look into the eyes of the American school board and scream, incandescent, 'defend our children'.

But in truth, it is not only the school board which has failed. It is all of us.

Chapter 4
School's Out

On 18 March 2020, in a broadcast without precedent, Prime Minister Boris Johnson took over the airwaves to announce '[A]fter schools shut their gates from Friday afternoon they will remain closed... for the vast majority of pupils until further notice'. The objective, he explained, was 'to slow the spread of the virus.'

For many children that Friday marked the last physical contact they were to have with their schools until September 2020, and we now know that announcement was merely the first in a series of shockwaves whose tremors, some two years later, are still carving through the educational system.

Between 23 March 2020 and the end of the summer term in 2021, the average pupil in the UK was out of school for more classroom days than they were present and schools were closed in England for longer than any other country in Europe bar Italy.*[129,130]

In the period between those full nationwide closures,**

---

* The timeline of school closures was:
  March 2020: Schools in England were closed to most children, remaining open for children of critical workers and vulnerable children.
  Summer term 2020: Some pupils in priority year groups were encouraged to return to in-person schooling.
  August/September 2020: Most pupils returned to in-person schooling.
  January 2021: Primary and secondary schools and colleges closed to most pupils, with vulnerable children and children of critical workers able to attend. Special schools and alternative provision remained technically open although attendance remained below 50% for much of that term.
  March 2021: Pupils began returning to schools.
** We are aware of the line of argument that schools 'were never closed'. While it is true that schools were open for children of critical workers and vulnerable children, this allowed only a very small fraction of children to attend. The reality for most children was that school was closed. The terminology we have adopted throughout this book reflects that reality.

schooling was subject to a sustained, at times near-continuous, barrage of disruption with county-level closures, local authority closures, individual school closures and swathes of often perfectly healthy children being required to stay at home.

Even when schools were technically open, children faced prolonged and severe degrading of the school experience and a generalised and potentially lasting narrowing of the school curriculum: they were able to play less or no sport, opportunities for music, drama and arts were reduced, hobbies were curtailed and friendship circles – both inside school and outside – became smaller.

With a few notable exceptions, the situation in the UK has mirrored that globally. As at September 2021 schoolchildren worldwide had lost 1.8 trillion hours, and counting, of in-person learning, a number which Unicef calls 'unfathomable'.[131] School closures have left virtually no child untouched – 1.7 billion children across 188 countries have been affected.[132] In Mumbai, primary schools and secondary schools have only been open for three weeks and three months, respectively, since March 2020;[133] in Uganda schools reopened only on 10 January 2022, after a full 22 months closed.[134]

At the time of writing some 616 million students worldwide are still affected by full or partial school closures. The global situation is so dire that Unicef, in a haunting statement timed to coincide with International Education Day on 24 January 2022, commented:

'In March, we will mark two years of COVID-19-related disruptions to global education. Quite simply, we are looking at a nearly insurmountable scale of loss to children's schooling.'

Geoff Barton, the General Secretary of the Association of School and College Leaders, described to us the moment he learned that schools across the UK were likely to close.

'I remember going in to see Gavin Williamson with my colleague, Paul Whiteman, expecting that he was going to say "we're going to have to cancel exams in the summer because we can't guarantee them." And instead what he said was "we're going to have to start closing schools down". And that was a moment where suddenly it felt like events were overtaking us and the seriousness of the whole thing suddenly crystallized for many of us.'

This sense of shock was reiterated by many we spoke to. Anne Longfield, former Children's Commissioner for England, recalls the first school closures and seeing children going home from school on the last day with bags full of books and thinking it 'was just such a big, significant thing,' before going on to explain that 'the thing that struck me at the time was... the kids had the rug pulled out from under them. They always thought they were going to be at school. They always expected to go.' She adds 'it was incredible for me to sit and just listen to it because I thought we'd all agreed – since about 1870 – that actually [schools] were a decent thing, actually we want them. We might all carp about little bits here and there, but actually they're a force for good; kids generally should go to schools and that's how we are; and it seemed at that point it was almost draining away – as if people were forgetting how important schools were. There was a point where they almost seemed to be disposable.'

As Professor Lucy Easthope, a disaster planning expert, explains to us, 'The idea that school was first and foremost a place of education was quite an elitist view – the framing of the school as the educational environment is the last thing it becomes in a disaster: it's a place of safety – where children are fed, kept warm, given a respite from abuse and safeguarded.' She adds 'The idea of homeschooling blew my mind and was all part of this idea that it was something that could be dispensed with'. A teacher we interviewed lamented, 'Schools stopped being a place of education and stopped being a kind of safe haven and protectorate of children last March when they closed them.'

Parents, too, speak of a profound reaction. 'My jaw was wide open and has stayed open', said one, while another told us she was 'stunned; we didn't believe it could actually happen, it all seemed completely unreal, a body blow.' Others recalled the immediate alarm bells that rang for them about safeguarding risk, vulnerable children and families who relied on school for essential respite and structure. One headteacher, who has asked to remain anonymous, recounted how the worry about those children would keep her up at night. 'I would worry perpetually throughout the lockdowns because I do have a very vulnerable demographic in my school and I knew that there were lots of families who weren't coping,' she says.

These comments reflect an instinct that schooling is sacrosanct, something essential for children.

We now know that instinct was, tragically, correct.

Learning losses

After close to two years of school disruption and closures, in low-and middle-income countries learning losses have left up to 70% of 10-year-olds unable to read or understand a simple text, up from 53% before the pandemic.[135] In Ethiopia, primary school children are estimated to have learned only 30 to 40% of the maths that they would have done in a normal school year. In Brazil, where one study estimated that school closures had wiped out a decade of educational progress,[136] 1 in 10 students aged 10–15 reported that they are not planning to return to school once their schools reopen; in South Africa, where schoolchildren are between 75% and a full school year behind where they should be, some 400,000 to 500,000 students are reported as having dropped out of school altogether between March 2020 and July 2021.[137]

In England, the most recent data we have show that the percentages of children in Years 2 to 6 who are achieving at or above the standard expected for their age dropped by approximately one-fifth between autumn 2019 and summer 2020,[138] and learning loss for secondary pupils is estimated at around 1.2 months in reading by the summer term 2020/21,[139] but these averages hide significant disparities. Learning losses for disadvantaged pupils and disabled and SEN children have consistently been higher and there are significant regional variations even within the UK. By the second half of the autumn term in 2020, the average learning loss for maths for primary pupils was 5.3 months in Yorkshire and the Humber compared with 0.5 months in the south-west.[140]

A common retort when bringing up the damage caused by school closures is 'so what, it's only a few months of lost learning'.

This could not be more wrong.

Even in narrow economic terms the potential losses are huge: some £40,000 in loss of lifetime earnings to each individual, which equates to £350 billion for the cohort.[141] The World Bank has compared the global impact of school closures 'to a bomb which destroys only one capital – the human capital.'[142] The World Economic Forum, in a paper headed 'The global education crisis is even worse than we thought', has stated that 'students now risk losing $17 trillion in lifetime earnings in present value, or about 14% of today's global GDP, because of COVID-19-related school closures and economic shocks.'[143]

Beyond learning loss

Severe though they are, the educational and economic impacts of school closures will, for many children, be a footnote to more serious harm.

For, while school provides education, school is much more than education: it is the heart of most children's lives, a place where they go to learn, play, be. For some children, school is everything, an essential safety net without which they are unlikely to survive.

Jay Bhattacharya is Professor of Medicine at Stanford University in the US and a vocal critic of school closures in America. He explained to us that 'literature in health economics very carefully documents the long-term health consequences of missing even short periods of school for children. That literature is unequivocal. It shows that children who miss school even for short periods of time lead shorter, unhealthier and poorer lives'. One study published in November 2020 suggests that the spring 2020 school closures could be associated with an estimated 13.8 million years of life lost based on data from US studies and an estimated 0.8 million years of life lost based on data from European studies. Crucially, it notes that the loss 'was likely to be greater than would have been observed if leaving primary schools open had led to an expansion of the first wave of the pandemic.'* [144,145]

Each tragedy of a life derailed has effects which ripple out beyond the individual. Uneducated children make not only for poorer adults, but also unhealthier adults, who tend to be more expensive for the state throughout their lifetimes. At multiple touchpoints they cost more both in terms of lost

---

* While the authors of that study acknowledge significant limitations in the modelling estimates used, it is beyond doubt that higher educational attainment has a knock-on impact on health – a paper prepared by UCL for Sage in February 2021 warned that 'The well-documented links between education and health mean that school closures during the COVID-19 pandemic are likely to be associated with significant health harms to children and young people'.

revenue and additional investment.[146] There will be Big Ideas that will never happen and societies that fail to flourish. For the world's poorest countries, pre-existing conditions mean that an intervention of this kind of duration will not only deal children a severe blow at an individual level, but will affect the countries themselves. If that sounds melodramatic consider India, where the World Bank warned that by October 2020 school closures had not only cost the Indian economy an estimated £6.5 billion, but also that the loss of earnings and skills development was set to devastate Indian economic growth in the long term.[147] As Jay says, 'Poor countries followed the advice of epidemiologists from rich countries. They shut down schools for nearly two years in some places. The consequence will be a lifetime of illiteracy, poverty, and poor health for a generation of poor kids in poor countries.'[148]

The single biggest inequity-generating policy of all time

A social media meme circulating during March 2020 cautioned 'we are all in the same sea but in different ships'. As applied to school closures, the subjectivity of each individual child's circumstances meant that the same intervention was experienced differently, and unevenly.

In what was a bad situation for many children we must be careful not to minimise the experiences of more fortunate children: only for a very few children were lockdown and school closures a net positive. For the rest, at almost every touchpoint imaginable, inequalities were not only entrenched, but deepened.

According to the Social Mobility Commission, disadvantaged pupils in England are now as much as seven months behind their more privileged peers at school, including the gaps that grew in the last year.[149] Almost a third of children in the UK now live in poverty and some regions have seen staggering increases during the pandemic. A recent IFS report notes: 'The immediate effects of the pandemic are particularly likely to increase three types of inequalities: income inequality, socio-economic inequalities in education and skills, and intergenerational inequalities.'[150] Research from the Education Endowment Foundation estimates that the progress made since 2011 in narrowing the attainment gap has likely been reversed.[151]

School closures had a disproportionate impact on women worldwide, either because women picked up the lion's share of homeschooling,[152,153] or because school closures themselves had a gendered impact on health, protection and education. Worldwide, only 49% of countries had achieved gender parity in primary education even before the pandemic, and at secondary level that gap widens.[154] School closures have further deepened that inequality.[155]

'It's important for us to recognize the truly disproportional impact the pandemic has had on the education systems of children living in poor communities or poor families, and children with disabilities', says Robert Jenkins, director of education and adolescent development at Unicef.[156]

It is for these reasons Jay Bhattacharya says he believes school closures to be 'the single biggest generator of inequality I've seen in my lifetime from a single policy'.

Children are resilient, but only to a point

It has been a constant feature of the last two years that those warning of the serious harms which they felt would flow from school closures were accused of catastrophising. 'Children are resilient,' was a common view, especially during the early days of the pandemic. It is a phrase we hear less often now. We are mindful of the need not to do down the life chances of a generation of children, but we must also recognise the gravity of the challenges we face.

Outside of war, the last two years have seen the most sustained onslaught on children's schooling, security and stability known in modern times. For many this situation is ongoing: in January 2022 some 616 million students remained affected by full or partial school closures.[157]

To tell children they are resilient demeans the serious, and in some cases life-changing, injuries that some have suffered as a result of school closures. As we have seen, there is a lasting impact on health in later life from even relatively short periods of school disruption, and as we shall see in the next chapter, for many children the last two years leave a legacy of obesity and reduced fitness which without intervention may prove lasting. The president of the British Paediatric Neurology Association has spoken of an 'explosion' of children with lockdown-induced disabling tics disorders and Tourette's syndrome;[158] studies also show permanent eye damage in children from increased screen time during the pandemic.[159,160] There is an unarguable permanence to the cycle of lost life chances and educational losses which passes from generation to generation, and of the 100,000 children now missing from the education system many will have little realistic prospect of escaping the consequences associated with such absence, including long-term under-attainment and crime.[161]

Just as the language of resilience hides harm, the language of 'recovery' bandied about throughout the pandemic has been unhelpful, too often appearing to provide a justification for continued harm.

On 3 February 2021, in the middle of the second period of school closures, the Prime Minister announced the appointment of Sir Kevan Collins as 'Catch-up Tsar', to 'oversee a comprehensive programme of catch-up aimed at young people who have lost out on learning due to the pandemic.'[162] Johnson assured the public that Collins's 'experience and expertise will help ensure every young person is supported to catch up on their education and gain the skills and knowledge they need to be able to seize opportunities in future.'[163]

For a few brief months the public bought into the idea

that an ambitious and far-reaching package of recovery might ameliorate at least some of the educational harm done. National print and broadcast media showcased frequent and often heated debates about the shape and form of the magic bullet required.

Fast forward a year and we now realise something that was obvious to many from the start: there's no magic bullet.

Collins resigned in June 2021, after being offered only £1.4bn of the reported £15bn[164] that he and key education stakeholders had calculated as necessary to meet anything approaching full 'educational' recovery (incidentally, a mere £22 per child in the average primary school, compared to a reported £1,600 to be spent per young person in the US, or £2,500 a head, in the Netherlands).[165] Talk of an ambitious recovery package was quietly replaced by far more limited plans for targeted tutoring, which itself appears to have met an ignominious end when chronic missed targets and accusations of poor quality tuition led to the cancellation of the contract with the tutoring contractor.[*166,167,168]

The degrading of education

In the wake of the last two years, the biggest victim might yet be education itself.

Whereas going into the pandemic in 2020 education was a right, in 2022 it is lesser: a privilege, or, in the words of Chris Whitty in February 2021,[169] a 'benefit': conditional worldwide on an array of medical interventions and concessions in some cases deleterious to the mission – and children – it is designed to serve.

It is no surprise that by treating children's schooling as on some level optional, increasing numbers of children (or

---

* Robert Halfon MP, Chair of the Education Select Committee, has said 'Our Committee heard that it is not reaching the most disadvantaged children, there are significant regional disparities and there is a real risk of failure through Randstad as the delivery partner. Moreover, it is not reaching the hundreds of thousands of "ghost children" who have not returned to school.'

their parents) now see it as such. In the UK close to 100,000 children have almost entirely disappeared from education since the pandemic. Nearly 800 schools have an entire class-worth of 'lost' children,[170] and children still in school register poorer than average attendance.[171]

One headteacher we spoke to told us of the 'families who now have decided that school is almost optional'; another teacher told us that they felt the secondary school children were more detached than he could recall seeing previously 'we now have swathes of kids – top set kids – who are completely apathetic and passive. They're not misbehaving; it's not a behavioural thing. They're just kind of quiet, disinterested, detached.'

Worldwide, the OECD recognises the dangers inherent in school disruption, saying in the middle of the 2020 closures that 'other elements that happen in the absence of traditional schooling, such as the curbing of educational aspirations or the disengagement from the school system, will have a long-term impact on students' outcomes'[172] – something which in labour economics is called 'hysteresis' – and is reflected by a gradual disengagement from the system which, they note 'may be more prevalent among students from less privileged backgrounds.' The grade inflation and U-turns that followed the teacher assessments after the cancellation of exams risks a self-defeating devaluation of the currency of education.

The university experience, too, has drifted from pre-pandemic norms. Two-thirds of universities are still not providing full face-to-face teaching, and online lectures and 'blended learning' are the norm for thousands of students.[173] Despite noise from Education Secretary Nadhim Zahawi[174] and Universities Minister Michelle Donelan[175] about the imperative for universities to return to full face-to-face teaching, there appears to be little political will to force this to happen, and the reality is that students are faced with ambiguity and uncertainty as to whether their teaching will be online or face-to-face in the 2022/23 academic year and beyond.

A historic blunder?

Even if we were to accept the idea that screen-based learning could be an acceptable replacement for school, the UK's poor digital infrastructure for online learning, including inadequate access to digital devices and a significant digital divide, was known about before March 2020. As Anne Longfield says 'The digital divide was vaguely known about but there was little sense of any urgency about that in the initial days,' and in fact that may have been a generous assessment. In early 2020, Ofcom's Technology Tracker estimated that 'between 1.14 million and 1.78 million children under the age of 18 lived in households without access to a laptop, desktop or tablet in the UK', and that between 227,000 and 559,000 children lived in homes with no access to the internet.[176]

That basing a remote learning experiment on this foundation would lead to a profound deepening of educational inequalities was an inevitability so obvious[177] that in our view it is one of the more unforgivable aspects of the way in which school closures came to be seen early on as an acceptable policy lever, and a bitter irony for a Government elected on a 'levelling-up' agenda. There was no obligation at all on schools to provide remote learning until October 2020[178] – up until this time many pupils simply received printed handouts, with little to no formal education. Even after that, and despite providing a total of 1.35 million laptops and tablets, and 77,000 routers by September 2021, the reality was that this help came far too late for most. Despite union pleas, DfE was initially slow to react and had only delivered 212,900 laptops and tablets, and 49,700 routers, by 13 July 2020.[179,180]

It should also have been obvious that even with suitable technology there were children for whom remote learning was so fundamentally unsuitable that it simply should never have been on the table – primary children, SEN children and disabled children in particular. As Anne Longfield said of primary children, 'keeping primary schools closed until literally the last couple of weeks of term was in my view, absolutely unnecessary. It added a huge additional detriment to those children and was completely irresponsible and virtually criminal for those children.' Noting that children with disabilities had essentially been 'incarcerated' in their homes, Dame Christine Lenehan, director of the Council for Disabled Children, noted 'There are some who have barely had any formal education since lockdown began.'[181]

The verdict of the World Bank in August 2021 was: 'Despite countries' laudable and indispensable efforts to provide remote education, which involved rapid adjustments, many countries are aware that remote learning has been a weak, unequal, and very partial compensation for face-to-face education. The evidence of that is mounting'.[182,183,184] This should have surprised no one.

Most damning of all was the predictability of the significant and serious welfare issues which were the inevitable result of school closures. For all children it was obvious that closures would equate to a dearth of the socialisation crucial to child development. 'When we close schools we close their lives', Professor Russell Viner, then President of the Royal College of Paediatrics and Child Health (RCPCH), told the Education Select Committee in January 2021.[185] Likewise, data published by the Department for Education within weeks of the first lockdown had shown that only 29,000 out of 723,000 children known to children's social care services in 2019 attended school in the week before the Easter holidays.[186]

There was a general sense from many we spoke to that there was no other option but to close schools in March 2020. While we recognise the force of public opinion at the time (see Chapter 9), and the impact of the lock-stepped, panicked reaction of much of the Western world, at policy level there was always a choice, as is demonstrated by the differentiated practice of those countries who kept schools open (see Introduction). The relative lack of benefit in epidemiological terms appears to have been known about from the end of April 2020 onwards.[187] As Professor of Infectious Disease Epidemiology and member of SAGE Mark Woolhouse notes:

'To recap, the arguments for closing schools were that the children were at some risk, the staff were at high risk and that schools would drive community transmission, thereby raising the R number. None of these concerns were supported by the epidemiological data and surely we should expect compelling evidence before we took such a serious step as closing schools. Sadly, this remained a minority view and none of the advisory committees were willing to recommend re-opening schools, so they stayed closed for the rest of the summer term.'[188]

In our view, school closures were the single most impactful measure of the pandemic – an impact which was almost entirely negative in its devastating reach. Jonathan Chait, in a haunting piece published in the *New York Intelligencer*, suggests that school closures were 'an error of judgement that was sufficiently consequential and foreseeable that we can't just shrug it off as a bad dice roll. It was a historic blunder that reveals some deeper flaw in the methods that produced it and which demands corrective action.'[189]

Many would now agree that prolonged school closures were a grotesque mistake. However, this collective understanding is worthless unless it is translated into meaningful action to ensure that in any future emergency, schools are safeguarded as the essential infrastructure they always were.

Chapter 5
Childhood Gone Backwards

Many readers will be familiar with the game of Jenga. Players take turns to remove one block at a time from a tower, creating a progressively more unstable structure. It is a sadly fitting metaphor to describe what we've done to child health during the pandemic.

School closures – for good reason – have attracted the lion's share of commentary. However, hugely significant though school closures have been, their impact has been exacerbated by an array of other restrictions, each of which has chipped away at the essence of what it means to be a child. In this context, the intense focus on education – to the exclusion of wider childhood impacts – has often bewildered us. As parents we want our children to achieve, but more fundamentally we want them to lead happy and healthy lives, a point reflected by Neil Leitch, CEO of the Early Years Alliance, when he tells us, 'when I hear and I listen to the focus, almost being exclusively on literacy and language, I can't help feeling that you'll get that as a result if you get a developed emotionally stable child.'

Many of the measures rolled out to curb the spread of the virus seemed instinctively to be at odds with healthy child development. Asking children to spend long periods behind a screen, stopping or severely curtailing their social interactions and their exercise, and even restricting their ability to play – such an essential building block of 'a good life' for a child that it merits its own Article in the UN Convention on the Rights of the Child – seemed counter to everything we knew. Furthermore, many of the aspects of life that until 2020 were considered essential or strongly beneficial for children – sports, music, drama, arts – were cancelled.

Children at home were instead, if 'lucky', asked to spend long periods behind a screen, and for those children in school, the school environment would have likely been very different to the one children had left behind on 23 March 2020. 'My child cries so much these days as he can't see his friends', said one message from a parent in the summer of 2020. 'He wants to go to school. He can't go swimming, he can't even go to the park. He's pretty much housebound unless I take him out for a walk. But all he wants to do is play in the park.'

Another message read:

'I have three children.

My youngest – aged four – is expected to be old enough to do her schoolwork online. Though if she'd been 30 days younger, she'd still be at nursery and considered too young to learn remotely. She has no interest in lessons on a screen and has no idea of who these 'new' teachers are. She struggled to settle in the first time starting school; the longer she is now away the harder it will be again for her. She misses having friends – and girls especially – to play with. SHE IS NOT COPING.

My six-year-old son is diligently doing his work every day, though needs constant one-to-one assistance. He also desperately misses his friends, his social network. He gets upset and stressed in a way he didn't before lockdown. It's been five weeks since he was able to play with his friends. His routine, his structure, his life has effectively been put on hold indefinitely and HE IS NOT COPING.

My eight-year-old is fairly independent. He is an excellent rugby player – prior to lockdown he was training at an elite level. He desperately misses his friends. His routine, his structure, and his life have effectively been put on hold indefinitely. And potentially his rugby career. He often breaks down crying for long periods of time. HE IS NOT COPING.'

Rod Grant is a headteacher who was one of a handful of school leaders to speak out unambiguously about school closures. These are his words, written during the height of the 2021 nationwide shutdown.

'In the last three months, in my school and schools like it, I am witnessing mental health issues unlike anything I've seen in my career. This is not me trying to be dramatic or to overplay what lockdown actually does to children. I am seeing children being diagnosed with clinical depression, increasing rates of self-harm… Suicidal ideation and, something I haven't seen for at least 20 years, a resurgence of eating disorders. …Children need to be with their friends. They need to play. They need to develop their social and academic skills. How dare we have created an environment where a five-year-old can say, I can't play with Freddie because he's not part of my bubble. It is the stuff of nonsense and it is our children who will end up being this lockdown's collateral damage.' [190]

Sir Al Aynsley Green was the first Children's Commissioner for England and is a lifelong champion of children. At the time we interviewed him, he'd spent the last few months gathering the accumulating data on the impact of the last two years. He estimates he's now sitting on a daunting collection of 500 pieces of evidence. 'The extent of what's happened is simply staggering', he tells us.

We do not attempt to provide a comprehensive summary of that evidence here: even if we could, too much is still unknown. As Sir Al Aynsley-Green notes, 'much of the hard evidence of what actually has been the impact in the medium to long term on children is yet to be uncovered.' However, it is becoming clear that some of the consequences we intuitively feared – and indeed witnessed first-hand – are materialising.

A *BMJ Paediatrics* narrative review, published in 2021, relating to the period of the first lockdowns globally, reads:

> *'A decrease in physical activity and increase in unhealthy food consumption were shown in studies from two countries. There was a decrease in the number of visits to the emergency department in four countries, an increase in child mortality in Cameroon and a decrease by over 50% of immunisations administered in Pakistan. A significant drop of 39% in child protection medical examination referrals during 2020 compared with the previous years was found in the UK, a decrease in allegations of child abuse and neglect by almost one-third due to school closures in Florida, and an increase in the number of children with physical child abuse trauma was found in one centre in the USA.'*[191]

As for the UK, one-third of children now fail to do the bare minimum of 30 minutes exercise a day, and childhood obesity is a grave and worsening public health problem. In reception, according to the Government's own National Child Measurement Programme, the prevalence of obesity has increased from 9.9% in 2019/20 to 14.4% in 2020/21. In Year 6, the prevalence of obesity has increased from 21% in 2019/20 to 25.5% in 2020/21.[192] One lecturer writes on Twitter: 'updating my obesity lecture notes with the most recent data from England's National Child Measurement Programme. The data are so shockingly upsetting I have to share'.[193]

School readiness is a key child public health metric, yet half of pupils are now thought to be unready to start school at age four. Many of them are unable to pay attention or feed themselves and a third are unable to hold a pencil.[194] Last year over one million referrals were made to specialist child mental health services – an increase of 15% from pre-pandemic levels[195] – creating a paediatric mental health emergency so severe it has overwhelmed child mental health services to the point that there are now three-year waiting lists for treatment.[196] The number of children waiting for eating disorder treatment has tripled.[197]

We do not yet know the long-term impact of the last two years on child development for very young children, but we do know that many of these children have lived the majority of their lives under pandemic strictures.

In April 2022, an Ofsted report into early years children recorded that:

'The pandemic has continued to affect children's communication and language development, and many providers noticed delays in their speech and language progress.

The negative impact on children's personal, social and emotional development has also continued, with many children lacking confidence in group activities.

Some providers continue to notice delays in babies' physical development… There were delays in babies learning to crawl and walk. Some providers reported that children had regressed in independence and in self-care skills.

Children have missed out on hearing stories, singing and having conversations. One provider commented that children appear to have spent more time on screens and have started to speak in accents and voices that resemble the material they have watched.'[198]

Dr Sunil Bhopal, of Newcastle University, and Pasco Fearon, of University College London, foreshadowed these disturbing observations when they wrote of the critical role of the early months and years for a child's long-term health, development and wellbeing:

'Development takes place at an extraordinary rate during a baby's first year, when the brain doubles in size. This

early development depends crucially on experience, and particularly social experience, which stimulates, tunes and hones the brain's unfolding architecture. A stimulating, varied and responsive environment supports the development of language, cognition and emotional and social competencies. This dependence on environmental input makes the brain exquisitely flexible and capable of adaptation. But, by the same token, it also means that babies are highly susceptible to the negative impacts of adversity.'

They continue,

'There are good reasons to be concerned about infant and early child development during this time and, like so many other things, these risks will not be evenly distributed.'[199]

Indeed, it has been suggested that developmental progress at 22 months serves as an accurate predictor of educational attainment at 8, 26 and – incredibly – 53.[200] As the House of Lords COVID-19 Committee points out,

'The unique set of circumstances that the last 18 months have presented also means that there are aspects of these experiences where no one knows what the long-term implications might be. This seems particularly true in relation to child development. As one witness stated: "In a two year-old's life they have been locked down more than half their life. In a four-year-old's it is 25%. It is enormous; it is massive. I do not think we can underestimate it."'[201]

Sally Hogg is Head of Policy and Communications at the Parent-Infant Foundation and coordinates the First 1001 Days Movement. In her view the impact on babies and very young children is diverse: some will be absolutely fine and some 'exposed to horrendous abuse, neglect and poverty.' Sally points out that between these two extremes there's a third category of young children – those who 'have had a mix of exposure to more stress at home but also to more quality time with their parents but perhaps a lack of enriching activities'. She goes on to explain that 'Whilst we don't yet know what the longer-term outcomes for these children will be, we do know there have been some dips in development outcomes around children's social and language development on a population scale.'

As CEO of the Early Years Alliance, the UK's largest early years membership organisation, Neil Leitch has a uniquely wide insight into that sector. He tells us that in his view, 'children have literally forgotten how to play. In some instances they have forgotten how to share. I spoke to one manager that said to me, and she literally was in tears when she said it, "I'm tired of having to console my staff who are fed up of being bitten and kicked by children who really have not developed appropriately." Generally, child development has just stalled.'

In Disney's film *The Little Mermaid*, Ariel so much wishes to be human that she gives up her voice to Ursula the sea-witch, in exchange for legs. Robbed of her ability to speak or sing, she cannot express herself.

Throughout the pandemic, children have had their voices suppressed, not only metaphorically, but literally as lockdowns and isolation have contributed to a staggering increase in speech and language difficulties. The issue has received less airtime than the explosion in child mental health problems, but is no less terrifying given the significance of language development and good communication skills in growing healthy children, and healthy adults.

Language development at age two is predictive of children's 'school readiness' at age four.[202] Vocabulary at age five is a very strong predictor of school-leaving age qualifications, while language and communication skills are essential for forming strong relationships with caregivers, teachers and colleagues.

It's notable that singing is a cornerstone of language development in the early years and is routinely used pedagogically in primary schools. Yet singing was prohibited in schools during the period of phased reopening from May 2020, and the rule reappeared in Northern Ireland in 2021.[203] Even as recently as December 2021 in England, there were examples of educational settings discouraging singing, with one parent telling us, 'Asked my five-year-old daughter why she's not been learning any Christmas songs in school. She said they're not allowed to sing – it spreads germs. She was also told the same thing last year and they did a silent Nativity. This year there is no Nativity. I'm so angry.' One school wrote to parents saying that singing was permitted, but only at 'moderate' levels, while another parent told us that her child was unable to sing in his reception class for the entire year.

While by no means the only contributing factor, this is an example of a measure which may have seemed inconsequential to those enacting it from their offices, but may nevertheless have disrupted early language experiences for millions of children; not only during the period when the guidance was in place, but also during the 'long tail' of the post-pandemic aftermath. The perception that singing is a 'germ-spreading', 'dangerous' activity persisted for months.

Mask-wearing by caregivers may have been another inhibitor to early years language skills development. An Ofsted report[204] published in spring 2022 observed that a number of early years providers felt that wearing face masks continued to have a negative impact on children's communication and language skills, adding that, 'Children turning 2 years old will have been surrounded by adults wearing masks for their whole lives and have therefore been unable to see lip movements or mouth shapes as regularly.'

There are deep and lasting impacts for children who are not supported to develop strong language skills. Up to 66%

of secondary school pupils who are at risk of permanent exclusion have some form of language or communication issue and lower language abilities are correlated with reduced health quality of life.[205] One study shows 66–90% of juvenile offenders had below-average language skills.[206]

In essence, the foundations of language development established in early childhood during the critical pre-school years underpin a child's future experiences. They influence that child's outcomes in adulthood as well as childhood. With the right interventions, prospects can be greatly improved, though it is essential to intervene early to avert a cascade of difficulties further down the track. During lockdowns and social distancing restrictions, the opportunities for children to both acquire the experiences to develop language, or to receive the appropriate interventions for already diagnosed issues, were severely curtailed. The need for intervention is so widespread that therapists report they are unable to keep up with demand, with Kamini Gadhok, the chief executive of the Royal College of Speech and Language Therapists (RCSLT) saying, 'Our members tell us that growing lists and waiting times for speech and language therapy are dramatically impacting on their ability to provide the support which children need for the best start in life'.[207] The burden of these effects, if not urgently addressed, will be borne not only by the children themselves, but by the entirety of society.

One of the unspoken fallacies of the pandemic was that it would somehow be possible to 'press pause' on child development and recover losses at a later date. This is a false and dangerous supposition, not least when it comes to vital speech and language development. As speech and language therapist and author of the book *How to Raise a Chatterbox* Sandy Chappell explains, 'around 80–85% brain development occurs in the first three years and as children get older, the neural connections in the parts of the brain that are not used, will start to be lost. This is why early intervention is crucial.'

Unfortunately, the speech and language therapy (SLT)

needed for this early intervention was, like so many other child health services, vastly reduced during the first lockdown. A study by the RCSLT showed that during the period between March and June 2020 62% of children previously in receipt of interventions had no SLT and 81% had less than usual.[208]

Sandy explained that she is now seeing a devastating impact on her caseload and in the nature of issues. Her referral rate is around four times higher than it was pre-pandemic, and she tells us that children seem to be presenting with more severe problems than they did before. She said, 'I have had a lot more children referred who are not using any words at age two, and in the past two weeks alone I have had two referrals of 3–4-year-old children who are still only using single words. I am also seeing children with more severe speech sound disorders. A couple of them are so difficult to understand that they don't speak at all at school. I have never had so many children with such severe problems on my caseload at any one time.'

Sandy also notes an increase in stammering referrals. This chimes with data from the Action for Stammering children's charity, which reported that the number of calls to their helpline had increased by over 50%.[209]

What must not happen is denial of the issue. However, troublingly, in January 2022 the USA's Centers for Disease Control and Prevention (CDC) quietly updated its speech and language information. The move has been criticised by some as an attempt to 'lower the bar' for speech development expectations. The organisation has introduced a new 30-month milestone and indicated an expectation of 50 words at this age, while in contrast the American Speech Language Hearing Association stipulates that fewer than 50 words at two years old is a sign of a 'language problem'. Whereas pre-pandemic the CDC advised that two-year-olds should be repeating words and speaking in two-to-four word sentences, in the revised guidelines the milestones major on pointing and gesturing with an expectation of only two words together.[210]

It should concern us all that these opportunities to identify and address issues may be squandered. Sandy tells us that she has noticed children now being referred to her at age four, rather than at age three. We have received numerous reports from parents telling us that their child's two-year health visitor review – which assesses development against milestones – has either not happened at all, or been conducted over the phone. Indeed, a *Babies in Lockdown* report from August 2020 found that only 1 in 10 parents with children under two had seen a health visitor during that period of the pandemic.[211]

An inscription in her book, given to us by Sandy, reads 'As an SLT, I believe every child deserves a voice.' It really should be as simple as that.

When we think of childhood milestones, our minds often turn to the early years, when so much brain development occurs. Yet one topic which has come up time and again within our parent community is the dispiriting sense that our adolescents have had their vital paving blocks on the course towards adulthood removed. This cohort has borne the brunt of mental health issues – from depression and anxiety, to eating disorders. They have also suffered the effects of pressing the 'pause button' at a critical transition time when they needed to be making friends, planning their futures, and striking out towards independence away from the family unit.

We spoke with educational psychologist Claire McGuiggan about how the pandemic has amplified her prior concerns for adolescents.

She observes that young people of 15, 16, and 17 were already becoming less independent, saying, 'That transition of separating from parents and family a little bit, going out into the world, exploring your identity in real life and coming into contact with other people different from you... having the confidence to travel around the country or to follow your football team, all those sorts of things... increasingly young people were doing those less and less.'

In Claire's view, this trend was affecting this cohort's mental health in the years before Covid. Now the pandemic has built on this pre-existing pattern, with the limited opportunity for interaction with the outside world at a time when this age group needed to separate from their families resulting in foreseeable effects. 'When you put young people into the position of all they are allowed to experience is the environment of their home, or the relationships within their families, and the only access to the world beyond that is online. Then it was entirely predictable that what you would see is a real rise in fearfulness.'

Parents reflect this sentiment and experience, sharing their worries about what they have seen with their own children. One tells us, 'We recently went to the college open evening and my daughter afterwards admitted being extremely overwhelmed and nervous. She hasn't had exposure like that. I'm currently arranging our own work experience in a bid to increase her confidence – she's missed many confidence-building opportunities.'

Another explains, 'My 18.5-year-old had just started a very promising apprenticeship. The company liked him, he was doing well there and at college. They were about to take him abroad to see clients. He then spent 18 months locked in his room, online college and occasional contact from his office. Saw no friends or colleagues. He waited a year to take his driving test. He's slowly regaining confidence but still has bouts of depression which is heartbreaking for a boy of 20 who is just starting out.'

Of the numerous reports detailing the devastating mental health toll of lockdown, many speak directly of the toll on university students. One[212] considers nine systematic reviews globally and notes that 'Only one review concluded the evidence does not suggest a widespread negative effect on mental health in COVID-19 compared with previous years.' It sums up 'The overall impact of COVID-19 on the mental health and wellbeing of university students is substantial.' Another report found that participation in activities seemed to have 'fallen substantially,' and that this 'loss of connections, social learning and student development opportunities will dent students' confidence and preparedness for life after university'.

And here is the crux of the matter. Removing foundational elements of children's and young people's experiences has consequences.

As Claire explains: 'All those incidental challenges of life and little steps of separation haven't occurred. When the restrictions are lifted and it's like, "right, back to where you were", they're not back to where they were. They're placed in a situation that's seen as appropriate to their age group having presumed that their age group would've been through those incremental steps of separation and building independence, and they haven't.'

Without this recognition, and with a lack of appropriate support systems, some young people are floundering in situations for which they have – through no fault of their own – not developed the skills. In this vein, one parent tells us of their child's failure to settle at a top-tier university, saying that they 'really struggled', and pointing to the lack of support structures appropriate to the development stage of her child after two years of lost experiences – 'not one face-to-face meeting with a tutor or any other staff, after two years of not being able to socialise, it was too much and he quit'.

At the most extreme end of withdrawing, young people who found socialisation difficult before the pandemic may have initially found the removal from anxiety-provoking situations a relief. However, according to Claire, this is counterproductive, creating cycles of avoidance rather than facing them in small steps voluntarily with support in place. Lockdowns, school closures, and removal of all other social situations have now created a situation where some young people have, in Claire's words, 'withdrawn from the world, haven't even emerged from their bedrooms or their homes'. For families and children in that situation, the future can feel bleak. As Claire says, 'You can't start talking about relationships or friendships or building interests until you're able to engage with the world. None of those things seem like they're possible parts of your future. And that's a hopeless place to be.'

Naturally, there is a continuum of those affected, from those who will need one-to-one support, to others whose social skills have been damaged but who are ready to recommence the route towards independence, and those for whom different support structures and enrichment opportunities designed to rebuild the lost experiences will be required.

Research from the Prince's Trust of over 2,000 16–25 year olds found, troublingly, that over half of young people (52%) agree that they've 'lost confidence in themselves', with this rising to over 60% among those from lower-income backgrounds.[213] As always, the most disadvantaged suffer the most.

It's essential for our society that our adolescents are given the tools to recover their confidence, and their losses are treated with the same respect and consideration as those of our youngest children.

'Three weeks to flatten the curve, two years to flatten the kids', is a meme flying around social media. It reflects the fact that, as is now acknowledged by report after report, childhood has 'gone backward across virtually every key measure'.[214]

Given what we now understand about the wide-ranging impacts on children and their health and wellbeing, investment in support services is now crucial. However there is scant public acknowledgment or acceptance among policymakers of the scale of the damage.

A letter from the Lords Covid-19 Committee to Vicky Ford, the former Children's Minister, in relation to early years children,[215] reads:

'We agree with witnesses that we cannot wait until the effects of the last 15 months are established before taking action. The Government should take steps to mitigate the potential long-term impact of the pandemic on babies and their parents, including through the provision of 'catch up' Health Visitor appointments and additional funding for services that support new parents, and establish a robust mechanism to monitor the impact of the pandemic on the emotional, social and physical development of babies born since the start of the pandemic.'

That letter was dated 23 June 2021.

Since then, the 'recovery' package for older children – in itself grossly underpowered – almost entirely excludes early years children and babies. As the House of Lords Covid-19 Committee *Living in a COVID World* report[216] notes, 'we were particularly struck by the lack of attention and resource that is being devoted to helping pre-school children recover and 'catch up'. The UCL Institute of Education, among others, has raised concerns about the lack of a coordinated national response to address 'the mounting evidence from Ofsted and others that the disruption in early years services is likely to widen the achievement gap in the emotional and developmental progress of disadvantaged children and their peers.'[217] Such talk as there has been of 'recovery' in the UK has focused on education. However, the deficit in children's welfare goes far beyond this and includes physical health, mental health and speech and language. But paediatric services are now threadbare.

At the time of writing in spring 2022 waiting lists across

NHS child health services from community paediatric and nursing services to speech and language therapy are soaring.[218] Waiting lists for planned hospital care for all age groups are up; but children's more markedly than adults (22% versus 17% for all ages).[219] A Nuffield Trust report notes 'The number of patients joining the waiting list for planned paediatric hospital care is consistently higher than the number starting treatment.' Waiting times for children with suspected cancer to be seen by a consultant have worsened and in some 15.7% of cases exceed required maximum wait times; measles vaccination rates have dropped to their lowest level in a decade,[220] mirroring a global trend that saw essential childhood vaccination programmes sharply decline.[221]

Across the world, reduced access to antenatal and maternity care has led to an increase in stillbirths[222] – alongside this birth rates have declined still further from already historic lows,[223] something which is likely to store up issues for economies in the medium to long term. Infants, born to stressed mothers, and with postnatal support and new baby friendship groups cancelled, appear in some cases to have reduced cognitive capabilities relative to their non-pandemic siblings.[224] Mothers' rates of postnatal depression were consistently higher than average for much of the pandemic.[225,226]

One mother told us, 'I had a baby on 1 April 2020, had to make my own way into labour unit, husband out in the car until I was confirmed in established labour. Then he had to leave shortly after the birth. My baby and I were both in hospital for about five days due to an infection, my husband wasn't allowed onto the ward during that time. In terms of follow-up, we' had trouble establishing breastfeeding, had a video call suggested with no face-to-face breastfeeding support allowed. Had my first health visitor appointment over Zoom (no one came to the house to actually check on us). Then for my daughter's MMR jab at one year, the doctors said they couldn't give us an appointment as they were too busy doing Covid jabs.' She is just one of many with similar stories.

As the House of Lords' *Living in a COVID World* report[227] notes 'The way that the pandemic confined many families to their houses, and restricted interactions with friends, family and services, has had severe consequences for some. There will be a lasting legacy of increased need for mental health services, domestic abuse services, Local Authority Children's Services, third sector family support services and others, but the evidence we received suggests these services are nowhere near having the capacity to respond to this.'

In March 2022, draft terms of the UK's public inquiry into Covid were published. Although subsequently amended under pressure from us, children's charities and Anne Longfield CBE (and others),[228] those original terms did not mention the word 'children' once. This was a narrow, blinkered focus which is indicative of one of the key failings of policymaking for children and which stores up problems for individual children and for society at large down the line: poorer child health leads to worse life outcomes. Conversely, early interventions, especially for disadvantaged children, which incorporate early education, nutrition and health, have been shown to have dramatic long-term benefits.[229]

There is an urgent moral imperative to nurture our children and young people back to good health, but how as a society can we possibly hope to do that, if we cannot even recognise what has been lost?

Chapter 6
Apex of Harm

Sara is an eight-year-old child. She has cerebral palsy, epilepsy and complex needs that require input from a range of therapists and healthcare workers. She has severe learning difficulties and is behind academically.

As Sara's father says,

> *'My daughter did not see a physiotherapist, a paediatric consultant, an epilepsy consultant, an occupational therapist, an orthopaedic surgeon, an optician or a GP for the best part of two years. She was denied the right to attend school for almost an entire year. She was deprived of the health benefits and pure joy normally afforded by her weekly sessions of hydrotherapy and riding for the disabled. Her mobility declined. Her mental health suffered terribly. Her seizures got to the point where they lasted so long that she was turning blue and choking. We have almost lost her several times.'*

The blunt instruments of lockdown, social distancing, and school closures have been indiscriminate in the breadth of their effects and most, if not all, children will have been shaped to some degree by those experiences. However, for some children and their families, the impact was little short of barbaric. On the frontline of the childhood lockdown casualties, pre-existing issues for the most disadvantaged and vulnerable combined brutally with the pandemic response, with tragic consequences.

Before we continue, a few words of context and explanation. We could not have written this book without attempting to highlight the shameful treatment of some of these children and their families. Their suffering holds up a mirror to haunting legacy failings as a society, as well as to the specific inadequacies of the pandemic response. However, in writing this chapter, we must also acknowledge our relative lack of on-the-ground knowledge and expertise in this sphere. While we have borne witness to stories from parents struggling with some of these difficulties, we recognise that there are a host of charities, individuals and advocacy groups who have been working to advance the interests of the most vulnerable children for a long time. Our role can only be to amplify their crucial work, and we have been been privileged to meet and speak to some of them in recent weeks and months.

It is a painful reality that the most powerless children are often unseen, and unacknowledged, until they have already been failed by the system. This is especially the case for those children who are silent victims of abuse and neglect.

In April 2020, just a month after the first lockdown and school closures, SAGE published a report entitled 'The role of children in transmission'.[230] At the back, tucked away in its blandly named 'Annex A The Wider Impact of School Closure', lurked some revealing insights. One chilling and prescient paragraph read: 'the risk to vulnerable children's welfare has increased significantly as a result of school closures. Vulnerable children not in school are most likely at home. The risk of harm and abuse in the home is likely to be higher due to isolation, financial stress and based on experiences in other countries. For example, incidents of domestic violence in China tripled over the course of the epidemic...'.

As we now know, 94% of children who were designated vulnerable at the time of the initial school closures were not in school, despite places ostensibly being available for them. In this context, the SAGE report authors ask, 'where are these children? What are they doing? How are they being supported, and importantly, safeguarded? How are schools accomplishing safeguarding functions when most children are not in schools?' These were questions with no answers.

Two months later, in June 2020, Arthur Labinjo-Hughes, a six-year-old boy from Birmingham, England, was brutally murdered by his stepmother, Emma Tustin. His tragic death, described by the judge, Mr Justice Wall, as 'one of the most distressing and disturbing' cases he had ever dealt with, followed months of 'cruel and inhuman treatment'[231] at the hands of his stepmother and father since moving in with them at the beginning of the first lockdown on 23 March 2020. Several extended family members tried to raise the alarm over the course of several months, but on one occasion his uncle was allegedly threatened with arrest for breaking lockdown rules.[232]

The horrific death of this innocent child is the full responsibility of Arthur's stepmother and father. However, many have asked whether this little boy might have been saved were it not for the circumstances of lockdown that hid him away from view and removed his access to services that might have come to his aid.

In the aftermath of the case, Anne Longfield, Children's Commissioner at the time of the first lockdown, told the *Guardian* that Arthur's vulnerability had been exacerbated by lockdown, saying that, 'a lot of the services went on to the screens for children, and this child in particular, Arthur, wasn't in school. And it's much easier for families who want to evade view to do that when they haven't got someone in the room'.[233]

Also out of view was 16-month-old Star Hobson, who died in September 2020 from catastrophic injuries, following months of cruelty and maltreatment by her mother, Frankie Smith, and her mother's girlfriend, Savannah Brockhill. Child protection officers had received five referrals in relation to the toddler, but social workers closed the case a week before the child's death.[234]

Sadly, the cases of Arthur and Star reflect a wider increase in child abuse and neglect during the restrictions, as foreseen by the SAGE report, and by many of our expert contributors who tried to raise the alarm (see Chapter 7). Between April and September 2020, there were 285 reports of child deaths and incidents of serious harm, representing a rise of more than a quarter on the same period a year before.[235]

The House of Lords, as part of its recent report, heard evidence from charities and service providers about the impacts on families and children, and corroborated these outcomes,[236] saying, 'We heard about an increase in domestic abuse, and an increase in the number of children witnessing domestic abuse, increases in child safeguarding concerns and the potential for increasing numbers of children needing to be taken into care.'

Undoubtedly, the pandemic response has amplified pre-existing fractures and underinvestment in children's services. Before the pandemic, the Local Government Association estimated that children's social care was facing a £3.1 billion funding gap by 2024.[237] Indeed, in 2018, the former Children's Minister Tim Loughton, who served in David Cameron's cabinet, staunchly criticised the 'woeful underfunding by government of a proper breadth of social care interventions'.[238]

Any public inquiry must address how these historical shortfalls contributed to the deepening crisis during the pandemic.

Long before Covid swept through the country, poverty was already casting a long shadow over the prospects of millions of UK children. In the years 2019/20, 4.3 million children in the UK were estimated to be living in poverty – a shocking 9 in every classroom of 30.[239] The pandemic has now both increased the existing gap between advantaged and disadvantaged pupils, and pushed ever more families over the poverty threshold. This bleak reality has been highlighted by recent research from Loughborough University,[240] which found that in London and Birmingham, cities which encompass the greatest concentrations of child poverty, there were a dozen constituencies 'showing the majority of children living below the poverty line.' Even more disturbing is the fact that this data didn't yet account for the widespread job losses and economic volatility resulting from the pandemic. Also distressing are figures from the Joseph Rowntree Foundation,[241] which highlight that around 1.8 million children are growing up in what is known as 'very deep poverty', in which the level of household income is inadequate to even cover the basics. That children in one of the wealthiest countries in the world are living in these circumstances is shameful.

The pandemic has now brought these prevalent and urgent issues into the forefront of the public consciousness. Drawing on his own childhood experiences, footballer Marcus Rashford highlighted the issue of child food poverty through his free school meal campaign, and subsequent initiatives to support disadvantaged children.[242] And as Geoff Barton, the General Secretary of the headteacher's union ASCL, pointed out, during remote learning, educators often had a stark window into the circumstances of their students' lives. He told us of the distress and horror provoked by this view into these often narrow and deprived worlds. 'What you found from teachers teaching online through Teams and Zoom and so on is they suddenly were getting a glimpse into the worlds of these young people. And in some cases seeing the absolute depth of the kind of impoverishment there. And I think that was for some very upsetting.'

The consequences of this impoverishment are far-reaching in terms of opportunity, life chances for the children themselves, and for our society as a whole. As we saw earlier, since schools reopened in September 2020, 100,000 children have all but slipped out of sight from the school register.[243] While the reasons for these severe absences are clearly multi-factorial, figures from the Centre for Social Justice highlight a correlation with poverty. They note that 2.4 per 100 pupils eligible for free school meals were severely absent in autumn 2020, compared to 0.7 per 100 pupils not eligible for free school meals, representing a significant disparity.[244]

In her impassioned final speech as Children's Commissioner,[245] Anne Longfield spoke powerfully of the overarching effects of poverty, and how, without addressing its spiralling effects, it would be impossible to make meaningful inroads in terms of 'recovery' after the pandemic. Alluding to the impending reduction in Universal Credit uplift, she said, 'If the Government is really focused on educational catch-up, it wouldn't even countenance pushing 800,000 children into the type of devastating poverty which can have a much bigger impact on their life chances than the school they go to or the catch-up tuition they get.'

Another group whose interests have been historically sidelined and disregarded is disabled children. We started this chapter with the account of a parent of a disabled child, Sara, because the reality of the pandemic response was almost invariably to make life unthinkably hard for families with children with particular needs. However, it was one of the very features of the pandemic that often what went on within families happened behind closed doors, making it hard for the outside world to fully appreciate the painful reality 'from the inside'.

In an effort to advance understanding of these unique and devastating challenges, in its report 'Living in a COVID World'[246] a House of Lords committee reported testimony from families of disabled children. It concluded that 'for the parents of disabled children, the pandemic has had a particular and often catastrophic impact. Some who had previously received support from a range of professionals 24 hours a day were left to look after their children almost entirely alone. Others feared that cancelled health and social care appointments had resulted in deteriorations in their children's conditions that may be irreversible. The parents of disabled children that we personally heard from felt that they had been abandoned during this pandemic, with damaging consequences for their own wellbeing and for their children.'[247]

As with the other vulnerabilities we have highlighted throughout this chapter, this abandonment of parents of disabled children was less a new issue than a worsening one. A SCOPE report in 2014 found that 9 out of 10 parents of disabled children felt isolated, while 47% had seen their GP due to stress.[248]

However, the pandemic response cast these abandoned families even further out into the wilderness. In May 2020, the Disabled Children's Partnership published a report detailing how disabled families and their children had been impacted by the pandemic. It was called 'Left in Lockdown',[249] a title that sums up the haunting treatment of disabled children and their families over the last two years, its findings reflecting the lived experiences of children like Sara. Over three-quarters of these families had had vital care and support suspended altogether.

The first-hand testimony from the House of Lords report reveals the impossibility of what was asked of disabled children and their families: 'Not only were we in lockdown and were shielding, but we also had to get rid of our care and support that we normally have. She has overnight support, so a typical night for me would be staying up until 4 or 5 o'clock in the morning and then getting up the next day and having to do three children's home-schooling, and also having to work as well and keep the household going'.

The sheer exhaustion families faced was clear: 'To say that I'm absolutely exhausted would be an understatement… How can you have a year with no sleep and all the other things that we have to do on top of that and then be okay at the end of it. I feel like I've aged 10 years in a year, basically.'

Another parent said, 'Don't get me wrong, I know that's life for a lot of people, but add that on to the 24-hour exhaustion. A couple of days ago I couldn't even remember my own name. I just couldn't think beyond anything. I was so ashamed, that's the word I want to use, because I couldn't eloquently get across what I needed because my brain just wouldn't connect, and so I went back and just sobbed afterwards because I felt like such a failure for not being able to advocate the way I should have been because of exhaustion.'

The report also contains harrowing examples of children who have missed key developmental windows, with one comment reading: 'She has Botox in her wrist because her spasticity is very high. The Botox should be every four months; the last time was in August, before that it was in January, before that in January 2019. We've got no hope of getting it now. The longer the spasticity remains the less effective it is next time because of the contractions in her muscles. This is irreversible damage that she's getting because we can't get the treatment that we need.'

Another parent quoted said, 'My daughter has now developed scoliosis over the last year which she didn't have before. She was starting to walk independently before lockdown, and now she has a developmental problem with her hips. This is in the space of a year.'

Of the distressing reports we have heard ourselves from families with children with additional needs, none has affected us more than the story of a parent of a severely autistic child whose behaviour deteriorated to such an extent during the prolonged periods of isolation and confinement associated with lockdown that the child ended up being taken into residential care. Breaking down as he spoke to us, the parent said, 'Lockdown put the cherry on the cake'.

Many of the issues for these children pre-date the pandemic and stem from a chronic underinvestment in children's services. However, during the pandemic, such help as does exist was – incredibly – often turned off.

Families were, with very little notice, abandoned by the state. Many disabled children have education health and care plans (EHCPs); during the first lockdown the legal obligation to provide these plans was withdrawn, resulting in the loss of all formal support for these children: school, essential therapies, care. At the same time, access to informal support from families and friends ceased. In many cases that left parents and young siblings taking on around the clock care responsibilities, in some cases including for children who need 24-hour support for basic needs such as toileting, feeding and administering medical treatments.

In addition to the suspension of essential support and therapies, there has been a failure to acknowledge the fundamental unsuitability of Covid mitigations for some of these children. As one report notes, 'providers and parents reported how use of face coverings by staff or pupils can act as a trigger for many pupils, resulting in behaviours which would present more immediate risk (to adults and pupils) than potential cross-infection',[250] and we heard repeated complaints from parents of children with special needs within our own network, dismayed at the impact of mask-wearing by others and social distancing on their children. 'My child has an aversion to face masks. We already know that. He will attack people wearing them, scratching and punching them', said one parent. 'There is just absolutely no way he can social distance. He doesn't get it, why would he? He doesn't understand personal space at the best of times. That's why we don't go out. So I just cannot see him getting on back at college,' said another.[251]

Even as normality has been restored to the rest of the population, at the time of writing many of these families have not, according to Stephen Kingdom, Campaign Manager of the Disabled Children's Partnership, had their full support reinstated. Given that many of these children have seen their conditions regress over the last two years, this is deeply troubling. As Stephen explains, 'we are really concerned about that backlog and what level of unidentified need is stored up in the system – for example, if children haven't been attending their usual settings, will their needs have been picked up?'.

In this respect the House of Lords report is sobering. 'It is clear to us that one of the long-term implications of the pandemic will be many more families needing various kinds of support. But it is also clear that, as things stand, this support is not available.'[252]

A fact which is too little discussed, but was raised clearly and passionately by Anne Longfield, is the *interconnectedness* of these vulnerabilities. There is, in fact, a group of children facing a combination of challenges and disadvantages including an 'unstable home environment, poverty, social and emotional health problems, communication difficulties, or caring for family members.'[253]

For these children, school represents an anchor. For children in poverty, school represents structure, a hot meal, and a chance to improve their life chances. For those at risk of abuse or neglect, it is a chance to be seen. For disabled children and their families, the loss of school, structured services and support may be make-or-break in an already precarious balancing act.

We end this chapter with one more piece of witness testimony given to the Lords Committee:

'I wonder how as a society we can justify this in years to come, because just looking at the little cross-section that we have here of how detrimental it's been, not just to our own health, but the siblings that don't have any problems, to the children that have these disabilities and the life-long impact it's going to have on their lives... I wonder how as a society looking back we'll ever be able to justify the neglect of these children who are human beings.'

We wonder too. This failure of our most vulnerable children and families must not be brushed under the rug of post-crisis selective memory. It wasn't a pandemic blip, or an oversight made in a state of emergency. It was the painful culmination of long-standing blindness and sheer indifference to their plight.

Chapter 7
An Ear-splitting Warning Siren

'Have I missed the mark, or, like a true archer,
do I strike my quarry? Or am I prophet of lies,
a babbler from door to door?'
Cassandra, speaking in Agamemnon, by Aeschylus

The harms which have arisen from lockdown and school closures are now so overwhelming and so incontrovertible that many of those who originally advocated for them now distance themselves from that position.

For those of us who expressed concern from the beginning, this is a bittersweet pill to swallow.

If, in the spring of 2020, you thought that lockdowns and school closures were a bad idea, you would have been unlikely to have been foolhardy enough to voice that position publicly. Those who did were variously slandered, smeared and de-platformed – some are yet to recover their careers.

However, a brave few did stand up, and regardless of consequence warned with urgency, courage and conviction about the inevitable consequences of a pandemic response which prioritised one type of harm and failed to consider all others.

No one was better placed to understand the breadth and longevity of potential harms than Anne Longfield, Children's Commissioner for England at the time the pandemic first struck. Anne retired from the role in February 2021. An article published in the *Guardian* around the time of her retirement reads:

'At midday today applications close for the next children's commissioner for England. There was never greater need for a fearless defender of children to take over from the admirable Anne Longfield, whose six-year term ends in February. After a decade of destruction there is a crisis in every children's service. Taking on this job will be a dauntingly dispiriting task, as report after report from every quarter chronicles rising numbers of children falling into deprivation with dwindling help. The post carries a Cassandra curse: to see all that's happening, to keep waving red flags of irrefutable evidence, but with no power to act.'[254]

As parents who spoke out relatively early in the pandemic about what we perceived as the near-certain harms that would arise from locking down – really, 'locking in' – children, we too felt that Cassandra curse, and we are not alone. Many of those people we interviewed for this book, and others we didn't have the chance to speak to, expressed severe misgivings about the pandemic response based on their years of experience and knowledge of what is needed to keep children safe.

It is one of the great tragedies of the last two years that as a collective, those voices failed to cut through.

Through her role as Children's Commissioner for England, Anne Longfield's robust interventions often challenged policymakers.

In April 2020, just weeks after the first lockdown, a paper authored by Anne's office poignantly questioned 'We're all in this together?',[255] the aim of which, it explained, was 'to better identify vulnerable children who need help both during the lockdown and beyond'. The paper cautioned that 'the loss of support networks, alongside the anxiety and financial pressures caused by Covid-19', was likely to push certain families to crisis point, and it warned, paragraph by paragraph, of the particular categories of children who were likely to be at most risk: those in families under increased pressure, those with SEND, those facing abuse and exploitation by criminal gangs, those in care settings and especially unregulated settings, those living in poverty, with poor internet access and in poor housing conditions.

'There are many hundreds of thousands of children in England living in households where there is domestic violence, adult mental ill health and substance abuse', said the report. 'Many of them are not known to social services. For those who are known to services, during the current crisis, there is a real risk that many more will become "invisible".'

This paper now looks hauntingly prescient.

We spoke to Anne about her recollections of those first few weeks of the pandemic. She reflected on her worries 'for those kids that had had particular vulnerabilities in their lives… because they wouldn't have other people around them that they could talk to, they wouldn't have that stability of school. They wouldn't get the services of support they might get in school. And also their families wouldn't get the support that they would normally get.'

She recalled, too, her 'dismay' on hearing that only some 6% of vulnerable children[256] had attended school in those early weeks, rightly realising that this marked a *de facto* failure of the vulnerable child attendance regime, which we now know had tragic consequences. She recalls arguing that there would be huge numbers of children exposed to 'hidden vulnerabilities' and that the parameters for that regime should be widened beyond simply children with social workers to all children 'in need'. It was her view that the situation for especially vulnerable children warranted a national effort involving 'schools plus social workers and an army of volunteers if needs be.'

'That was the level of priority it needed', she recalls, 'I was constantly nagging about it.' Her office had been 'watching the attendance figures very, very closely. We were analysing them.'

Anne acknowledges what is by now well known and discussed in Chapter 4 – that in fact it was known relatively early on that schools could be reopened safely, pointing to a piece of research around nurseries near NHS hospitals which had shown that it was possible to develop secure environments free from outbreaks.[257]

There were 'weeks and weeks and weeks where I was arguing that kids should be back in school', Anne tells us. She became so concerned, in fact, that she made a very public intervention on 16 May 2020,[258] imploring Government and the unions to 'stop squabbling' and commissioning a laudable paper in which she pointed out that a number of other countries had sent their schools back, and that while the scientific evidence on the safety of reopening schools was limited, 'there is overwhelming evidence that prolonged periods out of school is extremely damaging for all children, but particularly so for vulnerable and disadvantaged children.'

Anne explained, 'At that point I'd been arguing quite loudly for probably about three weeks that kids should be back in school. If you think they went out in March, they'd already been at home for two months. It was pretty obvious at that point that it [schools opening] could work, especially primary school-aged kids.'

That was 16 May 2020.

It is sobering to think how much harm might have been avoided had the Government properly weighed this unambiguous warning from the one person who, above all others, they had specifically tasked with the role of guarding children's interests.

Dr Rosie Gray is a forensic child psychologist with two decades of experience in child safeguarding and social work. As she explained to us in the context of discussing the increase in child trauma and abuse cases during the periods of lockdown and school closures: 'Arguably many of these harms were predictable. There were effectively fewer "eyes and ears" on children at a time that known risk factors for abuse and neglect were heightened. They were spending more time in the digital world, often with less supervision, during a period that online offending was increasing. Early evidence of educational disengagement and increased absenteeism was also seemingly ignored. Furthermore, it was already well-established that certain groups of children are more vulnerable to abuse, though such research appears to have been overlooked in the pandemic strategy. Infants, for example, are known to be a 'high-risk' group and might therefore have been offered additional protections from the outset. Sadly, however, they were not and, in England, there was a rise in reports of abuse amongst this group between April and September 2020.'

She concludes, 'It seems to me that we went into a period of uncertainty in terms of the virus, but we had a lot of certainty and a very well-established evidence base concerning child safeguarding risk factors for child maltreatment and what works in reducing that risk and all of that evidence was somehow overlooked or not used in the way that it could have been.'

A succession of other voices raised the alarm about what appeared, even then, to be safeguarding red flags, including:

Childline, 27 March 2020 – even in that very first week, reported a 10% rise in calls.[259]

NSPCC, 2 April 2020 – 'The impact of the coronavirus lockdown has increased online risks and brewed a perfect storm for offenders to abuse children.'[260]

NSPCC, 11 May 2020 – 'at the NSPCC we are becoming increasingly concerned about the safety of some children who may be hidden from sight during the coronavirus crisis.'[261]

Letter from cross-party MPs to Priti Patel, Home Secretary, 16 April 2020 – 'A terrible and disturbing aspect of this pandemic is that illegal activity online, including child abuse, appears to be escalating.'[262]

A *BMJ* **editorial** in April 2020 – entitled 'A shift in focus is needed to avoid an irreversible scarring of a generation', the paper pointed out that a perfect storm of factors: the locking of children in 'pressure cooker' environments, the absence of external oversight, a 22% increase in alcohol sales since the start of the lockdown – risked a 'secondary pandemic' of child neglect and abuse.[263]

In the context of the third lockdown, in January 2021 express warnings were also given about the likelihood of more young people being put at further risk of exploitation from county lines drugs gangs, with the Children's Society saying: 'And learning from previous lockdowns we know that when children are not accessing education they're often at more risk from perpetrators looking to control and exploit them'.[264]

Professor Ellen Townsend has been one of the most vocal advocates for children throughout the pandemic, from the earliest days of restrictions. A respected academic, leading the Self-Harm Research Group (SHRG) at the University of Nottingham, Ellen has worked extensively with vulnerable young people.

In speaking with us, she recounts how her initial reluctant acceptance of school closures as a short-lived emergency measure soon turned to desperate concern.

'I was worried straight away with schools closing, but I was willing to say three weeks was OK if we need to get stuff sorted. As soon as it was clear that they weren't going to start rolling it back pretty quickly, my "spidey-sense" told me this is not going to be great. Because of the work that I do, I work with children who have been abused and neglected and had really difficult lives. My immediate thoughts went to them, and thinking that those children are going to be the ones who suffer the most. I worried that if we didn't get out of it really quickly, what would happen to them?'

Professor Townsend says the lack of broader questioning within academia and wider society inhibited her input initially, though in the background she concentrated on developing a child-focused social media presence to highlight the impacts. Then, in June 2020, in a blog for the University of Nottingham, she urged policymakers to release young people from lockdown as early as possible, specifically highlighting the mental health impact of the response.[265]

The fact that she felt the piece was 'risky' says a great deal about the prevailing sentiment at the time. At that point, these wider issues of children's wellbeing had barely featured.

Shortly after, on learning that most children wouldn't in fact be going back to school before September, despite the growing evidence of mental health harm, she told us that 'something snapped'. She worked with academic colleagues to coordinate an open letter to the Secretary of State for Education Gavin Williamson, robustly calling out the 'neglect' of children in government policy. Published in the *Sunday Times*, the milestone comment piece slammed the 'dangerous omission' of scientific expert input on SAGE concerning young people's mental health and urged the government to 'prioritise children and adolescents in the release from lockdown as a matter of utmost urgency in order to prevent a national crisis and the decimation of their futures.'[266]

Despite media traction from this letter, and Professor Townsend's subsequent interventions, there was little sign of engagement from policymakers themselves. The academics called-for summer playschemes never materialised, schools were closed for the second time in January 2021, and lockdown restrictions were re-imposed – despite the ample evidence base of harm by that time.

Ellen points to society's overall deprioritisation of

children and the absence of early data, as well as the lack of a cabinet-level children's minister as likely reasons for why her warnings were not heeded. She adds, 'I think they [Whitehall] are squeamish about mental health. I think there's something deeply odd with the way that they seem to want to deal with mental health.'

Her own compulsion to speak out was informed by her role as a parent as well as her work with young people. 'I often reflect on whether I would've been as brave standing up for young people as I have been if it weren't for them (my children). I spent my most of my academic career working with vulnerable young people. I have had sleepless nights thinking about them, just knowing all the stories that I've been told over the years. So I really hope I would've been, I really hope I would've been brave and still stood up for them, but I think being a mum has been a huge part of my advocacy.'

And now? 'I'm still worried', she says. 'I'm worried about general cognitive development across the board because of lack of interaction, lack of socialisation, lack of face-to-face contact and lack of education. We know that missing out on a decent education is life-limiting and by contrast having a really good education is a way to move yourself out of poverty. We know this, we've known this for years, so I do worry about that.'

Furthermore, the safeguarding outcomes warned of by so many are on her mind. 'We've got over a hundred thousand children missing from our education system now because of the lockdowns. And we've got no handle on where they are or what's happened to them. I find that extraordinary that we seem to be quite happy to live with that.'

Professor Townsend continues to 'shout' – as she says – for children and young people's interests.[267]

We must ask ourselves, why did such a highly qualified psychologist need to shout at all?

* * *

Dr Ellie Cannon, known as 'Dr Ellie', is a GP, author and broadcaster who is a familiar and reassuring presence in the UK media via her column in the *Mail on Sunday* and appearances on mainstream outlets such as Sky News, ITV News and Radio 4.

Her experience at the intersection of parenting, media, and healthcare gave Dr Ellie a unique window into the horrifying risks facing children as a result of lockdown and school closure measures. And she has spoken up vociferously for them, especially regarding the disparity between adult and child restrictions, the impact of self-isolation, and mental health.

She told us of her frustration at the lack of societal insight into the issues children were likely to face. In particular, she challenges the early-held notion that because 'vulnerable children' were permitted to access school places, this would mitigate risks effectively. In fact, according to Ellie, it should have been glaringly obvious that children would slip through the cracks – sometimes irrevocably so.

'I recognise this being a parent and also being a GP. People were very quick, early on, to say, "well, it's fine because the vulnerable children will be in school". Even though we know that many vulnerable people didn't opt for the school place. But the perception was – you have the vulnerable children, then you have everybody else. That's not actually how life works. You have the known vulnerable children. And then you have the unknown vulnerable children, who are perhaps more at risk because nobody knows that they're vulnerable. Those children were hidden the whole way through the pandemic, whether they were vulnerable in terms of their physical health, their mental health, abuse, social harms, whatever it was.'

In speaking with us, her voice reflects shock at society's blindness to this danger. 'Nobody was looking at this group of children who we didn't know would be at risk. It was amazing to me that people couldn't see that there weren't simply two categories of children – vulnerable or not. There's actually an entire spectrum. '

It's painful to recognise how closely her comments echo the concerns of Anne Longfield, Professor Townsend and Dr Rosie Gray. The harms to a large cohort of children were both intuitive and foreseeable. Importantly, while children from disadvantaged backgrounds were likely to be most affected, Dr Ellie highlights the fact that all children were in fact at risk of these collateral harms. She adds that as a parent, she felt terror about how swiftly a child could change from thriving to struggling and the 'children who one could easily pass off as being not vulnerable, who very quickly become vulnerable.'

In October 2020, along with other GP colleagues, she wrote to Secretary of State for Health and Social Care Matt Hancock, warning of the harms of lockdown, including the impact on babies, children, and young people, highlighting among other issues the 'concerning signal that child suicide death rates in the UK increased during lockdown and amongst those reported after lockdown.'[268]

These were serious matters, but the response by Matt Hancock to the healthcare professionals' carefully thought-out letter was underwhelming. At the time Dr Ellie wrote in her column of the 'belittling' way in which the Secretary of State had 'cut and pasted' sections from a previous article of his own, as well as one by junior health minister Nadine Dorries. She had initially been optimistic that the letter may have sparked dialogue, but was left 'seething' at the lack of empathy.[269]

When we spoke, she seemed more despairing than furious, attributing the failure to heed warnings to overwhelming apathy. This is a bleak judgement, but one which many of us can relate to. We too experienced the same brick wall of silence, or if we were lucky, cut and pasted replies. She said, 'Whether you spoke to people on the street or whether I spoke to people when I was on television or when I wrote to the Secretary of State... The general narrative was that people were just not interested'.

Dr Ellie's own sense of urgency was prompted by her children. 'The truth is... I was trying to save my own children's lives.... I don't mean that dramatically. I was trying to save and protect their lives and I could see what was happening in my own household, but it was mirrored, everywhere else – in my GP surgery, nationally, absolutely everywhere. And I shouted really very selfishly because I just wanted to protect my own children. And I could see that I couldn't.'

It is a damning indictment that this healthcare professional of public standing, with years of loyal service to the NHS, was unable to make her voice heard to policymakers.

Robert Halfon MP is Conservative MP for Harlow and the Chair of the House of Commons Education Select Committee that scrutinises the work of the Department for Education, including children's social care, schools, colleges, the early years and higher education. He has often described himself as a 'school-down sceptic not a lockdown sceptic', and he confirmed to us that he opposed school closures 'from day one'.

'I thought it was a disastrous decision to close the schools for most pupils. They said that most vulnerable kids could go – but we know in the first lockdown, over 90% of vulnerable children didn't go to school.'

He goes on to explain the other foreseeable catastrophes that are now all too clear. 'I've described it as the four horsemen of the education apocalypse galloping towards our children in terms of lost educational attainment, mental health problems on the rise, safeguarding hazards... and of course damaging their life chances in terms of earning as good a living...'.

In highlighting these issues through broadcast and print media as early as June 2020, Robert Halfon described the UK as a 'strange country' for opening pubs before enabling all children to return to school.[270]

Yet, he told us, the reaction to his advocacy was mostly critical in these first months when the battle to reopen schools was still raging. 'At the time when I first started to campaign to keep schools open, which was quite early on, I had a pile of **** on my head from so many people, from even my local press, and all kinds of people, who said it was outrageous.'

Halfon remains adamant that schools should never have closed, particularly because of the impact on disadvantaged children, and describes it as a 'wrongheaded decision that should never have happened… and it must never happen again.'

He acknowledges the fear that surrounded the decisions in the first lockdown even if he, unlike others, believes school closures were always the wrong choice. 'I remember going to my local Sainsbury's and it was like something out of a horror movie, there was nothing on the shelves. I can sort of understand… there was panic.'

The decisions that followed, when the impact became clear, and the warnings were becoming starker, were, he felt, less justifiable. He says 'as it went on and you realised the remote learning wasn't working… that it was a complete lottery. So why was it allowed to continue? I don't know the answer to it.'

We finally come to the parents, including ourselves. We came together initially in May 2020 together with our third co-founder Christine Brett as tentative voices united by a firmly held conviction that something was very wrong. The early days of our campaigning were marked by urgent phone calls, and hastily written but heartfelt letters to state and third sector children's organisations, including the Children's Minister, the Secretary of State for Education and the Children's Commissioner. We instinctively felt that children's wellbeing was threatened and we were horrified to see protections such as the UNCRC crumble.

Over the first few weeks of the campaign, we were overwhelmed as our band of three very quickly grew to thousands: parents, professionals, paediatricians and experts, all sharing a sense of deep unease about the potential reach and impact of the pandemic response on children. In those early days, we had hoped that a collective of that volume would at least be listened to by policymakers, though as has been expressed by others we quickly became disillusioned as letters – to ministers, departments, MPs, and officials and organisations – went unanswered or were summarily dismissed.

As one parent writes, 'The first few weeks felt like an adventure for most people. The weather was fine, and we spent much of our time in the garden, and walking around the neighbourhood spotting the teddy bears our school friends had placed in their windows, for other families to find. But, as the weeks dragged into months, I grew increasingly concerned not just for the welfare and mental health of my own children, but for their classmates. One little girl in particular, who I knew went through hell at home. So too were most of the parents in my circle. This wasn't right, and we all knew it. In April 2020, I started a two-year long correspondence with my Labour MP. This was back when I believed that MPs could be appealed to with reason. When I believed that if I presented a strong enough argument, they would do the right thing. I argued that the school closures were a breach of the UNCRC, something I believe in even more strongly today.'

From the very start, there has been a tendency to dismiss the view of parents as being insufficiently expert to comment on the public health disaster unfolding. However, parents are uniquely placed to understand what is and isn't best for their children. That expertise is borne out of years of first-hand experience in child-rearing. We are now starting to understand the implications of so readily dismissing that instinct in favour of narrow scientific credentialism.

Cassandra, doomed to be disbelieved, didn't just want to be vindicated about the veracity of her warnings, she wanted to stop Troy from falling.[271] Similarly, none of us ever wanted to be looking aghast at the myriad impacts of school closures and restrictions on children in the rear-view mirror. We wanted to change the course of events before the harms took root. Looking on helplessly at the destruction of everything she loved, Cassandra's prophecies brought her only despair. Our conversations with advocates suggest that many are now haunted by similar feelings as what they feared has unfolded: day by day, report by report, child by child. In such circumstances, there is no comfort in warnings being proven correct, there is only sadness and anger.

Breaking away from the analogy, in our modern-day tragedy those sounding the alarm about the catastrophe unfolding for children were not seers. They were simply observing what was predictable, based on their knowledge and experience, which amply qualified them to speak up.

Despite their knowledge and experience, these individuals could not engage with policymakers to ensure that their valid concerns flowed through to timely action: especially in the first months of the emergency. Parents, safeguarding experts, concerned politicians, GPs, and even the Children's Commissioner were either not in the room where critical decisions were made, or not heeded. In some cases, academics and campaigners were actively silenced.

The shortfall of the state and society's response to these prescient warnings reflects a complex societal and structural failing that we explore in later chapters.

One conclusion, though, is simple. It was not the advocates' failing; it was the failing of those who, for whatever reason, did not – and still do not – listen.

Chapter 8
Playing Politics with Children's Lives

'Unlike other groups, children don't vote or have unions.' When we set up UsForThem in May 2020 and began drafting the copy for our overarching goals, the above message rang clear in our minds. We had an uneasy sense that children were largely voiceless, and structurally underrepresented in a crisis dominated by more powerful political bodies and special interest organisations. It was no accident that our mission statement somewhat acerbically pointed out that fact.

What we didn't know, though, was the extent of the fierce battle that was already in full swing between teaching unions and the government as Gavin Williamson, the Secretary of State for Education, ineffectually attempted to reopen schools. Nor did we understand the context of school closures in March 2020 – an unprecedented break with disaster planning that many struggle to comprehend even now. Yet, even in our naivety, we intuitively grasped that children had become political footballs amid the fear and panic, and that their interests were unrepresented.

An unedifying battle often raged over the top of children's heads, and rarely did any adult break off from the altercation to ask how the children cowering beneath the metaphorical cross-fire were faring.

This conflict – with the twin disasters of ensuing school closures and excessive mitigations – has been mired in partisan politicking in the UK, and even more extremely in the US. There are no easy answers. However, we must reflect on how a cocktail of pre-existing tensions between the left and right, narrowly-focused but politically engaged unions, a febrile atmosphere of fear, and an increasingly politicised and ideological scientific debate have contributed to a devastating array of impacts on children and young people. In this chapter, we are specifically discussing the role of teaching unions, as opposed to headteacher unions which navigated a more nuanced path throughout the pandemic.

School closures framed primarily as workers' rights instead of child welfare

In the UK, since as early as February 2020, the teaching unions have been a constant party to discussions about school closures and mitigations, including the vocal National Education Union (NEU), which represents 460,000 teachers and school staff across the UK. The push-pull dynamic between the union leaders and the incumbent Secretary of State for Education often dominated the discourse.

A similar dynamic played out in the US.

Unions are undoubtedly a positive and necessary force to protect workers' rights. Pre-pandemic, the NEU had played a valuable role in the ongoing debate about wider education issues such as educational budget funding, league tables, child poverty and the role of exams and assessments. Education has been historically underfunded – a failure of successive Conservative governments – and the frustrations that many in the teaching profession have felt about the undervaluing of their roles has been valid. A lack of value placed on education over the years can only have contributed to a climate of bitterness and resentment, and we have seen how funding cuts have disproportionately affected the most disadvantaged areas.[272]

However, throughout the pandemic response, the teaching unions revealed a different guise that may not have previously been apparent to the public or their own members. The NEU itself highlights the 'powerful voice' it brings to bear and has an overt and acknowledged political role. While not affiliated to any party, it does run a separate political fund which, according to *SchoolsWeek*, was established to 'allow the union to undertake campaigning of a political nature.'[273]

This background suggests a wider remit of the NEU, which during 'peace time' may not have directly affected children, but which became dominant during the 'war' of the Covid response. At times, it became difficult to unpick the NEU's defence of legitimate principles of workers' rights from a much broader conflict between a self-styled politically interested group and its instinctive foe, the incumbent Conservative government.

As we learned more about the nature of the crisis, we began to question – first privately, and then more publicly – the extent to which the actions of the NEU represented an opportunity to advance a political agenda, as well as genuine concern for its members.

First-mover advantage and a series of unfortunate events

In business, the 'first-mover' advantage describes the competitive benefits enjoyed by the first occupant of a market. In the pandemic discourse around schools, the teaching unions entered the fray early, and thus influenced the terms of future debate. Their first-mover status in March 2020 seemed to shape the discussion about school closures in terms of school and staff safety. In this frame of reference, school closures were viewed through the same lens we would use to consider the closure of any other workplace.

Ben Irvine, an independent writer, provides a helpful chronology of events[274] from the earliest days of 2020. He notes that as early as February, the GMB union wrote to local authority chief executives about the evolving situation, noting their responsibilities for sick pay in the event of isolation. At this point, there were only a handful of identified cases in the UK and the trajectory of the pandemic then accelerated quickly.

On 4 March 2020 Italy ordered the closure of its schools and on 14 March 2020 the NEU made its first intervention in a letter to the UK government, which asked why we had not done the same:

> *'Every day we are getting increasing numbers of questions from teachers and support staff asking why the Westminster Government isn't following the pattern of other countries in calling for periods of school closure.*
>
> *Those questions are increasingly asking why schools aren't closing if mass gatherings are to be suspended.'*[275]

Of course at this point, we were in the middle of an escalating spiral of fear and anxiety, with commentators looking especially to the situation unfolding in Italy. While in hindsight most now agree that school closures were a devastating mistake, the NEU's advocacy for its members was at this point understandable.

However, this early communication immediately draws a comparison between schools and 'mass gatherings'. To us, this seemed to be reductive language, which didn't distinguish between the uniquely important role of schools and other plainly 'non-essential' gatherings of adults. It was an early signal of the asymmetric framing of the discourse that considered schools primarily in terms of adult staff, rather than the children in them.

Of course, schools are not the same as other mass gatherings or workplaces – this was always a false premise. They are essential wellbeing hubs for children and families, providing sanctuary, social interaction, and community. As we now know, the impact of school closures on vulnerable and disadvantaged children and families was stark.

However, without a balance of strong voices at the very outset, advocating for children's welfare versus the initially legitimate concerns about school safety, the UK Government set out on a destructive course of action.

And in the absence of an initial acknowledgement of what schools actually represented, a skewed decision-making framework persisted throughout the pandemic.

On 17 March the NEU called formally for school closures, referring once again to the 'contradiction'of mass gatherings.[276] The following day, on 18 March, Gavin Williamson advised that schools would close for all but keyworker and vulnerable children. We may never know how much the NEU's letter influenced the final decision, which was made among increasing clamour for school closures from the public, parents and the media. However, what we do know is that closing schools proved to be a far simpler matter than getting them open again, especially since the Government had accepted the 'mass gathering' fallacy. Meanwhile, around the country, children were suffering – and few stepped forward into the political arena to speak up for them.

Professor Paul Dolan, a specialist in behavioural science at the London School of Economics, tells us of his surprise at the lack of intervention from left-wing politicians about the plight of vulnerable children behind closed doors. He described his reaction to the initial March 2020 lockdown and school closures: 'You would expect some of the voices on the left for example, that would typically be speaking up for disadvantaged, underprivileged kids of people to come out and say, hold on a minute, if we're going to do this, if, which is in itself questionable, have we put any measures in place that would ensure that the impact on those children is at least mitigated?'.

Instead, there was a void, since much of the school closure discussion from the left had already been framed in the context of perceived lack of safety for adults rather than the implications for children.

Further, as we saw, especially in the political narrative from the US, there was a sense that the only reason the 'right'wanted to reopen schools was for economic objectives:

productivity, not education and safeguarding. There may have been some truth in this perception, but this was no reason to override considerations of children's welfare.

Robert Halfon MP, Chair of the Education Select Committee, told us of the problem of this uneven weighting of the political debate, saying:

'There wasn't enough leadership at the time. I think the government was scared. You had active opposition to schools opening from the Labour Party at that time and the unions. And some of the scientists were saying that the schools should be shut. So, there was a whole load of pressure, but not enough was being done to look at the overall impact on children. And it was like a weighing scale weighing everything in one direction rather than [considering] what are the other bigger risks to children in terms of mental health, safeguarding, lifetime chances, educational attainment, impact on the disadvantaged and so on.'

Putting the toothpaste back in the tube

The following months saw a painful process in which the Department for Education attempted to put the toothpaste back in the tube and bring children back into school. As we began to learn more about the risk stratification of the disease, the role of teaching unions and scientific activists in dictating the course of events became less easy to justify.

By May 2020, schools in France and 22 other European countries had begun to open. The UK's Education Secretary, Gavin Williamson, stated his aim for a 'phased reopening'.[277] The NEU described the proposal, which pinpointed 1 June as the date for reopening to Reception, Year 1, and Year 6 pupils, as 'reckless'.[278] But in the nations where schools had already reopened, there had been no sign of any meaningful impact on infections.[279]

In a Zoom meeting on 14 May 2020, Dr Mary Bousted , the Joint General Secretary of the NEU, aired her views about this recklessness in a now notorious exchange. She especially condemned the government's decision to prioritise younger students for return, saying that these smaller children would be unable to observe 'social distancing – who are mucky, who spread germs, who touch everything, who cry, who wipe their snot on your trousers or on your dress'.[280] In response to the report, an NEU spokesperson said that the 'Government is putting an unbearable strain on school leaders and the wider education workforce'.

In fact, a body of evidence at the time compiled by UK Research and Innovation indicated that while the role of children in transmitting the virus was 'unclear', children were 'less likely than adults to acquire infection, and less likely to infect family members in the household'.[281] And even at that early stage, the data also hinted that younger children were probably less implicated still. For example, a study from Iceland in April 2020 found that younger children were less likely to test positive than adolescents and no cases had been found in children under 10 years old in random population screening.[282]

Dr Bousted's other comments during this meeting are also revealing. She notes – fairly – that the UK has some of the smallest classrooms and least favourable teacher/child ratios in the developed world, which would impact social distancing. Nevertheless, this could have had no immediate bearing on the active emergency of school closures with their immediate effects on children. Realistically there was no possibility of the Government addressing class sizes and classroom sizes at this point, whatever the failures of the past.

Kate Green, then Shadow Education Secretary, made similar comments later in the year during the Labour Party conference, for which she later apologised, saying:[283]

'I think there's obviously a real immediate pressure to address these funding needs for the crisis. But I think we should use the opportunity, don't let a good crisis go

to waste. We can really see now what happens when you under-resource schools, when you under-resource families and communities.'

We believe that the terror stoked by the Government and the wilful blindness about the risk-stratification of the disease must surely have contributed significantly to the school opening delays. It seemed to us at the time that no matter what data were presented to confirm that teaching staff were at no greater mortality risk than other populations, it was insufficient to overcome the emotional reaction of fear.

At this juncture, the unions were representing the concerns of their members, since many teachers did not feel it was safe to return. Nevertheless, this period marked a low point in adults' apparent inability to put their differences aside. The impasse between the Government and the unions was the context in which, as we saw earlier, Anne Longfield, the Children's Commissioner, urged them to stop 'squabbling'.[284]

When schools eventually reopened in early June 2020, it was only to a handful of primary school year groups, and 'full' reopening – though with an array of safety measures – only occurred in September. Local councils, too, took it upon themselves to obstruct even this meagre compromise position.

It should be a matter of shame to all involved that by summer 2020, most UK children were unable to attend school while adults queued outside Primark or went to the pub. A Children's Commissioner blog from this period strikes at the heart of the matter:

'...we have seen some people celebrating the decision not to proceed with a wider opening of schools as a victory over the Government. It was not for the Government's benefit that schools were re-opening, it was for the benefit of children.'[285]

Indeed.

Nadir of political decision-making

The political dynamic quickly deteriorated again after the September 2020 reopening – which lasted for only one full term – when the government elected to close schools for a second time in January 2021. Having full knowledge of the harms at this stage, this decision surely represented the nadir of pandemic decision-making. And here, in our view, linking events to union influence is a far simpler matter.

With cases and hospitalisations rising, murmurings about school closures had begun over the course of the autumn term. The NEU called for an October 'circuit breaker', which would have effectively shut children out of classrooms for an extra week.[286] As the Christmas holidays approached, tensions mounted and on 3 January 2021 the NEU wrote to its members saying that 'it would, in our view, be unsafe for you to attend the workplace in schools and colleges which were open to all students.' The following day, Boris Johnson announced a third national lockdown that included school closures.

The response of the NEU to this U-turn was quite extraordinary. It effectively claimed 'victory' in a widely criticised email to members:[287]

'We want to start by congratulating you all. It is never easy to stand up and be counted. It takes nerve and courage. But you did it. You stood up for your own safety, for your pupils, their families and your communities.'

The triumphant tone was echoed by Labour MP Zarah Sultana, who Tweeted:[288]

'This U-turn, like the ones before, didn't happen because the government suddenly saw the light. It was because the @NEUnion relentlessly fought for their members' health & safety & made history in the process.'

No matter what your views about the wisdom of the decision, it was surely not a cause for celebration that millions of children, already suffering the ill-effects of previous closures, should be locked out of the school gates once again.

As before, the process of reopening schools fully to all pupils in March involved significant pain and conflict. This time, the agreement to reopen appeared to be conditional on additional restrictions in the form of masks in classrooms.

For much of the following nine months until the time of writing, the tensions between the government and unions centred on the demands for additional measures to make schools 'safer' – circling back to the original framing. Again, this framing failed to consider that restrictions such as 'bubbles', mass isolations, temporary closures and universal masking created further harms for children.

Restrictions effectively became bargaining chips, and once again, in January 2022, masks were reintroduced in classrooms, with Jonathan Gullis MP writing in *The Times*, 'face masks have been a central demand of teaching unions.'[289] To us, this presented a false transaction of school closures or schools open with masks in classrooms.

Given the scant evidence for the benefits of these measures, it's difficult to shrug away the thought that the union stance may have been as much about politicking and 'winning' as the safety of their members.

Similarly, the Government response was often cynically political; choosing to capitulate on 'low cost' measures such as masks that gave the impression of safety, but which did not require the deployment of public funds.

All the costs, after all, were borne by children.

Independent SAGE and the Zero Covid agenda as applied to schools

'Zero Covid' is a pandemic strategy that aims to eliminate the virus.[290] It was modelled most dramatically by China, which was still pursuing stringent zero-tolerance policies by May

2022. In raising the question of scientific evidence, we must touch on how Zero Covid-adjacent groups such as the UK's Independent SAGE often aligned with the interests of those advocating for school closures or gold-plated mitigations in educational settings.

Independent SAGE was established in May 2020 by former Chief Scientific Advisor to Tony Blair, Sir David King. The body quickly established itself in the media with a range of strong and plausible voices, including former WHO advisor Anthony Costello, Susan Michie (who also sat on SAGE), and Christina Pagel.

A genuinely independent scientific group would have been a valuable counterpoint to help shape the pandemic response. Yet, in reality, behind the scenes it was reported that 'the founders and producers' of Independent SAGE were an activist group called 'The Citizens' whose mission was to 'use impact journalism to hold government and big tech to account.'[291]

From inception to as late as January 2021, Independent SAGE members were espousing a Zero Covid strategy;[292,293,294] at one point in July 2020, Sir David King stunningly proposed that schools should not reopen until the UK reached a state of Zero Covid.[295]

The NEU quickly established engagement with Independent SAGE. An interim report produced by the scientists during the fractious period after the first school closures noted that it 'was requested in the context of ongoing disagreement between education unions and the UK government on the reopening of schools in England.'[296]

Independent SAGE and a Zero Covid philosophy also appear to have shaped the NEU's calls for further school mitigations, especially masking. In May 2021, the union coordinated an open letter to Gavin Williamson[297] disputing the lifting of mask guidance, saying: 'while there is significant community transmission (Independent SAGE's suggested threshold is 10 cases/100,000 population/week with strong test, trace isolate and support systems, while Victoria, Australia was successful by targeting <1 case/100,000 population/week), we view face coverings (along with other measures such as improved ventilation, air purification, using outdoor spaces, and mass testing) as an essential part of the wider system of control in schools.'

It is telling that the global Covid Action Group – whose aim is to eliminate Covid – hosted this letter on its website. Indeed, the NEU open letter was signed by several non-UK members, including Prof. Yaneer Bar-Yam, New England Complex Systems Institute, and Dr Zoë Hyde, University of Western Australia, Perth, Australia.

Thankfully, most scientists long ago moved on from discussing Zero Covid as a serious proposition. We can argue over whether or not it was ever a realistic option at all. Still, the firm opinion of the authors is that the extreme and often punitive measures it involved were never compatible with a compassionate, holistic or reasonable public health response, most especially for children.

Red/Blue divides and Trump-mania

The political tug of war and inversion of left/right priorities has been reflected even more starkly in the US than in the UK. The political situation in many US states concerning schools and school closures has been extreme. It is a 'fair is foul' and 'foul is fair' world where masking toddlers and closing schools for almost 18 months is the 'virtuous' position. While we have our impressions as outsiders, we have turned to US parents for their insights and experiences of speaking up as #openschools campaigners.

As in the UK, support for school closures, lockdowns and extended restrictions such as masking came primarily from the left and 'blue states' such as California, while a drive to open schools and oppose restrictions was seen most in 'red states' like Florida and Texas.

The situation around schools in the US was particularly febrile for two reasons: Donald Trump, and election year.

In summer 2020, Trump began calling for schools to reopen, writing in characteristic all-caps on Twitter that 'SCHOOLS MUST OPEN IN FALL.'[298] His support of open schools had one disastrous outcome for children – it entrenched opposition to reopening among Democrats. As in the UK, teaching unions shared this stance, and Trump was criticised for his recklessness and prioritising the economy over lives.

The headlines at the time from UK and US publications speak volumes:

'Reckless, callous, cruel': teachers' chief denounces Trump plan to reopen schools Guardian[299]

Donald Trump's mind-bending logic on school reopenings CNN[300]

Trump wants to reopen schools. Hint: It's not just about education. Politico[301]

Whatever Trump's motivations, the response was telling. To what extent did Democrats' inability to engage with the incumbent administration on this single issue deepen the school closure crisis and extend it beyond reasonableness? As parent Jessica Hockett[302] told us: 'So much in 2020 was caught up with Donald Trump... and that it was a presidential election year, there was so much anti-Trump vitriol built upon, on one side it was always political here.'

Democrat states and Republican states were polarised in terms of the scope of school closures, their length, and then the nature of restrictions in schools. Even more than in the UK, where closures applied in the independent and state sectors alike, a gulf opened up regarding access to in-person schooling between public and private schools.

Professor Jay Bhattacharya documented this division:

'In the US there's really been a big divide between Democrat-led states and red states in how we've treated children through the pandemic. I think almost all of the US shut down schools for some time including just remote learning. But even from early in the pandemic, what happened was there was this rich/poor divide. So public schools were shut down preferentially early in the pandemic and especially in poorer areas, there's no way to substitute… Then as the pandemic wore on many of the 'red' states opened their schools like Florida, for instance, kept at schools 100% open over the objections of teachers' unions who sued the Governor over that decision to open. Whereas where I live in California, the public schools were closed more or less continuously for 18 months.'

This divergence can be attributed not only to Trump-related tensions, but also to the close links between the response in Democrat states and the strength of teaching unions. A study from 2020 documented the correlation between stronger teaching unions and longer closures,[303] and Jennifer Sey, a campaigner and writer, corroborates this from her own experience in California – a hub of heightened restrictions:

'The more uniform politically a particular geography is, and the deeper blue it is, generally speaking, the more power the teachers unions have in those places. And that also drives it… because the teachers' unions have so much power and influence. And my issue from the beginning was teachers' unions are there to protect teachers and fight for teachers. Who's fighting for the kids though?

That's not the union job so in a sense, I guess I can forgive them. But in San Francisco in particular, the Board of Education is supposed to fight for the kids, and they fail to do that. There's no daylight between the Board of Education and the teachers' unions, and so there's no one, but parents like us that are fighting for the kids.'

The effect of this politicking has been to vastly widen existing inequalities in the US through lengthy school closures. Even though schools are now open, in May 2022, some US cities, like New York, have continued with measures such as masking for two-year-olds in daycare while releasing restrictions for all other groups[304] – UK paediatricians and parents have looked on aghast.

It has also upended traditional alliances and tribes, with many formerly Democrat-leaning parents, concerned about the impact on their children, finding themselves politically homeless. According to Jennifer Sey:

'There is not an insignificant portion of parents, that are independent or that are willing to vote that might be registered with one party, but are willing to vote either way... as we saw with the Governor's election in Virginia. A lot of the moms in the suburbs who had voted for Biden, who had voted traditionally Democrat, voted for him solely on the issue of schools... he ran on an open school ticket.'

This dynamic and the fracturing of traditional left/right roles recalls Paul Dolan's comment – why did so few on the left feel able to speak about the likely impact of school closures on children, especially the most vulnerable? This has not only been to the detriment of children, but perhaps also ultimately to the long-term interests of political parties and teaching unions themselves. By leaving a vacuum of discourse, we did not keep more extreme actions and positions in check.

Revisionism

And so we come to the inevitable revisionism. Some have said that, in time, school closures will be akin to the Iraq War – no one will admit to having supported them. At the time of writing, we do seem to be becoming closer to that point.

In March 2022, Jonathan Ashworth MP, the Shadow Work

and Pensions Secretary, was asked whether he thought school closures had been a mistake. He answered: 'We were always very clear that school closures had to be absolutely the "last resort". We never wanted to see schools closed',[305] despite Labour leader Keir Starmer having insisted in January 2021 that school closures were 'inevitable' and should be part of a package of 'national restrictions'.[306]

As Jonathan Chait says, in his thought-provoking article for *New York Intelligencer*:[307] 'Most progressives aren't insisting on refighting the school closing wars. They just want to quietly move on without anybody admitting anybody did anything wrong.' On the other side of the political coin, Jeremy Hunt MP, who demanded in January 2021 that 'all schools should be closed', and regularly spoke in favour of restrictions, appeared on TV in May 2022 saying he thought 'we could have avoided all lockdowns'.[308]

It does no good to try to rewrite history.

When we come to reflect on the consequences of the pandemic response on children, society should honestly appraise the role of teachers' unions, the silence on the left (and indeed much of the right) and the politicisation of science.

It's not only progressives who need to admit their mistakes. Politicians across the ideological spectrum must take a look in the mirror. In a time of emergency, we rely on the government to lead with courage and compassion. Irrespective of the role that activist scientists, the opposition and unions played, ultimately, in the UK, the Conservative government orchestrated a climate of terror, exploited events to children's detriment, and failed to engage effectively with teaching stakeholders.

We leave the final words of this chapter to MP Robert Halfon, chair of the Education Select Committee: 'At the end of the day, the unions will do what they do. The Government has got to lead, they're responsible.'

Chapter 9
The Madness of the Herd

'Men, it has been well said, think in herds; it will be seen
that they go mad in herds, while they only recover their
senses slowly, one by one.'[309]

Charles McKay, *Extraordinary Popular Delusions
and the Madness of Crowds*

By the time UsForThem formed in May 2020, the pandemic
measures had already been in full swing for two months.

By that time, and as Laura Dodsworth vividly explains
in her book, *A State of Fear – How the UK government
weaponised fear during the Covid-19 pandemic*, the British
Government, enthusiastically aided and abetted by much of
the British media, had used a variety of means to effectively
grab control of 'the narrative'.[310] Aggressive public safety
measures had been relayed to the public on near-continuous
loop, via evening press conferences, daily publication of
terrifying death and infection statistics and 'STAY AT HOME'
messages. A willing media had, it seemed at times almost
gleefully, been caught up in the hysteria – as broadcaster Sue
Cook tells us, the media 'like ratcheting up the fear – perhaps
as it gains them more viewers and listeners.' As the saying
goes, 'If it bleeds, it leads.'

Alongside the escalating terror, it seemed that a small
group of scientists was being elevated to such a degree that
they appeared to be effectively dictating public policy. As Jay
Bhattacharya explained in the context of US policy, 'a small

group of very, very powerful scientists and public health officials in effect worked together to create the illusion that lockdown was the only reasonable path forward,' a situation which was not dissimilar to that in the UK. The wise men and women of SAGE were catapulted to unprecedented public prominence: how many of us would have been able to name, let alone readily identify, the Chief and Deputy Chief Medical Officers prior to 2020?

'I think what surprised me', says David Paton, Professor of Industrial Economics at Nottingham University Business School, recalling the days of the first lockdown, was 'the independent scientific and medical advisors and the very public role, which seemed to take on quite an activist role. So instead of being in the background, providing the government with data, which they would use and incorporate from different sources to make decisions, the scientists were put right up front on the press conferences, and it was clear that data were being used to match an agenda, to match policy as opposed to providing advice.'

There is of course another interpretation of the dynamic between SAGE and the Government – that the questions posed by ministers were skewed in a particular direction to yield the results they wanted: so-called 'policy-based evidence making'. Insight in support of this point of view came to light in December 2021 as a result of an extraordinary and revealing social media exchange between Fraser Nelson, editor of the *Spectator*, and Professor Graham Medley, Chair of SAGE's modelling group. Medley revealed, 'We generally model what we are asked to model. There is a dialogue in which policy teams discuss with the modellers what they need to inform their policy.'[311] Even more bizarrely, on being questioned by Nelson as to why the modelling group had not included a scenario of lower virulence of Omicron included in another model by JP Morgan, he added, 'Decision-makers are generally only interested in situations where decisions have to be made'. This head-scratching comment implies such a startling embedded bias towards lockdown measures and interventions that it would be unthinkable for it not to be addressed by the public inquiry.

An inherent government preference for draconian policies is also implied by the apparent blind-eye turned towards the costs of implemented measures, and a lack of rigour in weighing the effectiveness against the potential harms. As David Paton says, 'Where is the evidence that this will lead to an improvement in those deaths? That's never been evaluated properly and rigorously, but then the other side... what are the costs of doing this? What else could we do? What's the opportunity cost of doing that? We've not had that approach still to this day.'

Sue Cook recalls that 'all they were concerned about was stopping the spread and reducing the numbers of deaths and that's all they could think of. So, they didn't think of children. They didn't think about old people...'. Of the media presence at the government briefings she added, 'The journalists were always asking, why aren't you being more strict, more draconian? I've never heard a journalist ask at one of those press conferences, what about children? Not once.'

'It seemed very quickly to me that children just weren't being referenced in national dialogue', comments Anne Longfield. Indeed, to the extent that schools were featuring in national debate it was often because loud voices had, very early on, expressed forthright opinions calling for school closures. For example, Piers Morgan questioned on social media on 16 March 2020 how the Government could justify its position of no longer supporting mass gatherings due to transmission risk, but keep schools open. He asked,

'What does the Govt think happens when 100s of adults go to drop off or pick up their kids from schools?'[312]

Around the same time a *Daily Mirror* headline in huge, bolded letters, asked 'IS IT ENOUGH?' saying of Boris Johnson that 'he refuses to close schools and ban crowds'. The headline ran alongside articles showing pupils themselves calling for school closures.[313]

These calls, as we now know, were not based on robust evidence of effectiveness, and failed altogether to take into account the huge costs associated with such a drastic intervention. Nonetheless, they created a sense of inexorable momentum towards school closures as the next step in pandemic control.

There was much controversy and discussion during the pandemic about the concept of 'herd immunity' – the resistance to the spread of an infectious disease within a population. Another 'herd' concept, less discussed but equally emblematic of the period, is the concept of herd or crowd behaviour. As research into emergency evacuations has found, 'when under highly uncertain and stressful situations, an individual tends to follow others almost blindly.'[314] Similarly, during the emergency of the Covid crisis we saw multiple examples of herd behaviour – some positive, some destructive – from panic buying and clapping on doorsteps, to advocating for ever-more draconian restrictions.

Opinions about school closures formed quickly and decisively, with positions driven by social media hashtags and soundbites: stay at home, #closetheschools, save the NHS. Against this backdrop, and with the crowd moving largely together, it became excruciatingly difficult for parents, professionals and other members of the public to challenge the discourse around the initial school closures, reopenings and then subsequent measures for children. As we discussed in Chapter 8, the first-mover advantage of discourse had framed schools as a dangerous place, and the virtuous position as at least accepting, if not supporting, school closures and mitigations.

In fact, there was a view that if you wanted your kids back at school you were heartless – take this comment printed in *The Mirror* from influencer Charlotte Church, for instance:

'Highly recommend if you can help it, not sending your children back to school tomorrow… this government doesn't give a flying f*ck about you, your children, your elders or your vulnerable.'[315] The same article reported that 46% of parents were expected to keep their children at home.

Those who did raise concerns often did so in caveated terms, accepting on some level that the public health emergency justified significant interventions. As headteacher Mike Fairclough recalls, 'at the very start of the pandemic I was, like most of my staff, really worried about what we were being told. I remember exactly the moment when I was in my car, listening to Boris Johnson's speech, and he said many of us will lose loved ones. And I'd been following press from Italy and then reports out of China and seeing all those things, like literally bodies piling and I think any kind of rational, logical person with any kind of empathy or just the tiniest bit of concern, would've heard the Prime Minister making that comment and looking at those reports and thinking, well, there's a killer virus that's coming. And we obviously don't want children to suffer. So let's close down schools. I had no reason to doubt anything that I'd been told and just thought, right, this is really apocalyptic.'

We were not immune to the ominous messaging. In the height of anxiety, having seen the impending crisis unfold in China, and then Italy, one of us recalls lecturing family members about 'flattening the curve'. A scribbled note from a notebook in March 2020 says, 'main thing is we all stay alive'.

However, as April wore on the initial panic ebbed away, and we witnessed first-hand the impact of school closures, the taped-off playgrounds and the mounting social isolation. We began to be deeply concerned – both for our own children, and for the children behind closed doors.

When government plans turned to phased school reopening, the anxiety of many parents in our respective circles was palpable. One acquaintance said they wouldn't send their child back to school until 'September at the earliest' for safety reasons. Within this atmosphere of concern, those who needed or wanted to send their children back to school were left feeling conflicted, and even guilty.

Even tentatively sharing factual, reassuring editorial[316] about the happily limited impact of the virus on children felt difficult and charged, but separately we were coming to our own conclusions that school closures and social distancing were a disaster for children. We started to feel deeply uneasy about the lack of discussion of how the measures were affecting the youngest, most vulnerable members of society. So when we met by pure chance, it felt natural to join our voices and begin speaking up together.

After we launched UsForThem and stood against the herd, we were met with a Marmite reaction: people either loved us or hated us. While there was a smattering of supportive comments on our first published news piece[317] ('The measures introduced by these schools are just awful and I support the mothers 100%') the overwhelming majority were damning.

'I would have thought that the health and safety of your children (like mine) was SO MUCH MORE IMPORTANT. Christ you all need a reality check'.

'Get a grip, it's 10 weeks of which close on 3 were half term & bank holidays'.

'They should be ashamed, and if they take this track they should be ostracised.'

Our experience chimed with that of independent journalist Katherine Jebsen Moore, who recounted in an article her experiences of starting an online petition in Scotland in favour of school reopenings. She shared it on the Edinburgh Facebook group Edinburgh Gossip Girl.[318] Of the experience she wrote,

> *'Within a few minutes my post had 62 angry emojis, six stunned ones, three sad ones, and only 26 likes – and one heart. The comments reinforced the mood. As well as the simple "that'll be a no" and "wouldn't dream of signing this", it quickly progressed to mud-slinging, strawmen and high tempers.'*

We learned quickly that the pack had the power to shame.

This period marked the beginning of almost two years often out of kilter with mainstream opinion. As campaign novices with no established platform, together with a growing band of parents, we relied on persistence and hard work to try to make our voices heard, often against the tide.

In the film *Sliding Doors*, the course of the main character's life hinges on a single moment – whether she catches a train, or not. From that instant, two parallel chains of events unfold. How much could an even subtle shift in discourse have changed the way that children were treated throughout the pandemic? Had the handful of voices been joined by multiple other credible peers, would that have changed history? Would it have emboldened others to speak up more forcefully? Would it have shifted the discourse and framed policymaking in terms of children, rather than adults? We can't know the answer, but it's a question that many of our contributors have reflected upon.

Professor Ellen Townsend was an early and clear voice in the early days, as we saw in Chapter 7. One of her disappointments was the lack of other academic voices joining her in her first, tentative calls to prioritise children and young people. She said, 'I would've liked a few more academics to speak out. I feel very sad that so many people have been frightened into submission... Into not speaking out because as I think actually the power of more voices could have made a difference.'

Ellen also alluded to the phenomenon of private support being more forthcoming than public endorsement. She said, 'I get emails all the time from people, some of them telling me off for what I'm doing. But mostly sort of saying thank you, which is lovely, but it always makes me think "you could be doing this. We could be doing this together". So, I think that's a sadness that more people haven't found whatever it was or found it necessary to speak out really.'

It's a sadness shared by educational psychologist Claire McGuiggan. She told us of her experience after the initial weeks of lockdown and her increasing concerns about the impact on children of not accessing school at all. She put all her thoughts and ideas into an article entitled 'Return to Childhood' and sent it to a professional educational psychology blog site.[319] They told her that they would publish the piece, but as they feared it might be too provocative they wouldn't share it as widely as usual. The 'provocative' article made what should really have been an uncontroversial statement, especially given the audience, arguing that children should return to school because, 'they are children: inquisitive, sociable, stimulation-seeking, sponge soakers of experiences, developing little people. Childhood development cannot be paused, ignored and then revisited at a later date. It is continuing for every child, kept home for the safety of the nation, but deprived of the essential elements for that development.'

McGuiggan's words testify prophetically to everything that we know has evolved since. We cannot pause childhood, and the professionals in her circle must have been fully aware of that fact. Having courageously staked out her position, she waited for the feedback, and the response took her aback.

She told us, 'I didn't get any positive response from people across my profession... And bearing in mind that my profession is educational and child psychologists. A profession you would expect to be at the forefront of being able to talk about child development, child mental health, children's learning and the essential role of schools within that, it would be education and child psychologists. That's our job. That's what we do. We are in schools supporting schools to meet all those needs of children.'

Not only was there an absence of positive responses, but she was also actively criticised, albeit in small numbers, by professional peers who disagreed with her position because their own children were coping well, and the family was enjoying 'quality time'. She said she was left 'floored' by the reception and with a sense of confusion because there could, in her view, be little disagreement with 'the premise that actually children's needs can't be met if they are not in school and they're all just at home and they don't see other children and they don't experience the world?'

The reaction was even more surprising, given the respondents'certain professional knowledge of, as McGuiggan says, 'the lived reality of lots and lots of children and families, and that it's not, for lots and lots of children, playing in the garden, planting carrots and making gingerbread.'

The whole experience has left Claire disorientated. Unlike other contributors, Claire wasn't subject to smearing or a witch hunt. Rather, it was some limited disapproval, then silence, from the group of professionals uniquely placed at the intersection of child development and the role of schools to speak up for children. 'That was the end of the discourse', she said.

Claire believes the reasons for this relative silence are complex, but rooted in the perceived 'political sensitivity' of the issue (See Chapter 8). Yet, as she points out, advocating for children needn't have been political at all: amplifying the needs of children, and sharing the legitimate concerns, could have been accomplished from a neutral standpoint by providing the information and allowing 'politicians to weigh that against all the other information they might have been getting economically, and from the epidemiologists and everybody else.'

Claire's disappointment at the lack of advocacy for children – at the time when it mattered most – is palpable. 'Somebody said that to me, just the other day, another education psychologist, that we were the champions of children and I had to really bite my lip in the situation I was in. We weren't the champions of children at all, and I think we didn't advocate for children when we needed to. And I think we weren't these champions of children as we sometimes like to style ourselves.'

The range of silencing effects was also starkly apparent in the inhibited media response. Healthy discourse begins with questions and debate, which allow views to evolve without fear or favour, and different perspectives to be heard.

Broadcaster Neil Oliver is one of a handful of television presenters to have consistently questioned the accepted lockdown wisdom. He told us:

'I think I'm saying very straightforward things, and other people are saying the same things to me in private, but for whatever reason, in the many rungs above me in this food chain up to the silverbacks of the jungle that I would've expected to take the lead role and would have expected to be saying, "hold on a minute here, okay, we've got a virus to deal with, but what we're doing in terms of the damage that we're inflicting on society, on civilization, on the economy, on people's mental and physical health, on children is by orders of magnitude over the score" – and yet deafening silence. And so somehow it's come down to someone like me – an archaeologist, BBC two eight o'clock TV presenter, and I hear myself on Saturday nights having a go at Joe Biden, and I think how, "how can this have happened?" But if nobody else will say it, I'll just have to say it.'

A senior news editor told us how, in their view, the lack of questioning contributed to the conformist approach, and ultimately failed children:

'I would expect an independent media in any country to question any government, which says, you cannot leave your home other than this reason, and you cannot meet your family at all. You can't see your loved ones in hospital. I would expect that to be challenged to a degree by the media and it simply wasn't. And that's as true for kids.'

Much is made in the corporate world of a 'speak-up' culture, which encourages honest discourse as the cornerstone of an ethical organisation. However, away from the memes of LinkedIn, and in the real world of actual, devastating consequences, we failed to follow through when it mattered most.

The Salem witch trials were a series of hearings and prosecutions of more than 200 people accused of witchcraft in colonial Massachusetts between February 1692 and May 1693. Thirty were found guilty, 19 of whom were hanged. The youngest accused was Dorothy Good, aged just four years old. It was the deadliest witch hunt in the history of colonial North America and is an infamous example of the dangers of mass hysteria.[320]

As we now know, the hold of the Covid-orthodoxy on public opinion has been strong, colouring much of the debate since the very first days. Arguing against the prevailing wisdom of lockdown, school closures and other measures has at times felt like a witch hunt. The fanaticism with which that orthodoxy has been propagated has taken on a quasi-religious status. Indeed, others have compared the outward symbolism associated with Covid – in particular face masks – to the vestiture of religion (see Chapter 8).[321] It has felt almost blasphemous to question that orthodoxy and those of us doing so have been viciously attacked and smeared. In the context of schools, it has not helped that the issue became politicised almost immediately. Those advocating for 'open schools' have often been perceived as anti-union and therefore – so the argument goes – 'right wing' or 'Tory scum' (see Chapter 8).

Professor Sunetra Gupta of Oxford University and Professor Jay Bhattacharya of Stanford University are two of the three authors of the Great Barrington Declaration (the third is Swedish biostatistician Martin Kulldorff, at the time Harvard Professor of Medicine). Signed in October 2020, the Declaration proposed an alternative way out of the pandemic: 'focused protection' i.e., investing substantial and targeted efforts into protecting the vulnerable while leaving the rest of the population to continue their daily lives. The Declaration attracted significant controversy, going as it did against the established pro-lockdown positions taken by most of the Western world at the time.

Jay and Sunetra have spoken extensively, to us and elsewhere, of their experiences of being targeted and smeared because of their authorship of the Declaration. Indeed, it's now a matter of public record that the three scientists were subject to an organised attack from senior officials within the US administration. Emails from Dr Collins, the head of the National Institutes of Health, to Dr Fauci, director of the National Institute of Allergy and Infectious Diseases, referred to the three 'fringe epidemiologists' saying, 'There needs to be a quick and devastating published take down of its premises'.[322]

Speaking of the attack and the campaign that followed, Sunetra told us: 'They decided to brutally demolish us, which was emotionally so damaging that I still have horrible dreams about being chased by people trying to kill me. It was just a horrible, horrible smear campaign.'

This is an extreme but by no means isolated example of the kind of public and hostile attack that many of those challenging the orthodoxy of the Covid religion have endured.

Take the case of David Perks – a headteacher who questioned facemasks in classrooms – 'It puts a psychological and physical barrier between staff and children that is just destructive',[323] he said, only to find himself under scrutiny by the Department for Education when Regional Commissioners wrote to his school saying they were 'concerned about the stance' he had taken.[324]

Julia Hartley-Brewer is one of a very few public broadcasters who challenged the orthodoxy. She told us about the consistent abuse she's faced for doing so:

'I was told I was a Covid-denier. I was told I was a granny killer, despite the fact that I was someone who would be adamant to my own parents in their late seventies that they needed to be careful, banning my father from attending my brother's 40th birthday, because it was too risky to him and really talking on air and on Twitter repeatedly in February and early March about how people needed to be careful. And then suddenly I was someone who was denying Covid, who was a conspiracy theorist. It was bizarre.'

Professor Ellen Townsend faced similar after acting as a signatory to the Great Barrington Declaration. 'We were called granny killers. We were called eugenicists. We were called a death cult. That's the sort of level of debate that surrounded those suggestions.'

Those speaking out have been threatened with loss of livelihood. Headteacher Mike Fairclough faced two internal investigations after he dared express his concern about the lack of long-term safety data in relation to Covid vaccines for children publicly (both investigations were dismissed). One senior reporter for a major news outlet tells us he'd proposed publishing a challenging, hard-hitting story. On calling a leading state organisation for comment, he'd been told 'We will destroy your reputation if you publish this.'

You might have thought those advocating against lockdown on the grounds of child welfare would have been spared such attacks. You'd be wrong. As Professor Ellen Townsend says, while 'I haven't had it nearly as bad as some of my colleagues, I think because I've tried to always couch it in terms of children – putting children first being my mantra – I've had some horrible emails and a lot of nasty stuff on Twitter; in fact, it got so bad that last year I left Twitter because it was so horrible. Some of the vitriol has been quite hard to bear'.

This very much reflects our own experience.

From almost day one of launching UsForThem we've been targeted by unfounded accusations of misinformation, disinformation, being – variously – a shadowy front for 'dark money', anti-vaxxers, granny killers, even, memorably, 'killer clowns': the animosity of these claims has often seemed to increase proportionately with the level of publicity the campaign has attracted.

The perversity of being slurred, and labelled 'extreme', for maintaining positions that until 2020 would have been entirely consistent with previous pandemic planning, medical ethics and public health practice, grates and confuses. As Julia Hartley-Brewer told us:

'It's not particularly nuanced to say people who are at a higher risk from a disease should take a vaccine, which will prevent them most likely from going to hospital or dying from that disease and saying that at the same time, that people who are not at high risk of this disease should make a decision for themselves (as everyone should)… And that children who are virtually zero risk should definitely not take a vaccine that is not there to protect them. And, that none of this should be mandatory and it should not be required that you show your proof because the vaccine is about you protecting yourself and it should be a personal choice. It's utterly bizarre that these sorts of normal positions were suddenly castigated as extreme and dangerous and ideological and libertarian.'

The seeming senselessness of many of the slurs we have faced hit home when we interviewed Jennifer Sey and realised that the same attacks – word for word in some cases – had been levied at parents in the US. In summing up her exasperation, Jennifer told us:

'I get the same that I'm making money and I'm funded by the Koch brothers. And I'm like – "by who?!" – I just spend all my time on this because I think it matters. Like it's so foreign that we could actually do this because we care desperately. That's what's crazy. It's sort of like, they can't even imagine that it's just done because we actually care and we make no money and we're willing to endure the slings and arrows. It's sort of unfathomable, right?'

Yet the personal slurs inevitably sting. As Jennifer says, 'I mean, frankly it's been awful to speak out on it. It's been a year and a half of just getting brutalised. I have fractured family relationships. I have friends that I've lost. My job is at risk. But at the end of the day, I can't help myself because I think about those kids and there's no one, but parents like us that are fighting for them. And it's so harrowing because you get demonised and called these awful names and they come for your job. It takes a lot of fortitude to keep going.'

There is a poignancy writing this. In February 2022, Jennifer's refusal to 'quieten down' ultimately cost her her role as Levi's brand President. In leaving, she turned down a USD 1 million severance package which would have required her to sign a non-disclosure agreement. 'I quit so I could be free', she writes.[325] It was a high price she paid.

The toll these witch-hunts take on a personal level is upsetting, but their impact on the arc of debate has been pernicious, deterring much-needed voices from speaking up. As Jennifer wryly notes, 'it's warranted to fear speaking out.' This 'silencing' is especially pronounced among professionals, whose voices are arguably needed most of all, but who have been unable to voice concerns for fear of losing their jobs.

As we saw in the context of the initial school closures, and as we've seen consistently since, these attacks limit the extent to which necessary and reasonable arguments about child welfare are heard in the mainstream, at the point when they might have influenced the debate. We have lost count of the number of messages we have received from professionals, often though not invariably employed in some shape or form by the state and its institutions, who tell us that they admire our stance but have felt unable to offer public support for fear of professional repercussions.

This is a dangerous place to be.

As Julia Hartley-Brewer comments, 'I'd always been brought up that asking questions is never bad.'

The Salem witch trials have been used over the centuries as a cautionary tale of the menace of persecution, intolerance and bigotry – witness Miller's *The Crucible*, which presented the trials as an allegory for McCarthy's campaign against communism. Two years in, and with clear evidence as to the damage our pandemic policies have caused children, we wonder how much of that might have been avoided if the voices who tried to speak had been spared the ducking stool of social shaming.

Chapter 10
Vectors

The pandemic response has been characterised by fear, and the weight of this fear has often fallen disproportionately on children. Not only have they been disregarded by policymakers, and burdened by pandemic restrictions, but all too often they have been demonised and stigmatised by adults who should have known better. It is one thing to be legitimately anxious about the pandemic threat; it is quite another to cast blame upon a specific group. How did we reach a point where society feared and othered its own children?

Throughout history, human beings have used labels to justify the degrading treatment of specific groups as defined by gender, race, sexual identity or other characteristics. Disturbingly, the examples of the pandemic treatment of children discussed within the pages of this book carry an undertone of discrimination. At the most extreme, children have been treated not only as lesser than adults but as less than human – such as in the instances we have described of children eating lunch outside in the rain 'like cattle'.

Our language matters, and the process of dehumanising begins with the words we use. At too many points during the pandemic, the language used to describe children and young people has framed them as a danger rather than as vulnerable members of society to be cherished, nurtured and championed.

There is no stronger exemplar of this than the ubiquitous use of the word 'vector' to describe children and their 'role in viral transmission' throughout the crisis. This is a word that we have rarely heard used to describe adults. Let's consider what it means and the implications of such language. The WHO explains, 'Vectors are living organisms that can transmit infectious diseases between humans or from animals to humans. Many of these vectors are bloodsucking insects, which ingest disease-producing microorganisms during a blood meal from an infected host (human or animal) and later inject it into a new host during their subsequent blood meal.'[326]

The comparison reduces children to a lowly status, portraying them as nothing more than walking carriers of disease.

In January 2022, a university professor in Michigan hit the headlines following a bizarre and angry video rant. Addressing his students, he said, 'You people are just vectors of disease to me, and I don't want to be anywhere near you, so keep your **** distance'. He went on, 'when I look out at a classroom of 50 students, I see 50 selfish kids who don't give a **** whether grandpa lives or dies.'[327]

This is an extreme example, but one which has been mirrored in other discourse, from social media commentators and mainstream news outlets, to respected academics.

As we mentioned in Chapter 8, in May 2020, teaching union leader Dr Mary Bousted came under fire for describing young primary school-aged children as 'mucky'.[328] A piece for the *Washington Post*[329] over a year later by William Miller, a respected professor of epidemiology, ran with the headline 'We teach kids to avoid germs. We should also tell them they are germ spreaders.' In fairness to Professor Miller, he is unlikely to have selected the inflammatory headline for the article, which discussed raising awareness of our collective responsibility for disease. It's revealing, though, that he believed that children needed to learn this lesson the most. Even more disturbing is the fact that the choice of headline demonstrates how 'safe' mainstream media outlets feel when propagating derogatory messages about children. Imagine if we were to replace the 'kids' of this title with any other specific group of people. Would the sub-editor have let it through?

In June 2020, a headline for Health Canada warned, 'Kids remain a petri dish of COVID spread.'[330] More commonly, schools, rather than children themselves, were alluded to as petri dishes. It is telling that schools, populated by children, have seemed to attract this description more than any other setting. Have we commonly heard of offices or restaurants described in this way?

In June 2021, Dr Julian Tang, Honorary Associate Professor/Clinical Virologist at the University of Leicester, was quoted by Science Media Centre as saying, 'the virus will eventually concentrate in this school-age population which will eventually become a reservoir and driver of any ensuing delta variant epidemic.'[331] Again, the use of the word 'reservoirs' characterises children as mere vessels of infectious agents.

What is the source of this fear? Certainly, the notion of children as walking transmitters of disease long pre-dates 2020. In 2017, an NHS communication foreshadowed the accusatory 'Don't Kill Granny' messaging of the pandemic and exhorted children to take up the flu vaccine to protect their grandparents. Professor Keith Willett said, 'there's still time for parents to get their "super-spreader" children vaccinated to help protect elderly relatives.'[332]

Indeed, the initial fear during Covid likely stemmed from the prominent role of children in other respiratory diseases such as flu. Amid March 2020 panic, newspapers reported that several Irish supermarkets had banned children from entering due to their status as 'vectors'. One of the supermarket signs said,[333] 'No children allowed. Children are deemed to be vectors of Covid-19.'

Though it quickly became clear that this was unlikely to apply to Covid-19, the narrative persisted. From the beginning of the pandemic, children's often asymptomatic status was frequently not accepted as a blessing and a relief; instead, it was a danger. So, the narrative went, children, by nature of their mild illness, actually posed more of a risk to adults than less – without symptoms, an adult could only assume that every child was an existential threat.

Indeed, in the same article about the Irish supermarkets *The Journal* helpfully signalled the danger to its readers, saying: 'The term "vector" can mean "an organism that transmits a pathogen", and in this case, people are using it to mean that children can pass on the coronavirus to adults.' It went on, 'Because studies in China have found that children can in some cases be asymptomatic, the fear is that children who don't appear to be ill could pass on the virus "silently".'

In August 2020, a paper in the *Journal of Pediatrics* revisited this initial perception with damaging effect.[334] A small study of 192 children ages 0–22, with 49 children testing positive for Covid-19, was widely reported to indicate that children were 'silent spreaders', playing a 'more significant role in the community spread COVID-19 than previously thought'.[335] Other experts subsequently criticised the study, including Dr Simon Clarke, who said, 'the study does not actually demonstrate that children spread the virus.'[336] In astonishment, Alasdair Munro, a paediatrician, pointed out that the study compared children's viral loads at their peak to adults' after seven days.[337]

In our opinion, the moral panic of the accompanying news articles reporting children as 'silent spreaders' was no journalistic accident; it was determined by the initial study press release from Massachusetts General Hospital, the headline of which screamed,[338] 'Massachusetts General Hospital researchers show children are silent spreaders of virus that causes COVID-19'. The communications department subsequently altered it 'to more closely reflect the findings of the study'.[339] But the damage was done. The tabloid-style initial message that children were indeed the stealthy threats of the public imagination had circulated widely. As the saying goes, the lie is halfway around the world before the truth can even get its boots on. The timing was catastrophic – and the inflammatory and divisive messaging fuelled further anxiety around the long-awaited school reopening in both the US and the UK. In Africa, it was reported that Unicef's Mohamed Fall intervened in response, urging, 'Let's not stigmatise children', adding that there was no scientific evidence for the claim.[340]

A year later, in an important article for *The Conversation*,[341] academics Rebecca Adami and Katy Dineen also stepped in to address the ongoing stigmatisation of children, calling out the impact of these terms as 'demeaning'. They highlighted the link between language and policy, which 'encourages us to consider children with COVID only in terms of the impact they may have on adults'. Their comments to some extent chime with those of Guibilini et al.,[342] who described in the *BMJ* in the context of vaccination policies how children had become 'mere means' to serve other people's interests or some form of the 'collective good'.

The pre-existing conditions for the treatment of children seem to have extended beyond their anticipated role in the transmission of a respiratory virus. In fact, fear already had a fertile ground in the prevalent dislike of young people that has permeated our culture.

Dr Ellie Cannon, GP, parent, and broadcaster, believes this antipathy towards young people explains some of the pandemic response failures. She says, 'I'm not sure if this is the UK or generally globally, there is a disdain, particularly for young people. With 16 to 25-year-olds, we tend to think of them as flaky or spending all their money on drink and drugs. I'm generalising obviously, but there isn't really respect for young people. There isn't respect for childhood in this country. You only have to look at how we underfund education, and sport for children and CAMHS [children and young people's mental health services] around the country to see that there is not a respect for childhood.'

She added that the importance of events in a child's life, from playdates to 'kissing a boy for the first time' to applying for university, have been deemed 'frivolous and trivial' by adults throughout the pandemic, reflecting a 'longstanding lack of interest'. In fact, these events are vital rites of passage, ironically established as significant milestones of a child's life by adults themselves, who were then quick to dismiss them.

Using an example from her own community, Dr Ellie recounts her disappointment and shock that her synagogue failed to acknowledge the sadness of many children who had been planning bar and bat mitzvahs during the first lockdowns, saying: 'It wasn't the missing out on a party. It was the loss of rite of passage that they had been made by us as adults to look forward to and anticipate their whole life. And yet when it was taken away from them, nobody even thought to apologise or offer anything else. That was another real illustration to me, of a complete lack of interest.'

Sir Al Aynsley-Green has written extensively about our nation's attitudes towards childhood. In an article for the *Mirror* in 2018, he wrote of his empathy for Scandinavian colleagues' view that English people 'hate' children. He alluded to the closure of youth services, the inability of ordinary parents to afford music lessons, and the lack of adult volunteers to support the Scouting movement.[343] He also referred to the government's refusal to regulate the 'Mosquito' ultrasonic device designed to 'repel' teenagers by emitting a high-pitched, irritating sound only audible to under-25s. There are echoes here of the 'vector' narrative that presents children as a scourge. The marketing copy for the 'Mosquito'[344] notes that the 'idyllic life we seek can become disturbed by unwanted youngsters who may not choose the best places to meet up and hang around'. It's hard to disagree with the conclusion of Jenny McCartney, who wrote in 2011 that 'Britain's essential contempt for childhood feeds through on a national level: the overstretched and fraying maternity wards, the desultory after-care for mother and baby, the historically abominable treatment of children in care, the patchy provision of adequate NHS dentistry for young children.'[345]

This contempt has been turbo-charged and amplified by the pandemic response, leaving children as a *de facto* underclass.

We have seen signs throughout the pandemic of a general feeling of dislike and fear aimed at children. Parents have told us how their children felt 'in the way' at school. One Year 7, having joined secondary school for the first time in September 2020, was informed by her form tutor that she as the adult was 'brave' for facing a class of wide-eyed 11-year-olds. Another parent told us how her four-year-old, having fallen in the playground, was told to give himself a 'virtual hug' and wipe his knee by himself. One note to a parent from a school during the same period reads 'if you have a younger child coming into school with laces... can you double knot them in the morning so staff do not have to tie them up when they come loose'.

There are also more extreme cases of demeaning and degrading treatment. On 26 February 2021, Australian epidemiologist Zoë Hyde put out a disturbing tweet – since deleted:

> 'I said that cases in children might be detectable for a shorter period. How can we get around that? One option is anal swab testing because faecal shedding is prolonged. A study in Wuhan found that about one-fifth of children had negative nasal swabs but positive anal swabs.'

Parents and fellow scientists reacted with horror at the coldness and dehumanising nature of the suggestion.

In the summer of 2021, footage circulated of an autistic child, who, despite his medical exemption from testing, was being forcibly tested by airline staff and was in a state of abject distress.[346]

Children who were exempt from wearing face coverings in England were frequently asked to wear a lanyard to identify their status to others. In a shocking and thoughtless move, a school in Kent asked children to wear yellow badges.[347]

We should make no mistake. Children do internalise the notion that they are feared. In 2021 youngsters in Ireland told a Joint Committee on Children that they felt stigmatised by the labelling.[348] One of the witnesses said, 'The fact that other people shunned us, and in many cases tried to walk in the middle of the road rather than pass us, left a bitter taste in my mouth and made me want to stay in rather than go out.'

A teenager wrote to us about their response to childhood vaccination, saying, 'If we are vaccinated, then adults might be less terrified of us. Maybe we won't get blamed for meeting up, and fewer people will call for restrictions in schools.'

This adoption of self-blame is profoundly concerning and dangerous.

It is hard to draw any other conclusion than that these undercurrents of discourse that have surrounded children amount to discrimination, as Adami and Dineen asserted, or childism. The language we have used about children has not been used to describe any other group, and in fact, it is hard to imagine how it would be permitted. Adults who have employed this demeaning language and participated in discriminatory behaviour, such as politicians allowing themselves to be photographed unmasked among a sea of masked children, have often shown an alarming lack of self-awareness.

There is another chilling perspective to consider here. Much of the pandemic narrative surrounding children has centred on their role in the burden of disease. Society often made concessions for young people because of some function of the pandemic; a realisation that children were not, in fact, primary drivers of transmission; that adults were vaccinated; or that cases were falling. These arguments made by well-intentioned people, ourselves included, aimed to persuade policymakers that facts meant that children should be readmitted to school, or have restrictions removed. But however valid these scientifically-driven points are, have we made the ethical arguments powerfully enough? The argument boils down to this. Shouldn't we as a society nurture and respect children, irrespective of their role in transmitting a disease?

Suppose there was a novel disease of which children truly were the horrifying 'silent spreaders' of the public psyche. Given the way young people have been shunned, restricted and burdened for a virus in which they are less implicated, it is terrifying to contemplate what the reaction might be to one in which they played a greater role. For this reason, we must engage more fully with ethical arguments as well as scientific ones when considering the failures of the pandemic response for children.

Chapter 11
Parental Conflict

John Morton was born in Dorset, England, in the early 1400s. In his early career, he practised law before joining the clergy. He rose through the ranks quickly and, in 1487 under King Henry VII, was appointed Lord Chancellor.

As Lord Chancellor one of his jobs was to organise the collection of taxes on behalf of the Crown. Then, as now, the nation's wallet was in an impecunious state, so this could be a challenging task. Morton is recorded as saying:

'If the subject is seen to live frugally, tell him because he is clearly a money saver of great ability, he can afford to give generously to the King. If, however, the subject lives a life of great extravagance, tell him he, too, can afford to give largely, the proof of his opulence being evident in his expenditure.'

And so was coined 'Morton's Fork', a kind of false dilemma in which two equally unpleasant alternatives lead to the same conclusion – otherwise known as being 'between a rock and a hard place'. It is, in fact, where parents have spent a great part of the last two years.

A perpetual state of dilemma and conflict

It was obvious to many of us from the outset that several proposed Covid 'protections' were potentially harmful to children: masks, homeschooling, isolation, bubbles, testing…

the list might go on. Yet, as a parent, the choice has often been to go along with the intervention or to watch your child face a worse alternative. An email received from a parent at the time that testing of children in schools was first being discussed sums it up perfectly: 'I do not want my children to be subjected to tests – but I do want them to have an education. What do I do?' Another reads, 'this is a trade-off of our children's education. How is this allowed to happen? I am utterly devastated. I am such a champion of children being in school but I will not subject them to daily testing and feel I've no other choice but to look at alternatives for them.'

This was during the Christmas break of 2020. It is a period that sticks in the memory because it was partway through the furore over whether or not schools would open at all in January 2021 – an on/off conflict that cast a dark cloud over that break for many parents, given how stark it was by then that homeschooling was not only a failed educational experiment, but for many children, a harmful one. 'I think I am still carrying the emotional scars of the first round of home-ed during lockdown 1.0 and still haven't really had time to process how difficult and downright disruptive it was to our home life and to the relationship I have with my children,' wrote one parent.

This conflict has been a near continuous feature of the pandemic for many parents. In fact, it had been neatly summarised in May 2020 in a paper published by the Children's Commissioner:

'Parents, meanwhile, are understandably concerned and conflicted. A recent survey found that only 1 in 5 parents would follow the government's public health advice, a similar proportion would only listen to the advice from teachers, while 1 in 10 parents were in favour of keeping their children at home until everyone at their child's school has been vaccinated. On the other hand, a third of parents responding to the survey indicated that they did not feel

confident supporting their child's learning at home. Parents were more likely to report being concerned about the effects of isolation on their child than the risk of someone in their family catching Covid-19.'[349]

This situation has been duplicated in relation to every intervention since then.

We saw it repeatedly in the context of masks, when theoretically voluntary guidance was often applied as law. While children were 'lucky enough' to be in school, they were often subject to an intervention that many parents felt uneasy about. When schools went back in summer 2020 it was to an array of medicalised procedures and a radically altered set-up that flagged alarm bells to many concerned with child welfare. At the very sharp end parents across the world now have an invidious choice of 'no jab-no school' or – worse still – 'no jab-no access to restaurants cinemas, softplays'[350] for children as young as five.

Sometimes the idea of 'choice' has been illusory. Consider homeschooling, where really the 'choice'was remote learning, or – for many – nothing at all. Technically we might call this type of conundrum 'Hobson's choice', more commonly recognised as the 'take that one or none' ultimatum and a phrase which can be traced back through the ages to Thomas Hobson, a Cambridge carrier who operated a livery stable providing transport to and from London in the early 17th century. As legend has it, Hobson offered customers the choice of either taking the horse in his stall nearest to the door, or taking none.

Regardless of nuance, this has led to a state of almost perpetual conflict that has left parents feeling battered, bruised and bitter, all the more so as often it has been set against a background barrage of upheaval and disruption to children's lives. This has been deeply distressing to witness and at times has felt nothing short of cruel. We have written previously about the context of the January

2021 school closures and how they came as a savage shock to many families. A message from a parent received at the time reads, 'Feeling heartbroken. The announcement tonight has just hit me like a ton of bricks'. Another wrote 'How to break this to my daughter again?'. These notes reflected the wider sentiment of our parent community at the time. The announcement in February 2021 that schools were to reopen on 8 March 2021 should have been a cause for celebration – as it momentarily was – until parents realised that a condition of the reopening was that secondary school children would be masked in classrooms. This postscript, buried in a 66-page operational manual for schools, came as a body blow to millions of parents and children alike.[351,352]

It's no surprise that in these circumstances many opted out of a regime they deemed harmful: 'until further notice I will be refusing to "homeschool"', said one parent; another says 'My child is just a mess. Feeling singled out for not wearing a mask... he is so anxious about going to school. I feel like just pulling him out but don't know where to start.' It's notable that both here and in the US rates of traditional homeschooling (as opposed to remote learning) increased sharply during the pandemic.[*] [353,354] 'It's clear that in an unprecedented environment, families are seeking solutions that will reliably meet their health and safety needs, their childcare needs and the learning and socio-emotional needs of their children,'[355] commented the United States Census Bureau.

But even for those who might have been desperately uneasy, removing children from the school environment was often not a viable option. For most parents, simply making ends meet during the pandemic was hard enough. There is little realistic scope in the 'average' domestic set-up for a

---

[*] According to BBC research published in July 2021, there was a 75.6% rise in home education in the UK between September 2020 and April 2021, compared with the averages for the same school terms over the previous two school years. Every nation and region of the UK saw at least a 50% rise, based on the councils that responded and for some, the rate was much higher.

child to be home-schooled in the longer term. This effective removal of the option of 'conscientious objector' only added to the sense of conflict at the helplessness of watching a child suffer.

The expectation of compliance in the context of a terrorised population also pitted parents against the state, other parents and, at times, even their own children. Take the example of the nursery parent who refused to wear a mask at the nursery gates. Many parents instinctively feel it to be inherently damaging for adults to wear masks around small children. In the climate of 2020 and early 2021, it is likely that those concerns would have been ridiculed, with 'there is no evidence that masks harm children' being a common retort. But, as sociologist Robert Dingwall observed a few months back, while there might have been 'little evidence that face masks harm children – few studies have been done, there is abundant evidence of the importance of facial engagement for child development from 50 years of research in psychology, linguistics and education. Harm is a reasonable inference'.[356]

As we now know, these words were prophetic – we saw in Chapter 5 that the Ofsted reports attribute speech and language issues for early years children potentially to the fact that they will have been unable to see lip movements or mouth shapes for an extended period of time.

Nevertheless, parents who trusted their instincts and refused to wear masks around their children would likely find themselves social pariahs in the playground. If they were especially unlucky, they may even have found the police called.[357]

At times, parents were even co-opted into the design of restrictive regimes for their children. 'People who may be willing to accept restrictions, themselves, may be less willing to do things that would distress their children. There are opportunities to involve children in the co-design process, enable their creativity, and inspire them to be agents of change for the alternatives they create',[358] reads one missive from the notorious SPI-B group in relation to the Christmas 2020 period. Worldwide, guides for parents detail how best to persuade reluctant toddlers to 'mask-up'.

'I will never forgive what they made me do', reads one post from a parent on social media. It expresses a complicated sentiment: the issue of parental responsibility in the context of a damaging, mandatory regime is difficult and at times unbearably conflicting. But it does reflect the central dilemma faced by parents during the pandemic – every which way you looked as a parent you were damned if you did and damned if you didn't.

Professor Sunetra Gupta eloquently expresses the bind that parents have found themselves in:

'I also feel though we should not make any judgements for the parent of the five-year-old who says I'm going to have no option but to send my child to school in a mask and that they will be eating lunch outside. I think that we have to be very careful in judging the people who submit, because that's the thing, there are very few of us who are in a position to say, this is wrong. What's been taken advantage of is the fact that most people need to make a complicated decision that maximises their children's benefit. And the way things have been set up is that a lot of people who don't believe in any of this will still send their children to school in masks and say, you've got to eat lunch outside, because that is better than the alternative. That's the tragedy, that human tragedy begins at that point where you are doing something that's terrible, but the alternative is worse.'

This onslaught of near-continuous conflict leaves parents demeaned and grateful for the smallest of blessings. A parent wrote to us to tell us of her joy when her child had, after much pleading, been offered two days a week at school. Parents had to accept any shreds offered.

Many parents we spoke to told us how hard it was to see

their children struggle and not to be able to do anything about it. As one mother wrote about her teenage daughter in the early days of remote learning:

> '*I watched her lie on the floor – it was April 2020 – after a day of remote learning. She just came down the stairs, stopped on the floor and didn't want to move. And I thought "Oh my god this was my bubbly, thriving child". I had no real power to help her, and that was the worst bit. And also thinking that this was a child who was in a good situation with a good family life and a good home. And was still in this state of pure apathy and misery. I just watched the colour drain from her face. And I became so angry that this is what my child had been reduced to and I could do so little to help her.*'

The parlous situation may also have criminalised large swathes of parents. Hard evidence is, for obvious reasons, not easy to come by, but anecdotally we have heard time and time again of otherwise law-abiding parents who took the view that various restrictions were so deleterious to children's health that a higher order duty dictated that they must be abandoned. 'I refuse to apologise for that', said one parent, in the context of driving their disabled child to the countryside for a much-needed walk during the height of the first lockdown.

The cumulative effect, even before the alleged law-breaking activities of the rule-makers themselves had surfaced, has been to foster mounting resentment, anger and disillusionment among swathes of parents. 'I am deeply fearful for the future of my children and their generation as a whole', wrote one mother in summer 2020. 'I did not become a mother so that the life chances and opportunities available to my children would be curtailed in such an atrocious way'. 'I am ashamed of what is happening to our children and their futures. This is incredibly sad', wrote another.

This anger has been compounded by the fact that often legitimate, serious and urgent concerns about child welfare have fallen on deaf ears. We have received thousands of emails and messages over the last two years expressing exasperation about the indifference of politicians and policymakers. Very few of the campaign emails and letters we and our army of parents wrote to DfE, DHSC and PHE were ever answered in a meaningful way. It creates a feeling of hopelessness and disengagement with a system wilfully closed to the needs of children, which is summarised by one parent who wrote: 'Thank you for all your hard work but I'm not sure what more can be done. No matter how loud we shout it seems to fall on deaf ears.'

That many of the rules which have been most detrimental to children have been introduced at the last minute, or after U-turns and after being leaked first to the press, or buried in reams of guidance often during school holidays, instead of being announced openly and transparently,[*][359] has likewise bred a hard-to-shake impression that children, their education, and their parents, are an afterthought.

However, there may yet be a silver lining.

If the last two years have been anything, they have been a clarion call to parents. One lasting pandemic trend may yet be a wave of parent activism – a significant ray of light to emerge from the darkness.

As we discussed in Chapter 8, in America the duration of school closures was – in some states – extreme,[**][360] and so-called 'blue' states often required even toddlers to be masked all day at kindergarten. It is no surprise that parent anger has

---

[*] Examples include the first announcement of the controversial 'mask-in-class' mandate – buried in a 66-page operational manual for schools on the day that school reopenings were announced in January 2021, or the reintroduction of the mandate announced late on New Years Day 2022.

[**] California is a notorious example. Over half of schools were shut for the entirety of the 2020/21 academic year.

reached fever pitch. A nationwide debate is ongoing regarding the role of parents in school life, with legal and political battles playing out across America. The mask mandates have sparked intense debate and some US states have seen a surge in parents enrolling on school boards,[361] with the issue becoming a key election topic. In Texas, Governor Greg Abbott has made parental rights a core issue in his reelection campaign. In pitching the idea that parental rights will be strengthened as an amendment to the Texas Constitution, Abbott declared: 'Parents will be restored to their rightful place as the preeminent decision-maker for their children.'[362] President of the conservative American Principles Project, Terry Schilling, in the context of US school closures and the mask mandate there, said 'This whole regime is at war with the parents. They just want to raise their families according to their values and take them to church and not have people interfere, but they're interfering with that and that's why there's a big conflict right now.'[363]

In the UK too there is growing recognition among the public (if not yet policymakers) of the hugely detrimental impact the last two years has had on children. A renewed and collective energy to put the world to rights is the one positive we see emanating from this period. As sociologist Robert Dingwall says, 'I think that's the sort of reframing that needs to go on and it will take academics and journalists and other thinkers to do more, to articulate that vision and it will need parents to demand it – the parents who are coming to see the damage that has been done to their children, and wanting to do something about it.'

For our own part, our children were 3 and 6 (Molly) and 13 and 11 (Liz) when the pandemic began. We share every single one of the sentiments expressed by parents in this chapter. We have spent two years watching as four happy children by turns became sad, angry, demotivated, confused, had rites of passage and life opportunities taken away from them and friendships curtailed. We are very conscious that each of those four children was one of the lucky ones: we have been horrified and humbled by some of the testimonies we've heard and read.

In light of the way that children and their interests have been sidelined over the last two years, we now see that political complacency is a luxury we no longer have. One parent speaks for us when she says 'you don't get a second chance at being a child. I won't stop fighting until that is acknowledged and put right'.

Chapter 12
Shattered

During the pandemic, not only did Government appear to remain steadfast in its failure to properly weigh up the harms and benefits of its response, but at times its behaviour leaped rubicons many had previously believed uncrossable.

Nowhere is this clearer than in the context of the childhood vaccination programme for Covid-19, which from the moment it became a reality has been blighted by obscurity, U-turns, ambiguities and contradictions, and which at times has represented a profound break with established principles of medical ethics, leaving a great many parents and professionals desperately uneasy.

The sorry saga begins in earnest in April 2021.

Before then, the vaccination of children against Covid-19 had been robustly ruled out by both British politicians and the British medical establishment. In November 2020 the then Health Secretary, Matt Hancock, had said 'this is an adult vaccine, for the adult population',[364] words reinforced by the head of the UK's 'vaccine task force', Kate Bingham, who, on 5 October 2020, had said 'There's going to be no vaccination of people under 18. It's an adult-only vaccine, for people over 50'.[365]

To many, this appeared to make good sense, for on the face of it, while special considerations may apply to certain at-risk groups of medically vulnerable children, there seemed to be scant need to vaccinate children in general. As we have seen, the vast majority of children are not at great risk from Covid-19 and although some parents wanted their children to be vaccinated, many others, however supportive of traditional childhood vaccinations, had misgivings, based on the risks/benefits and lack of clinical need.[366] Plus, once it is understood that vaccination does not stop transmission,[367] the 'greater good' argument (i.e. that you are vaccinating the young to somehow protect the adult herd), falls away, even before one gets to the ethical considerations.

And then something changed: as with so much policymaking during the pandemic, the discourse turned towards the decisions of other nations and a narrative took hold that vaccination of children would be essential after all. Members of SAGE went on record as saying that children should be vaccinated 'as fast as we can' to keep them in school,[368] and suddenly the regulators in the UK were faced with the question of whether to approve the Covid-19 vaccine for children.

A word on the regulatory framework here.

MHRA is the regulatory body responsible for authorising a drug for use on the UK market. On 4 June 2021, MHRA, following a pattern set overseas, granted the Covid-19 vaccine approval for emergency use in over-12s. We do not pass judgement on whether this was the correct decision, though it is interesting to note that this decision was in itself controversial – experts worldwide argued that there was simply no emergency in children to justify the grant of such licence.[369]

Either way, the fact that a drug has been authorised for use is different from saying it should be recommended for mass use in a healthy population – take, for instance, the example of *varicella* (chicken pox) vaccination, which is authorised but not recommended for routine roll-out under NHS provision. The latter decision – whether to roll out a vaccine to the general population – rests with the Joint Committee on Vaccination and Immunisation (JCVI). These individuals are the Government's appointed panel of vaccine experts, and until 2021 it would have been unprecedented for a vaccination programme to be recommended without an express recommendation from JCVI.

Medical ethics

As with any medical intervention, vaccination carries risks as well as benefits. Occasionally, those risks can be severe. As such, foundational principles of medical ethics apply in decision-making about them.

While these principles evolve over time, the established orthodoxy in the UK has been that the treatment ought to be justified on a risk/benefit analysis for the individual concerned; a person's decision as to whether or not to accept the treatment ought to be based on informed consent and – as such – based on transparent data; and that consent must be given voluntarily and free from pressure or coercion.

Overstatement of benefit

JCVI first considered the question of whether the Covid vaccine should be rolled out on a 'mass' basis to children in July 2021. Its evaluation was clear: 'JCVI does not currently advise routine universal vaccination of children and young people less than 18 years of age.'[370] It went on to explain that 'The health benefits in this population are small, and the benefits to the wider population are highly uncertain. At this time, JCVI is of the view that the health benefits of universal vaccination in children and young people below the age of 18 years do not outweigh the potential risks.'[371]

This was a clear statement, one that parents could understand and rely upon. Seemingly that should have been the end of the matter. Far from it – this was just the beginning.

Against what appeared to be a backdrop of escalating

and unorthodox pressure from ministers and others in and around Government,'[372] the JCVI, a mere three weeks after its previous pronouncement, recommended the roll-out of one dose only to 16–17-year-olds, and to clinically vulnerable children in the lower age group, 12–15 year olds. Then, on 3 September, despite having failed to recommend a mass roll-out to 12–15 year olds, in a move which marked a profoundly usual break with precedent, the JCVI gave discretion to the Chief Medical Officers to effectively overrule the JCVI by considering 'the wider societal impacts of vaccination'. Shortly afterwards the CMOs duly authorised the roll-out on the basis it would be likely to 'reduce... education disruption'.[373] Authorisation of a second dose for 16–17-year-olds followed the first in November 2021,[374] then boosters, then a second dose for 12–15s (having declined to recommend a first).[375] On 16 February 2022, while again not expressly recommending the vaccine for 5–11 year olds, the JCVI advised 'a non-urgent offer'.[376]

These decisions marked a significant departure from the initial premise that the vaccines would not be for mass paediatric use, and they have been followed by campaigns of sustained pressure from, variously, the NHS and DfE, often using language which appears inconsistent with the carefully crafted JCVI advice. 'Vaccines give your children the best possible protection against the virus and help keep them in school', says one such missive from DfE.[377]

In passing the decision to the CMOs on 3 September, JCVI indicated that the clinical justification for vaccinating healthy children was weak, stating that 'the margin of benefit is considered too small to support universal vaccination of healthy 12 to 15 year olds at this time'.[378] From here, it is difficult to read the decision for younger age groups –

---

* In early June, Matt Hancock argued that vaccination of children would prevent disruption to their education, words echoed later that month by CMO Chris Whitty. In late July, absent a recommendation from JCVI, hundreds of jobs were advertised for 'school immunisation health professionals' across the whole of England.

5–11-year-olds – and understand where the benefit lies. By the JCVI's own calculation, under some scenarios some 4 million doses would need to be given to 2 million children to prevent just one paediatric ICU case and protect against a future unknown variant of the disease. As the JCVI acknowledges, 'The extent of these impacts is highly uncertain'.[379] In each case the JCVI's advice has been far from the kind of clear, non-ambiguous recommendation that one would expect, or is typically the case for other childhood vaccines.

We asked Robert Dingwall, as a former member familiar with JCVI protocol, why he thought this was. He said, in the context of the decision on 5 -11 year olds: 'Remember that JCVI are an advisory committee and this constrains the language they can use in any public statement. However it seems to me that they are trying to signal as clearly as they can that this vaccine is not being recommended to parents – but this still didn't stop the NHS and the BBC launching a campaign to promote it.'

We might compare the approach taken in this country to that of Norway. In deciding against recommending the vaccine for mass use in the 5–11 age group, Norway's Minister of Health and Care Services Ingvild Kjerkol said:

'Children rarely become seriously ill, and knowledge is still limited about rare side effects or side effects that may arise at a distant time. There is little individual benefit for most children, and the Norwegian Institute of Public Health has not recommended that all children aged 5–11 be vaccinated.'[380]

An admirably candid explanation.

Fitting intervention to policy

The argument that vaccination would save educational disruption raised eyebrows from the start.[381] It relied on an assumption that vaccination would help significantly reduce transmission, a claim undermined by the medical data[382] and which the JCVI itself had acknowledged to be very uncertain and, if it existed at all, 'relatively small'.[*][383]

David Paton, Professor of Industrial Economics at Nottingham University, has suggested that, on the basis of the central modelling scenario proposed by the CMOs, it would save just 15 minutes of missed school per child[384] ('less than the time that it is going to take them to have the vaccine', as pointed out acerbically by Caroline Johnson, an MP and paediatrician).[385]

More fundamentally, even, and as pointed out by a group of MPs writing to the Heath Secretary in September 2021, education disruption was a policy decision rather than an inevitable clinical consequence: 'disruption to education is not an inevitable consequence of rising COVID cases. Differential approaches to school closures internationally have demonstrated that school disruption is a policy choice not a public health consequence,'[386] they said.

Indeed, some six months later, the JCVI, in the context of the decision about 5–11-year-olds, 'considered that the benefits of vaccinating in preventing school absences were indeterminate',[387] effectively revealing what appeared to many to be the case from the outset – that the 'school disruption' argument was an artificial inflation of benefit. Not so much an automatic health sequitur, as a policy retro-fit to a desired-for-intervention: vaccination.

Downplaying of harm and the impossibility of informed consent

Vaccination – like all medical interventions – carries a degree of risk, and though that risk is small, for those affected in rare cases it can be serious, including death.[388] Though it is incredibly difficult to get an accurate sense of how widespread

---

[*] JCVI in the decision on 12-15s had said 'There is considerable uncertainty regarding the impact of vaccination in children and young people on peer-to-peer transmission and transmission in the wider (highly vaccinated) population. Estimates from modelling vary substantially, and the committee is of the view that any impact on transmission may be relatively small.'

serious adverse reactions to the Covid-19 vaccine are, serious questions have been raised by parliamentarians in the UK and beyond[389] about the scale of such events,[390] and concerns include the risk of myocarditis, particularly in young men.*[391] With any relatively new medical treatment there is the potential for long-term unknown adverse consequences: as the JCVI has noted there is 'considerable uncertainty regarding the magnitude of the potential harms'.[392]

For mass vaccination to be recommended for children, one would expect there to be a demonstrable benefit to the individual child that justified and outweighed the risk of that medical intervention. With some vaccines that benefit is large – take, for example, the polio or tetanus vaccines, which protect the individual against an illness which may well be serious or even life-threatening for many. Sometimes, the benefit on an individual level might be smaller – take, for example, HPV vaccination for teenage boys. HPV is often asymptomatic for males, so here vaccination is justified more by population-level benefits: reducing transmission and possibly eradicating the virus, but even so there is clear evidence that some males would clinically benefit.[393] Crucially, though, where the benefit to the individual is small, to justify a mass vaccination programme one would expect the risk to also be small.

For that, risks must be known, and yet, as one article, published in March 2022 in *New Scientist*, puts it, 'As the UK offers a covid-19 vaccine to children aged 5 to 11... we still have an uncertain picture about the risks to the heart.'[394]

Even if serious adverse events are rare, there is a fundamental question of whether proceeding despite such uncertainty around potentially unknown harm is tolerable in the context of a decision with such scant evidence of direct

---

* The CDC figures relied on by JCVI in its decision on 5–11-year-olds put this at less than 2 cases per million doses, but other studies notably from Hong Kong and Israel suggest rates considerably higher – 1/2680 (Hong Kong) from the Comirnaty (Pfizer) vaccine in male 12-17-year-olds and data from Israel show rates of 1/6637 in 16-19 year old males after the Pfizer vaccine.

medical benefit for the individual child.

What makes this yet more troubling is a perception that risks have been downplayed, misrepresented, or obscured altogether by those whose opinions were trusted – and yet accurate and transparent data is key to the ability of the individual to give informed consent.

In the context of a very finely balanced decision, consent becomes still more important, as the CMOs themselves said when recommending the roll-out to 12–15s: 'Issues of consent need to take this much more balanced risk-benefit into account' to ensure that 'risk-benefit decisions [be presented] in a way that is accessible to children and young people as well as their parents'.[395]

Troublingly, communications from trusted state sources have appeared to amplify the benefits, underplay risks and overplay the effects of Covid in children. On an episode of *Newsround*, a news programme specifically targeted at children, Professor Devi Sridhar of the University of Edinburgh, an influential academic with an advisory position within the Scottish Government, claimed: 'So far trials have shown the vaccine is 100% safe for children'[396] – a claim which could never be true for any medical intervention and which was at the time contradicted by emerging safety data.

On 2 December 2021, an article, entitled 'Pfizer boss: Annual Covid jabs for years to come' appeared on the BBC News website, featuring an interview between medical editor Fergus Walsh and the CEO of Pfizer, Dr Albert Bourla.[397] Having asserted in the context of the adult vaccination programme that 'People will be likely to need to have annual Covid vaccinations for many years to come', Bourla was then quoted as commenting on the childhood vaccination programme, saying that 'Immunising that age group [children under the age of 11] in the UK and Europe would be a very good idea'. At that time, the vaccine had not been included in the emergency temporary approval for use in children in this age group in the UK. The article reported that he also added

'So, there is no doubt in my mind that the benefits completely are in favour of doing it'. These statements seemed scarcely consistent with the findings of the JCVI in declining to recommend mass roll-out to the older cohort, and seem even more disconnected from the terms of the subsequent urgent non-offer for 5–11 year olds.

An NHS England video published online in February 2022[398] claimed 1% of children with Covid were hospitalised.

The video was taken down after uproar from child health professionals about the misleading nature of its claims, but the damage had been done, as paediatrician Rob Hughes wrote in a post in *Unherd*:

> *'Earlier this month, NHS England tweeted out a video to its half million followers to try to promote the Covid vaccine among children. The video cited a series of worrying, but inaccurate, statistics about the risks that Covid apparently represents to children; one in a hundred children will get sick enough with Covid to be admitted to hospital; 136 children in the UK have died of Covid-19, and 117,000 children are suffering from long Covid. The response duly "went viral", attracting re-tweets from some of the biggest public health influencers online, who shared the report with their hundreds of thousands of followers, endorsing it as "an important message", "an excellent piece", "a great video", and using it to lobby JCVI "when will be able to protect our children?".'[399]*

However, as Rob Hughes continued, 'As both a parent and scientist who has been involved in research on symptom duration and severity of Covid in children, the cited statistics didn't make sense to me. The idea that 1% of children with Covid are hospitalised for it didn't pass the "sniff test". I know how contentious the debates about prolonged symptoms after Covid infection have been, and likewise the challenges of estimating Covid mortality among children. So the idea of broadcasting confident numbers on this seemed odd, especially from NHS England... What's more, the powerful – and important – sharing of a story about "long covid" in an 11-year-old seemed at odds with current UK vaccination guidance, which does not currently advise vaccination of this age group.'

Such misleading claims create confusion in parents and they go to the very heart of the individual's ability to give informed consent – for which full, accurate and transparent data is a prerequisite.

Coercion

Another established principle of medical ethics is that consent should be voluntary and free from coercion.

'It is essential that children and young people aged 12–15 and their parents are supported in their decisions, whatever decisions they take, and are not stigmatised either for accepting, or not accepting, the vaccination offer. Individual choice should be respected,'[400] the CMO Chris Whitty himself had said in September 2021.

Offers that use incentives to entice parents or youngsters to be vaccinated do not sit well with this principle,[401] and certain statements and policies made in connection with the Covid vaccine in our view have breached it outright. Vaccine passports, in place for a short time in nightclubs in England as a means to encourage vaccine uptake among the young, and the suggestion that vaccination be mandated for students in higher education settings (a suggestion which faced such a resounding backlash it was swiftly dropped),[402] are just two examples. At a school and county level, differential treatment of unvaccinated pupils to their vaccinated counterparts, as was reported in the autumn of 2021, also put unsavoury pressure on youngsters to be vaccinated.[403]

There are many who might recoil from the idea of mandatory vaccination for children in any circumstance, but in the context of such a finely balanced risk/benefit it is hard to see on what basis this could ever have been thought justified.

Parental consent

According to the NHS 'Children under the age of 16 can consent to their own treatment if they're believed to have enough intelligence, competence and understanding to fully appreciate what's involved in their treatment'. The law in this area is complex, but before 2020 while there were circumstances in which parental refusal to a medical treatment could be overridden by the child, as a general rule these would have been considered appropriate in limited cases and only where there was an immediate safeguarding issue for the child involved.

However, on 26 August 2021, the *Telegraph* reported[404] NHS plans to vaccinate 12-year-olds from the first week schools went back, without requiring parental consent, relying instead on 'Gillick competence'. A blazing row transpired in which Nadhim Zahawi MP told *Times Radio* on 5 September that people in that age range could override their parents' wishes 'if they're deemed to be competent to make that decision, with all the information available', and in the autumn of 2021 vaccine uptake among 12–15s remained sufficiently low that Zahawi toyed with the idea of sending letters directly to that age group asking them to get vaccinated.[405]

These increasingly circuitous attempts to sideline parents and confuse children by relying on Gillick competence would have been unthinkable prior to 2021. At best, the discussion smacked of opportunism given the complex and marginal nature of the risk/benefit decision – impossible for a child to unpick – and at worst, it seemed like yet another strike by the government at the heart of family life, further destabilising already precarious parental authority after 18 months of interference (see Chapter 11).

Trials

Before a vaccine can be rolled out to a particular population, it must first be tested for safety and efficacy in clinical trials. As you would expect, the ethical bar for enrolling children in such trials is very high, and is set out in various well-known guidelines, declarations and conventions dating back to the Nuremberg judgements of 1946.

Nuremberg established that as a general rule 'the voluntary consent of the human subject is absolutely essential',[406] and later Conventions[407] elaborate the benefit/risk calculation for the individual subject where that subject – as with a child – is legally unable to give consent. For example, the Council of Europe Convention on Human Rights and Biomedicine states that while the inclusion of such subjects in clinical research may be acceptable, in addition to all other usual requirements, the following conditions should apply:

Results obtained should have the potential to confer benefit to the person concerned, or to persons in the same age category or afflicted with the same disease or disorder or having the same condition; and

The research should entail only minimal risk and minimal burden for the individual concerned.[408]

The same convention also states that 'The interests and welfare of the human being participating in research shall prevail over the sole interest of society or science.'[409]

Dr Alan Black is a retired pharmaceutical physician with 30 years' experience in the pharmaceutical industry. We spoke to him to ask whether, in his expert opinion, he thought this high ethical bar had been cleared.

He explained that in his view: 'There's never been any conclusive evidence presented that COVID-19 generally poses a significant clinical risk to healthy children (i.e. for these purposes, those without underlying health conditions which would make them potentially more vulnerable to serious health consequences from COVID). Thus, it has been unlikely from the early days that any benefit to a participating subject, in terms of clinically significantly reduced risk of severe disease, hospitalisation or death would be seen. It was also unlikely that any such significant benefits would be seen in groups of healthy children similarly-aged to that trial subject. Once this became clear, the focus of attempted justification for childhood Covid-19 vaccination moved to other speculative endpoints such as preventing lost schooling, preventing "long covid", preventing transmission to elderly or vulnerable adults and protection against some future, as yet unknown, covid variants. Some of these mooted benefits are not even clinical benefits at all. The decision to close schools or keep them open is a political decision, not a clinical one… There are always risks associated with vaccines, both known and unknown, and most of these are not serious. However, some of these, although rare, can be serious, or even life-threatening. I do not understand how exposing a healthy child to any such risk without at least a reasonable chance of significant clinical benefit can be considered ethical.'

He concludes: 'In my opinion, from an ethical point of view the potential benefits to healthy children, either as individuals or a population, from participation in COVID-19 vaccine trials, was, and remains, insufficient to justify the potential risks, both known and unknown, of their participation and to me appears not to come close to meeting the criteria for their inclusion as set out in the Council of Europe convention.'

In Alan's view, the matter may be different for children with underlying health conditions which could potentially make them more vulnerable to serious health consequences from Covid. Here, he believes benefit from vaccination may be clearer, making their inclusion in trials easier to justify ethically. Nevertheless, he points out that before the Covid vaccines received their conditional marketing authorisations for paediatric use, doctors were still free to prescribe their use for such vulnerable children if they thought it was clinically indicated.

* * *

Trust is the bedrock of public health.

It underpins each and every vaccination programme, including those critical to children's health such as polio, MMR and meningitis. In August 2021 Boris Johnson urged parents to 'trust the JCVI – they know what's safe and I think we should listen to them and take our lead from them'.[410]

Vaccinations are integral to childhood health and are one of the stand-out medical successes of the last century. In the UK, we have always traditionally enjoyed strong public support for childhood immunisations and low vaccine hesitancy. Like many parents we are fully supportive of childhood vaccinations in general, although we believe these should always be voluntary, resting on the informed consent of parents and transparent information about risks and benefits. Worryingly, data from early 2022 is showing that rates of uptake for MMR and measles vaccines have markedly dropped.[411]

In the context of the NHS video discussed above, Rob Hughes remarked on Twitter: 'My impression was that some, including influential "experts", felt that the accuracy of the numbers used was secondary to advocacy objectives, i.e. the ends (promoting vaccine uptake) justified the means (using inaccurate, and emotive, statistics and powerful stories). This feels like extremely dangerous ground to me, especially given what we know about the importance of trust in vaccine confidence and uptake, and the recent worrying falls in childhood vaccination.'[412]

This is tragic, as these long-established vaccines with well-understood safety profiles have brought immeasurable benefits to millions of children around the world in reducing death and serious disability.

While erosion of trust is unlikely to be the sole factor at play in immunisation drop off – presumably NHS resourcing has also played a part – it appears that the ham-fisted attempts to force the roll-out of the Covid vaccination to children, with its uncertain risk/benefit profile and the practical impossibility of eradication of the virus, has been allowed to compromise these other programmes. For this reason we believe it no exaggeration to say that the roll-out to children of the Covid vaccination – with the twists, U-turns, lack of transparency and absence of clear, clinical benefit – may prove to be one of the most short-sighted initiatives ever carried out in the name of public health.

Chapter 13
Rogue State

In 1981 author Toni Morrison told *Essence* magazine, 'I don't think one parent can raise a child. I don't think two parents can raise a child. You really need the whole village.'

It's a sentiment that too often contradicts the experience on the ground of parenting in modern Britain, in which degradation of support systems, and prohibitively costly childcare, makes child-raising an often lonely affair. It's sad, but not surprising, that the UK places only 14th in the Raising Children rankings, while family-friendly Denmark, Sweden and Norway take the top three spots with well-rounded public health and education systems.[413]

Yet, no matter how far from ideal, there is 'a village' of sorts in play, an ecosystem relied on by parents, children and families to support them both through normal times, and in times of hardship. From support networks such as playgroups and third sector organisations, to schools, local authorities, healthcare providers and social services, children experience multiple touchpoints throughout their lives intended to help them thrive, promote their interests, and in some cases meet their basic hierarchy of needs.

The significance of these touchpoints depends very much on the circumstances of individual children. For those children who cannot depend on the family as their primary source of support, or who have specific support needs, the wider structure of society must come into play. During the emergency of the pandemic we should surely have expected those systems and structures to act as a safety net.

Indeed, in non-pandemic times, for those children at risk of abuse, the 'village', in the form of neighbours, friends, schools and the wider community, is relied upon to flag up safeguarding issues, and look out for the most vulnerable children. During the pandemic, with lockdown measures in place in May 2020, the Welsh Government called for 'friends, neighbours, postal workers, delivery drivers and communities to act as the eyes and ears for victims of abuse who need help, but can't get in contact because they are under the watchful eyes of their abuser.'[414] As we will explore later, while easy to write, this proved hopelessly naive in practice, with tragic consequences.

Our responsibility to protect and uphold the rights of all children has been formally acknowledged and developed over the last century, and cascaded through institutions, although the concept of children's rights is actually a relatively recent initiative in modern history.[415] Children's rights were initially documented by the Geneva Declaration of the Rights of the Child, and adopted by the League of Nations in 1924. The context and history of this declaration, drafted by co-founder of Save the Children Eglantyne Jebb, is a poignant one. Her impetus was borne out of her experiences of working with refugees in the aftermath of the disaster of the First World War, and serves as a salutary reminder of how emergencies and conflicts degrade and endanger the lives of children most of all. The declaration sought to specifically recognise the special protections required for children, and following its initial foundation, it was adopted in 1959 by the United Nations General Assembly. Then in 1989 a new milestone was introduced in the form of the United Nations Convention of the Rights of the Child (UNCRC). This marked a step forward in safeguarding children's rights, by 'recognizing the roles of children as social, economic, political, civil and cultural actors.'[416] Today it is one of the most ratified treaties in the world – indeed, of the countries eligible to ratify it, only one has not: the USA.

The principles of the UNCRC are often taught in schools. Ironically enough, its tenets were taught to one of the authors' own children during a dispiriting day of remote online schooling during the second round of school closures in January 2021. The juxtaposition of extolling Article 28 – the right of every child to an education – while authorities had withheld face-to-face education for months on end, is a bitter irony.[417]

As Unicef lays out, 'children are neither the possessions of parents nor of the state, nor are they mere people-in-the-making; they have equal status as members of the human family'. Children's autonomous lives must be respected, honoured and nurtured – and they must not be treated as possessions, neglected, or merely used as a means to an end.

How we achieve that as a responsible society is quite another matter.

Usually, primary responsibility for meeting children's needs lies with parents and the family, but there are many instances where the state either has touch points with children's lives or in some cases must step in as 'primary duty bearer to find an alternative in the best interests of the child'. Much of what follows highlights the gulf between stated intentions and responsibilities and the realities on the ground. During the Covid-19 pandemic, children fell headlong into this chasm between words on a page and genuine commitment.

The systemic safeguarding failure of children

Protection of children, and especially the most vulnerable children, based on the principles of child rights, should have been one of our most secure priorities – even and indeed especially during a period of emergency.

In England the legal duty to safeguard is complex, relying on the state and its institutions, parents, and various non-state actors, such as charities. However, because the state and its various institutions and employees – schools, hospitals, nurseries – are, to a greater or lesser degree, central to most children's lives, the state necessarily plays a central role in the safeguarding of children. Statutory guidance sets out the duties of organisations, agencies and individuals working with children and includes schools and educational establishments. An overriding framework – 'Working Together 2018' – provides 100 pages plus of statutory guidance for anyone working with children, which expressly includes schools and early years settings. The *raison d'être* of the framework, 'Safeguarding and promoting the welfare of children', is split into four key points:

- protecting children from maltreatment
- preventing impairment of children's mental and physical health or development
- ensuring that children grow up in circumstances consistent with the provision of safe and effective care
- taking action to enable all children to have the best outcomes.[418]

It is impossible to reconcile the damage done to children by our pandemic policy responses with these aspirations. Not only did state organisations fail to protect and safeguard the most vulnerable children, but in many cases sadly their actions and inactions exposed children to a wider array of harms than they might otherwise have been, for virtually no child health benefit, and making more children vulnerable as a result.

As we saw in Chapter 6, abuse and neglect increased significantly during the pandemic; a record and quite staggering one million referrals for child mental health help treatment were made;[419] and rates of childhood obesity are soaring (see Chapter 5). The idea that child development has 'stalled', as Neil Leitch of the Early Years Alliance put it, is now starting to be borne out by emerging evidence.[420] Safe and effective care was actively halted for many children. Can we really, hand on heart, maintain that our pandemic response was action taken to 'enable all children to have the best outcomes'?

In reality, aside from not being protected, it's hard to see how children's needs featured at all in a pandemic response which hollowed out the system of procedures, legislation, regulations and guidance which had been painstakingly put in place to protect child welfare and which was, until 2020, thought of as inviolable.

'The Covid-19 pandemic and its "lockdown" has seen us bear witness to yet another betrayal. The needs and rights of babies, children, young people and their parents have been ignored while adult life was discussed to granular detail',[421] lament Sir Al Aynsley-Green and Dr Sunil Bhopal in their College of Medicine manifesto.

Vulnerable children

Nowhere is the state's safeguarding role stronger than in respect of the 80,000 children in residential care,[422] where the concept of the 'corporate parent' is used to describe the relationship of the state to the children in its custody. And, for the other 320,000[423] or so children who, though not in care, rely heavily on the state for critical services – because they have an EHCP, or because they have a social worker – the state, though not a guardian, is an important custodian. In addition to these vulnerable children supported by the authorities, there are many more – some 1.6 million[424] – who are not.

A child needing state support in March 2020 – in care, or with a social worker, or on a special needs care plan – would have found that support was withdrawn almost without notice when an array of protections designed to protect children at particular risk were 'relaxed' (aka suspended): some 65 separate legal protections were removed or diluted in relation to children in care alone, a move which Carolyne Willow of Article 39 called an 'outrageous assault on safeguards'.[425]

What was still worse about this episode, was that the standard 21-day consultation period, according to which a regulation would usually be published three weeks before coming into force, giving an opportunity for public scrutiny of the measure, was bypassed. Epitomising the lack of advocacy for children that plagued the pandemic period, Vicky Ford, Children's Minister and a person who might have been expected to defend children's interests most staunchly within government, defended the move: 'waiting 21 days will put extraordinary pressure on local authorities, providers and services', she claimed.

Children's Commissioner Anne Longfield protested that the changes had been made 'with minimal consultation' and that 'Children in care are already vulnerable, and this crisis is placing additional strain on them... If anything, I would expect to see increased protections to ensure their needs are met during this period. ...I would like to see all the regulations revoked, as I do not believe that there is sufficient justification to introduce them', she added.

Anne was ultimately to be proved right. Children's charity Article 39 subsequently won a Court of Appeal case in which Lord Justice Baker concluded the departure from the normal consultation process was not warranted and that the failure to consult the Children's Commissioner and other children's rights bodies had been 'conspicuously unfair'.

Alongside the suspension of the statutory duty to provide the services set out in critical protective plans, the myriad of services and safeguards designed to detect, prevent and respond to maltreatment were suspended or severely disrupted. Until 2020 schools, GPs, children's centres and health visitors had all been thought of as vital for detecting early signs of abuse and neglect, yet all were either closed or switched to remote during the first lockdown. Although vulnerable children were technically able to attend school, far fewer than anticipated did so. While the attendance figures for vulnerable children during the second round of school closures were higher than the dismal figures from the first lockdown, they still hovered consistently around a little under 50%.[426]

One report by Briggs, Telford, Lloyd, and Kotzé, in *Youth Voice Journal*, looking in detail at two social worker case studies, noted that 'already austerity-hit Children's and Young People's services moved almost all their service delivery online, preventing frontline child practitioners and youth offending workers from properly assessing, monitoring, and supporting vulnerable children and young people'.[427] In both case studies, the participants claim that repeated lockdowns have done irreversible damage to their client relationships, jeopardised potential progress out of vulnerable situations, and heightened risks for many of their client group. The report concludes: 'Essentially, these two examples indicate how Covid-19 measures close the door on protecting vulnerable children and young people.'[428]

Making children vulnerable

One of the particularly cruel facts of the pandemic was that not only did we fail to protect already vulnerable children, but our policy response also made many more children vulnerable, exposing a new cohort of children to potential abuse and harm. Take as just one example the 120,000 children now perpetually absent from school. 2020 absence figures represent an increase of 54.7% compared to the previous year.[429]

One of the most unsettling emails we received after launching UsForThem was from a child safeguarding expert. She first wrote to us over the summer of 2020, saying: 'The safeguarding issues are so many it's hard to comprehend how far we have come from protecting children. No one seems to be remotely interested in adhering to any of the legislation in place.'

That email reinforced a clear impression that had been developing in our own minds for some weeks. It was becoming increasingly impossible to reconcile what we by then already understood were the known impacts of lockdown, social distancing and school closures, with what we as parents and citizens had understood of society's duty to safeguard the young from harm. Our view then was as it remains today, that the fact an intervention *might* have some benefit to adults is insufficient to absolve society of its safeguarding duty to children. As we have seen, since early in lockdown many have warned that these measures were likely to be harmful – even fatal – to children. 'There appears to be a system wide dereliction of duty to protect children from harm', our expert concluded.

A number of aspects of the Covid regime inside nurseries, schools and universities might have been expected to raise flags from a safeguarding perspective prior to 2020. Indeed, one of the most troubling aspects of the pandemic for us has been witnessing how easily and completely school and educational settings – places which are meant to inspire and create, or at the very least protect children – became places of potential harm.

The Department for Education guidance, in place from the partial reopening of schools in June 2020, had stringent rules in place if a child became unwell while on the school premises. It said, 'If a child is awaiting collection, they should be moved, if possible, to a room where they can be isolated behind a closed door, depending on the age of the child and with appropriate adult supervision if required.'[430] This recommendation seemed inconsistent with 'best practice' as outlined by the NSPCC to have at least two adults present when working with children and young people.[431]

A newsletter from a school, typical of many that we saw during the pandemic, reads: 'At school, the safety of all of our pupils is of paramount importance. If you have any concerns regarding child protection or keeping a child safe, please contact the School Safeguarding Lead.'

Yet time and time again we have seen the dismissal of voices attempting to raise concerns, by school leaders, local authorities, and even directors of children's services.

In addition, we believe safeguarding questions should have been asked about the clear negative implications of so much screen time for young children and teenagers alike. 'To grow up healthy, children need to sit less and play more', reads WHO guidance published in 2019. As one headteacher commented to us, 'Schools would be up in arms if we actually said that they were on their screen that much time [prior to the pandemic] – it would be a safeguarding issue. Wouldn't it?'.

We have received sufficient emails and messages from teachers and staff inside school, nursery and university buildings as well, obviously, as parents, to understand that many have had concerns.

One primary school teacher we spoke to recalled her experiences of summer 2020 back in the classroom: 'it was an awful environment... it was Year Six sitting with their headphones, still Zooming, because most of the teachers were still at home. They would sit at their desks with their computers and headphones and then every couple of hours somebody would come and point a temperature gun at their head. It was just horrific.'

Another, writing to UsForThem in June 2020, said:

'Then slowly I started to see news reports of schools with yellow and black taped off areas and hoops for children to stand in outside. Stickers on the floor measuring 2m distances for children to subserviently stand on in order to keep them "safe" from a virus that affects them far less than the flu. I even saw a teacher on Twitter yesterday who was proud of his home-made shield for one-to-one reading sessions. This was an A3 plastic laminate across a table

for a Year 1 child. He was genuinely pleased and wanted to share it as a good idea. Even more horrific was the fact that other teachers did, indeed, think it was a good idea.'

Another email read:

'I am a cook in a primary school – key stage one children separated 1 or 2 to a dining table. It is very sad.'

That educational settings also closed their doors to parents and, often, school governors, may be considered a safeguarding failure in itself. Before 2020 it would have been unthinkable for a parent, especially of a nursery or a young primary school child, to have been denied the opportunity to visit the premises where their child spent their days, especially when these premises may have been radically changed since parents would have last been allowed on site, yet this became not only the norm, but an unchallengeable one. As one governor said 'as governors, we couldn't go in and visit and we couldn't pick up on any atmospheric changes in the school or anything that we might be concerned about. We couldn't do our job properly of holding the head to account.' The same governor also pointed out that although school board meetings did still happen on Zoom, worries around confidentiality issues prevented concerns about individual children being raised. As they stressed, being able to go into the school was key to preventative action.

While the risk associated with certain of these measures might have been lessened had they proved to be genuinely 'emergency' or 'temporary', many acquired a semi-permanent status over the last two years. While not all of these situations were the norm, neither were they isolated, and none should have come to pass had we genuinely hardwired protection of children, their welfare and wellbeing, into our processes and institutions.

Broken custodians

'Everyone who works with children has a responsibility for keeping them safe,'[432] asserts the Working Together statutory guidance. Yet, from the very first days it seemed incomprehensible that not a single one of the multiple local and national authorities tasked with 'working together' to safeguard children – local authorities, safeguarding partnerships, directors of children's services, Ofsted, the Department for Education, the Children's Minister, the Secretary of State for Education – had spoken publicly to question the impact of school closures and drastic social distancing and lockdown interventions on children. The only voice to have expressed concern was the Children's Commissioner, but her concerns – to put it bluntly – appeared to be sidelined.

The two posts with direct ministerial responsibility for children during the pandemic were the senior cabinet position of Secretary of State for Education and the more junior position of Minister for Children and Families, the latter with responsibilities spanning vulnerable children and those in care, early years, school sport, children, and young people's mental health and specifically the Covid response for children's services and childcare.

The posts were held in 2020 by Gavin Williamson MP and Vicky Ford MP respectively. We do not know what representations were made by these individuals behind closed doors, but we do have the hard evidence of their respective records in office.

Under Gavin Williamson, English children spent more time out of school than any other country in Europe apart from Italy. In the very first weeks of lockdown in England, on finding out that significantly fewer than anticipated vulnerable children were in school, Gavin Williamson commented simply that the figures illustrated 'the incredible effort families all over the country are making' by keeping children at home[433] – seemingly missing the clear and present danger that the actions taken by his department in closing schools had foisted on children and in sharp contrast to Geoff Barton, who was quick to point out that the figures were 'a very serious concern'.[434] Williamson's ultimate failure to stand up to union pressure has been well documented (see Chapter 8), as has his indecision over exams, which led to many children being denied university places, especially those from disadvantaged backgrounds.

Vicky Ford's defence of the bypassing of the standard 21-day consultation period in the context of the relaxation of care duties has been discussed above, and in our view is just one example of the lack of courageous advocacy for children which plagued Ford's time in office. Ultimately, though, we should let her time in office be judged by the legacy she leaves: recorded increases in cases of abuse and maltreatment,[435] widespread and well-documented deterioration in the physical and mental health of the cohort, and increased rates of language difficulties.[436]

Throughout the pandemic there has been a bitter irony in the fact that it was the Department for Education – whose almost exclusive remit is children and young people – which authored the potentially harmful rules and restrictions imposed on them. At times local authorities seemed to be engaged in a 'race to the bottom', a perverse competition to see who could impose the most stringent and inflexible requirements on children.[437] While Ofsted has now published a number of reports highlighting the harm caused by school closures, it was slow to mobilise: 'Ofsted weren't very interventionalist and vocal', commented Anne Longfield, before continuing, 'I did think Ofsted should [have] come in early as specialists to say "this is what should be rather than this is what is"... obviously subsequently they've done their reviews and said some of these things, but that didn't happen until October plus and the argument needed to be [made] earlier.'

While some school leaders voiced misgivings, they did so

in vanishingly small numbers and were even reprimanded for doing so. Though, as headteacher Mike Fairclough has pointed out, safeguarding training for school staff would have been expected to include examples of where staff have failed to report a child protection concern out of fear for their jobs and reputations: 'employers are responsible for... creating an environment where staff feel able to raise concerns and feel supported in their safeguarding role' reads the 'Working Together' guidance.[438]

Outside of the schools context those speaking out were likely to find themselves in a minority and often criticised – take the example of the social worker who expressed frustration at her colleagues who were not visiting due to the Covid rules, commenting that those still going about the visits were 'seen as the "rule breakers" because we actually do the visits when we shouldn't'. A youth offender worker talked about how isolated she felt carrying on home visits in the face of the rules and orders from her superiors – 'So really, I am on my own. I want to deliver a service, but I have no backing if anything goes wrong.'[439] The same youth offender worker referred to herself as 'someone critical' in a 'system of lemmings' – but isn't it precisely when the system fails under stress that whistleblowers need to be encouraged and protected?

Often those variously imposing or acquiescing in a potentially harmful regime were those in a position of trust. Trust, in fact, goes to the heart of any safeguarding regime: it is precisely because children trust adults that protection, at times, is needed from those adults. As one teacher reflected to us, 'those teachers have let them [the students] down... I get quite upset about the fact that adults who are in that position of power, so much power we have with the children in our care, and they didn't take that seriously.'

These are difficult issues to confront, because of course the state and its organisations are just groups of individuals. Thus failures of the state are at some level also personal failures: of parents, teachers, everyone in fact who was in some way a custodian of children – so many either complicit or did not speak out.

The failure of checks and balances

'There need to be more safeguards built across the system', remarked Anne Longfield in the course of discussing the events of the last two years.

We wholeheartedly agree. As outsiders, it has seemed to us that a key, largely unspoken issue, is that those charged with responsibility for advocating for or protecting children were employed or funded by the very state whose actions and oversights, from a child welfare standpoint, had turned rogue. To our minds this is a glaring and structural weakness which runs through the system, preventing not only effective advocacy for children from those within Government and the other arms of the state at the time it was most needed, but also adequate checks and balances afterwards.

However, we also need to recognise that there is only merit in talking about reforms if as a society we agree that protecting and nurturing children is a good thing to do. Such is the gulf between our written words and our actions that it's not clear to us that – at a communal level – this agreement exists. As Unicef states, 'translating child rights principles into practice requires action and leadership by governments.'[440]

Governments which ratified the UNCRC are obliged to report to the UN Committee on the Rights of the Child every five years. The last report, published in December 2020 by the combined Children's Commissioners amid the height of the pandemic, is worth reading in full.[441] Here we extract a number of key areas which represent a startling indictment of the failure to entrench children's interests at the heart of decision-making.

As we've discussed repeatedly, during the pandemic, the provisions for children to be 'a primary consideration' failed, with decisions that routinely neglected their interests, especially with regard to school closures. The report agrees, saying:

> 'In England, whilst there is now a priority for children to be in school, the initial pandemic response overlooked children's needs, reopening hospitality and shops first.'

We all remember that Primark and pubs were open, while most children were locked outside the school gates.

In terms of protection from sexual abuse, the report finds that:

> 'In England, most children who experience sexual abuse are not identified or supported. For those children who are, the investigative process, including significant delays in bringing cases to trial, is often traumatic.'

And what of the overt discrimination towards children which we discussed in detail in Chapter 10? This too was highlighted as unacceptable in terms of concerning public narratives about 'young people' and Covid-19 restrictions, echoing earlier discourse and measures around anti-social behaviour.

What we cannot measure, we cannot improve. Without knowledge of the impact on children of the pandemic response, across all touchpoints, how can we truly address their needs? The report notes that the 'significant' and concerning data gaps have made it 'challenging to assess the impact on children of the pandemic and State responses'.

All this is bad enough. But most damning of all, the report asserts that 'The UK government does not prioritise children's rights or voices in policy or legislative processes.'

Based on the experiences of the last two years, it is impossible to disagree with this conclusion.

Let's take, for example, an NHS February 2022 document

outlining its plans for tackling the backlog in elective care.[442] The strategy aims to lay out how it will 'transform services' and prioritise those in greatest 'clinical need'. The document mentions paediatrics once, and 'children' only twice. As our country's healthcare bastion, it should surely have a commitment to prioritising children's rights in recovering their health? See articles 3 (best interests of the child) and 24 (health and health services) of the UNCRC. Recall too that children's sacrifice – of their education, mental health and wellbeing – was in the name of protecting the NHS. Will the NHS return the favour?

In March 2021, the Scottish government under Nicola Sturgeon incorporated the UNCRC into domestic law, taking the country's supposed commitment to children's rights a step further than in other jurisdictions.[443] Despite this, secondary school children in Scotland remained subject to greater restrictions than the adult population, with a longer requirement to wear masks in classrooms and schools than in other parts of the UK.[444] Given the likelihood that this decision was at least in part influenced by the largest teaching union, the EIS, the nation cannot really claim to be making children a primary consideration when they are subjugated to adult interests.

Let's also consider that the MP Robert Halfon, having convened a parliamentary debate to discuss the critical issues of educational recovery following the pandemic on 9 March 2022, was faced with a virtually empty chamber containing only a handful of MPs. As our elected parliamentarians, do the 600+ MPs who did not attend the debate not take seriously their responsibilities under Article 3 (best interests of the child), and Article 28 (right to an education)?

To translate this into Ofsted-speak, we might categorise our commitment to prioritising children as 'inadequate'. The bitter truth is that while the UNCRC Children's Commissioner report was published in December 2020, and its findings were perspicacious, little has changed between then and May 2022 to close the gap between aspiration and reality.

It may seem cynical, but when an international treaty such as the UNCRC is simply a collection of words in a document and not a set of values that cascades throughout a society's organisations, then we must question the point of holding them.

Our children's welfare should not be a tick-box exercise, reduced to hollow words, action points that are never met, and emergency protections that vanish in the first moment of a crisis.

There is little point in brandishing our commitment to treaties, conventions and national frameworks, and it does no good to report on safeguarding failures after the fact. The mechanisms must be there to respond in the moment, protect children, and act with urgency: prioritising children must run through the veins of our laws and institutions in deed as well as in word.

Otherwise, all we have is a paper tiger.

Chapter 14
Surrounded by Darkness

'At the end of the day, what is manifest in the treatment of children I found hard to square with any kind of principle of the wellbeing, the welfare of society. It's revealed something very dark. And I hadn't realised how we could come to this point in two years. There are lots of things you can do to adults, but I really didn't think we could do this for young people or that anyone would be up for that. I just didn't think it was possible.'

We start this chapter with these words from Sunetra Gupta. Like Sunetra, many of us would have said it was society's first and foremost duty in any emergency to protect its young. To embrace the inverse reveals a void where there should be a soul.

The implementation of measures with limited or in some cases no evidence of efficacy, and the near to complete disregard for potential harms, may have been explained as mere oversight in the early days of 2020. As time wore on, the failure to carry out either randomised controlled trials or impact assessments invalidated that excuse. Instead, we are left reeling from the actions of leadership intent on pursuing a single-minded approach to public health – the reduction of transmission – however injurious that should prove to the wellbeing, mental health, life chances and physical health of society's youngest members.

We reflect on the words in the SAGE subgroup 'Annex A' from April 2020 that we referenced earlier in the book.

The authors wrote, 'Two urgent areas where experts are expressing concern, but require data to understand the impact are: a. Increases in child suicide. b. The impact of the lack of socialisation on pre-school children.'[445]

The dry words reveal a horrifying insight – the awaited 'data' meant injury or death.

Given the uncertainties, and catastrophic risks, we must ask whether a clinical trial would ever have been approved on non-pharmaceutical interventions that carried these outcomes – let alone an experiment involving millions of children at critical periods in their development.

The actions of the UK Government were mirrored by an international community which – whether by default or design – often appeared to act in lockstep: 'the treatment of children in the developed countries and in developing countries has been shocking', says Jay Bhattacharya. Any doubt that the measures pursued in 2020–21 were a one-off was quashed in April 2022 when PM Boris Johnson stated in a television interview 'I can't say that we wouldn't be forced to do non-pharmaceutical interventions again of the type we did. I believe that the things we did saved lives. I'm not going to take any options off the table.'[446]

We only have to look to China to see where the logical extension of the global health precedent set by the pandemic response might lead: a population exhausting its food supplies after weeks of continuous, unabridged lockdown; citizens screaming from blocks of flats; the forced quarantine of those testing positive in detention centres and the separation of adults from their Covid-positive children. In the words of commentator Neil Oliver, 'the next stops on the science-driven railroad to hell'.[447] US commentator and medic Vinay Prasad says this is 'fundamentally incompatible with a free society, democracy, human rights'[448] – but the same might be said for many of the measures taken in the name of public health by the international community and indeed the UK Government during the pandemic. Blanket and prolonged restrictions on liberty and free movement, vaccine passports, mandatory vaccination, segregation and the encouragement of stigmatisation of a subset of the community – all would have been thought unthinkable until the moment they were introduced.

As a result many parents have fought on two related, but distinct fronts during the pandemic. One is the immediate, clear and present danger to the health, welfare and education of children; the other is existential, striking at the freedoms we are honour-bound to bequeath to the next generation. Each battle extends far beyond anything we had imagined necessary in our lifetimes.

In a way, much of this book is a discussion of the failings – of public health, of discourse, of ethics – that allowed us to arrive at a place of such darkness.

However, we must emphasise two points.

The first is that, to an extent, our current situation reflects the pre-existing status quo of a 'gerontocracy', structurally biased in favour of older generations. It is a mark of how far England has strayed from the 'education, education, education' mantra of the Blair years that while education spending has mostly fluctuated between 4% and 5% of national income over the last 30 years, health spending has seen substantial increases, rising from 4% of national income in the early 1990s to over 7% just before the pandemic,[449] and to around 12.8% in 2020.[450]

As the IFS points out, what this means is that 'Over the whole period since 2010, by contrast, health spending will have increased by over 40%, education spending by less than 3%.'[451] In pointing out the disparity between increases over the last three decades in health spending and education spending, they say 'The cuts to education spending over the last decade are effectively without precedent in post-war UK history, including a 9% real-terms fall in school spending per pupil and a 14% fall in spending per student in colleges. While we have been choosing to spend an ever-expanding share of national income on health, we have remarkably reduced the fraction of national income we devote to public spending on education...'[452]

While life expectancy in the UK has been increasing steadily in modern times,[453] since the 1960s the physical and mental health of young people has – as a generalisation – been declining.[454] Obesity rates increased substantially for primary-aged children during lockdown, but in fact that merely marked an acceleration of a pre-existing trend which has continued for at least the previous 15 years.

The above consequences are to an extent the natural result of a long-term disregard for the young, but were exacerbated during the pandemic as the interests of the vulnerable elderly population directly conflicted with the legitimate needs of the youngest. To an extent the US administration exemplified the interventions made by the Western world. Biden and Fauci as the heads of that administration in relation to the pandemic response have a combined age of 160. Given the risk profile of Covid it is a bitter observation that while their mandated interventions were often diametrically at odds with healthy child development, they also did not extend 'healthspan' (as opposed to 'lifespan') in any meaningful way.*[455] Instead, they might at best have hoped to extend those end of life, lesser quality years. We are not alone in wondering how we reached a point where the dominant approach was to strive to extend the last years of adult life at the expense of children with their whole lives ahead of them.

Lord Sumption is a former Supreme Court judge, and a vocal critic of the Government's lockdown policies. He told us:

---

* Healthspan is the period of a person's life during which they are typically in good health and which generally is significantly less – up to a third – than lifespan. In the period 2015 to 2017, males in the UK had a life expectancy (LE) of 79.2 years at birth while females had a life expectancy of 82.9 years. By contrast, in the UK in 2015 to 2017, healthy life expectancy (HLE) at birth was 63.1 years for males and for females was 63.6 years.

'Children are special in two main respects. The first is that they are at virtually zero risk of becoming seriously ill as a result of Covid. And the second is that counter-measures that prevent them from going to school or associating with other people have an effect on them, which is longer term than its effect on adults. Its effect on some adults is very long-term indeed, but its effect on almost all children and particularly the less advanced children is both very damaging and very long term. It's likely that those who are most challenged in the learning process will suffer consequences for their personal development which will live with them for their whole lives.'

Beyond the tragedy for these children at an individual level, the shortsightedness of such an approach in terms of cost to the state is often obvious. As Paul Dolan notes, to take just one example, the 100,000 'ghost children' who we now know to have dropped off the school register: 'They're going to have shorter lives. They're going to have less happy lives. And they are going be a huge expense to the public purse, leaving to one side whether you care about their welfare. They're going to be costly because they're going to be coming in and out of the system for the rest of their lives.' Similarly, obesity – which already costs the NHS £4.2 billion a year. This figure, without 'urgent and radical action', in the words of the Royal Society for Public Health, 'will rise to £10 billion a year by 2050.'[456]

And, in all of this, one has to ask – who was it for?

We do not for a second suggest that the Bidens and Faucis speak for all of their generation: since starting UsForThem we've been deluged by messages from concerned grandparents beside themselves at the treatment of their grandchildren. 'Not in my Name'[457] wrote columnist Janet Daley in June 2020, saying 'It absolutely horrifies me to think that my grandchildren might be disadvantaged into the indefinite future, in order (possibly) to protect their grandparents' generation from – what?'. Her worries were echoed by Paul Dolan, who mused, 'I would be really interested to find out if anyone bothered asking what older people would've liked to have seen done. I know from some empirical work we've been doing and previous work as a health economist, that older people want quality of life, not quantity of life.'

This leads to the second point.

As we have alluded to above and throughout, Covid is a discriminatory virus. It is not denying the threat the disease poses to some adults to say that, by and large, it poses little threat to the vast majority of children and young people.

As Alberto Giubilini of the Oxford Uehiro Centre for Practical Ethics explains, 'Covid-19 is a serious disease for some parts of the population, and its risks are unevenly distributed across different age groups. As a result, it is important that we critically and ethically assess how we treat these different groups, carefully evaluate different risks and benefits, and are clear about why we make the policy decisions that we do.'[458]

However, it has been a consistent – and indeed ongoing – feature of the last two years that as a society we have refused to tolerate any serious public discussion about the ethics of our actions, even as those actions seem contrary to what many would previously have considered established principles.

This failure has manifested itself in different ways, but nowhere more vividly than in the lack of debate around whether it was ever legitimate to impose indiscriminate measures on the general population, including developing children.

As Giubilini says in the *Spectator*, 'we have heard a great deal about the policies used to manage the virus, but very little about the ethics. This is a mistake. We should be asking how we can critically and reasonably strike a balance between conflicting values and interests.'[459] It's a balance that we appreciate would encompass a range of positions, including those of parents of children for whom concern about viral protection was of greater weight than, for example, parents of children with SEN for whom maintenance of a normal school environment and access to therapies was often an overriding factor. However, school closures, an indiscriminate measure imposed with hugely damaging consequences on children not by and large at risk from the virus, exemplify the failure to consider this ethical balancing act. Writing in the context of the suggestion to shield the vulnerable, Giubilini notes in the *Spectator*: 'It might be a difficult policy to implement in practice – but it is one that should at least be explored calmly and rationally. Instead it has been met with hyperbolic fury.'[460]

This overarching ethical failure has been compounded along the way by further failures – for example the vaccination of children against Covid, which Giubilini has labelled a 'double ethical mistake' – first via the use of children as 'mere means', and second via the manipulation of school disruption as a necessary consequence of transmission. But in fact, as Giubilini himself acknowledges, the same mistakes are part of a broader failing, in which we 'attribute the harms imposed by the decision to close schools and to lock down society to the virus itself.'[461] It is, incidentally, for this reason that throughout this book we resist presenting harms to children as flowing from the virus, rather than the measures taken to combat that virus. In the vast majority of cases, the latter is true.

As we saw in Chapter 12, the framing of school disruption as an inevitable health sequitur artificially inflates benefits to children and so muddies any debate around the ethics of potentially harmful interventions on children. Similarly, a refusal to countenance open discussion of costs (harms) has also made honest discussion about the ethics of interventions impossible. 'In every slide show delivered during the Downing Street press conferences, we only ever see data about the virus. This is regrettable. To allow rational and ethical scrutiny, we would need slides showing how many will die from the effects of lockdown,'[462] says Giubilini in the *Spectator*.

The same might be said in the context of any number of interventions imposed on children: whether through censorship or self-censorship we have stifled public discussion to such a degree that at times it has become impossible to raise reasonable and indeed essential ethical questions about our choices.

Back in the haze of 2020 a conversation needed to be had: uncomfortable, difficult, but necessary. That conversation ran something along the lines of 'imagine a re-enactment of the clichéd, but apt, example of a crowded life-raft set to leave the shore with room for one other passenger. Standing on the water's edge are a five-year-old child and an 80-year-old adult. Which soul do you save?'

Naturally, this is a false dichotomy, as all such moral dilemmas are. As a society we should – and would – have sought to protect the elderly and vulnerable, but that ought to have always been contextualised against the respective harms to children. There is a simple equity to this that before 2020 few would have denied: children haven't yet lived their lives, but adults have, or, to put it another way, in the words of Norway's Corona Commission:

> 'To put it a little simply, we can say that children and young people are worse affected by restrictions than by infections and that there is a difference between what you miss out on over a year when you are 16 compared to when you are 46'.[463]

For these reasons our natural instinct is to protect children, but that instinct was denied. This conversation was never permitted in mainstream societal discourse, and that failure to face up to the realities of the distribution of harms set the tone for all that followed.

Chapter 15
The Way Forward

'We say: start with the child at the centre. Remember children
are precious and exquisitely vulnerable. Remember they
are the future of the very society that is letting them down
so badly. Put children at the centre of healthcare services,
schools, outdoor space, the built environment, care systems,
courts and job centres.'

Sir Al Aynsley-Green and Dr Sunil Bhopal, College of Medicine
manifesto, 'Hope for the Future'[464]

And so we come to the end of our inquiry, and the beginning
of the next chapter in our children's lives, as we look to
the way forward. In conclusion, we need to reflect on fixing
what was broken – putting the checks and balances in place
to prevent the same flawed and inequitable responses from
happening again in a future disaster. In the interests of repair
and recovery, we must also apply the national will and effort
needed for urgent interventions to mitigate the impacts
experienced by children and especially the most vulnerable:
those with disabilities, speech and language difficulties and
mental health issues who cannot wait a moment longer for
help. As we have seen, however, children's lives were not
a calm sea even before the pandemic. Beyond repair and
recovery we must aspire to do better: how do we reimagine
childhood to ensure children flourish?

It is our collective moral imperative to address these
questions.

How to protect children in the next disaster

From a child welfare point of view, our pandemic response was a national disaster.

Not only does it appear that the response conflicted with seminal principles of international children's law,[465] ethics and morality, it also appears to have contravened any number of key pre-established pandemic planning principles. A 2007 Cabinet Office pandemic management ethical framework[466] urged that 'those responsible for providing information will neither exaggerate or minimise the situation and will give people the most accurate information that they can.' The same document[467] included a 'reasonableness requirement'; and noted that decisions must be 'rational; not arbitrary; based on appropriate evidence; the result of an appropriate process…[468] And with respect to the principle of proportionality, 'decisions on actions that may affect people's daily lives, which are taken to protect the public from harm, will be proportionate to the relevant risk and to the benefits that can be gained from the proposed action.'[469] A 2011 planning document reiterates the same critical point – 'Proportionate response to pandemic influenza' reads the title to the key table in the document in big, bold letters.[470] Unfortunately, we seem to have parted ways with the principle of proportionality in March 2020.

Laura Dodsworth has written of the state's egregious failure in respect of the first of these principles and indeed the level of fear deliberately stoked by Government clouded all that followed – it was almost impossible to advocate for calm common sense over hysteria-fuelled blanket restrictions. Indeed, surely this sensible notion of responsible messaging was regularly breached by the failure to present accurate risk stratification alone. As for reasonableness and proportionality, our view remains as it was on the day we launched UsForThem back in May 2020: that the pandemic response as it impacted children was neither reasonable nor proportionate (or indeed rational), failing not only to prioritise children, but also in many cases to protect them at all.

As we mentioned at the very beginning, we live in hope rather than expectation that the official Covid public inquiry will look in detail and with a genuinely independent lens at these issues, but even if we are pleasantly surprised, the timeframe for any inquiry – at half a decade or more – extends far beyond what is helpful for the current cohort of children. What follows are our reflections on how to ensure that the next pandemic does not see the same crippling deprioritisation of children and their needs.

Inequitable trade-offs

'What you need to say is… If we are going to have a future, if we are going to get through this, we prioritise the children and their needs above all else.'

We have started this section with these words from disaster planner Professor Lucy Easthope, as we could have done worse than let this thought guide our pandemic response.

In any disaster scenario the interests of different groups must be balanced and trade-offs made. By its nature, there will often be only imperfect solutions. What really happened in the time of Covid was that the interests of one category of vulnerable citizens – children – conflicted with another: elderly and vulnerable adults, and perhaps, to a lesser degree, a category of very vulnerable children. As outsiders, we cannot say with certainty how those trade-offs were balanced, and one reason that the Covid public inquiry is important is to shine a critical light on these decision-making processes. We have, however, had the benefit of interviewing two people who have been intimately involved in disaster planning for the last two decades, Robert Dingwall and Lucy Easthope. It is with their insights and what we know of the impacts of the last two years that we can now say with some certainty that when vital decisions were made, it appears that children were not only not prioritised, but were barely considered at all.

We must ask why that was.

The failure to follow previous disaster plans

The idea that children should be protected was implicitly recognised by previous disaster plans, which appear to have been predicated on an underlying assumption that schools would, by and large, stay open.

As Robert Dingwall explains, 'When I was involved in pandemic flu planning around 2005, 2006 we were always very clear that the schools would never close, unless there were so many teachers off sick that you couldn't provide a safe environment for the children. We were thinking a threshold of maybe 30, 40% of the teaching staff.'

In fact, although legacy planning documents are not entirely consistent, this assumption was written into some of them: 'once the virus is more established in the country, the general policy would be that schools should not close unless there are specific local business continuity reasons (staff shortages or particularly vulnerable children)', reads the UK Influenza Pandemic Preparedness Strategy 2011.

In Lucy's view, this reflected the fact that the 'gravity of school closure was understood well beyond education... we just worked in a room where we always went "schools will stay open,"' a point reinforced by the 2011 flu pandemic planning document mentioned above,[471] which concluded that due to the substantial economic and social consequences of school closures, 'such a step would therefore only be taken in an influenza pandemic with a very high impact'. It said that 'although school closures cannot be ruled out, it should not be the primary focus of schools' planning'.

While in more recent years there appears to have been

something of a shift away from 'school as essential for children' to 'school as essential childcare', by the time of the coalition government in 2014 a Public Health England pandemic planning document incredibly contained only one reference to school: 'Examples of indirect impact may be closure of schools and children's nurseries, resulting in staff unavailability for child care reasons'.[472] Full, prolonged school closures were never really contemplated in these documents.

On the contrary: the most recent pronouncement on the matter comes from one of the learnings from Operation Cygnus, the practice pandemic planning exercise conducted in 2016. As is now notorious, those learnings were not made available to the public until 2020 and many, it appears, were never followed up.[473,474] This is unfortunate, as one of the key suggestions from our perspective – Learning 14 – was:

> 'DfE should study the impact of school closures and also examine the possibility of keeping schools open by getting retired teaching staff to return to support the profession and by the temporary upskilling of students. Any plans should include safe-guarding procedures, the allocation of appropriate roles and the legislation that may be required to allow staff to return to the profession.'

It appears this was never done.[475] We can only speculate as to why. Robert Dingwall has spoken in another context of the impact of 'the acute loss of organisational memory' in relation to pandemic planning:

> '...as a result of the slimming down of the civil service over the last 10 years as a result of austerity. I recall being on a committee where a civil servant came along and said, "well, I've been charged with producing a document to say how we'd deal with this contingency". And they clearly had no awareness that such a document had already existed,

and that whoever had written the previous document had actually looked at the experiences of emergencies back to World War II in developing it. But we had reached the point at which nobody actually knew that this document existed'.

In her book, *When The Dust Settles*, Lucy Easthope recounts how, in relation to pandemic planning exercises, 'as time went on, we received more and more declined appointments for the exercise from both senior clinicians and government ministers.'[476]

As Lucy says, 'the guidance [in early March 2020] coming out of central government on how to ready for the dead of the pandemic was woefully incomplete... government advisers in public health were telling local planners to use the "IFR", the infection fatality rate, to calculate the local need. But that is not how planning for deaths in a pandemic works. You also need to factor in the other harms: the delayed hospital treatment, the neglected maternal care, the beaten children.'[477]

Whatever the reason, it appears a regrettable failure and one which left both DfE and the wider community woefully ill-prepared to ensure continuity of children's schooling and safeguarding arrangements in the event of a pandemic.

It is a failure we must, this time, learn from. As Anne Longfield says, 'if you're looking for any kind of crisis of the future it would make sense to identify the core parts of government infrastructure that need to be prioritised. Clearly the economy would be one, clearly people, if it's health related, would be another. But I would say education needs to be on there. There needs to be some kind of crisis planning that needs to come out of the government review of the handling of the pandemic and then a strategy of readiness for a future pandemic that has to write education in and children's wellbeing in.'

Checks and balances

Whatever they do or do not say, disaster plans are only of any use if they are first found, and then followed. Legal and operational safeguards are critical to ensure protection and prioritisation of children in reality as well as on paper in any emergency. This question, at the heart of how we should protect children's interests in policymaking, is discussed further below, but is particularly important in an emergency situation where life and death decisions may well be taken under extreme pressure.

One practical strategy Professor Paul Dolan suggests is simple checklists for decision-making to highlight consequences. He says:

'What we ought to have done right from the beginning, if nothing else, is have a checklist of some of the important impacts and consequences that would follow from the quite significant measures that were put in place. One of the most obvious things that ought to have been at the forefront of policymakers' minds when deciding to close schools, for example, would be what impact school closures would have on children. In particular the impact on the most vulnerable and the most disadvantaged children in society where school the only place that they would've got care, comfort and attention – and food – and where the school would notice if there were any significant issues at home and where they would've got fed. There's something really significantly broken in the decision-making process.'

The UK Influenza Pandemic Preparedness Strategy 2011, published by the Department of Health,[478] sets out as one of its overall objectives: 'Minimise the potential impact of a pandemic on society and the economy by... supporting the continuity of essential services... and protecting critical national infrastructure as far as possible.'

If the last two years have taught us anything, it is that schools are essential for millions of children – not only for education, but for child wellbeing and safeguarding. For this reason, the bar for school closures must be set exceptionally high.

As currently defined throughout legislation, by and large 'critical infrastructure' does not include schools, and this absence sets an unhelpful tone, contributing to an assumption that schools are in some way non-essential and can, when push comes to shove – and unlike power stations, supermarkets or hospitals, say – be seen as an acceptable lever in the toolbox of pandemic management. In reality, school is just as important to a young person's life as a hospital may be to an elderly or unwell person's.

In this respect the Essential Infrastructure and Opening During Emergencies[479] bill tabled by Education Select Committee Chair Robert Halfon MP – a project with which we are proud to have been involved – is helpful, suggesting as it does a 'triple lock' mechanism before schools are closed. This would elevate the status of schools and education in public consciousness, and would provide an element of practical protection: a separate vote of Parliament would be required before schools could be closed, and advice from the Children's Commissioner would need to be taken. However it is done, a coherent, workable and realistic plan that considers operational constraints to keep schools safely open in scenarios where there are staff shortages should be considered urgent, and essential.

Safeguarding

The pandemic response involved a systemic weakening or outright suspension of the social work protections for children. The result was to make many vulnerable children less visible at a point at which risk factors for child maltreatment were heightened. Leaving aside the question of whether school closures were justified in this case, in the exceptional circumstances in which it is both a proportionate and necessary reaction for schools to close (for example, a virus that is of severe threat to children) we must ask what more needs to be done to bolster safeguarding mechanisms outside of schools.

As forensic psychologist Dr Rosie Gray notes, 'Support services for children and families that protect against, and can help to identify early signs of, abuse, neglect and/or exploitation, including health visiting, parenting support, youth work etc, to be recognised as essential frontline services should, wherever possible, be maintained during periods of crisis, since this is when they are likely to be needed most. If services absolutely must be restricted, we should use existing knowledge of high-risk groups to aid decision-making as to where best to direct resources and mitigations (e.g. children with disabilities, under ones, etc). More generally we must identify low-risk (i.e. low-transmission) activities as soon as possible and utilise this knowledge so that safeguarding and support services can be maintained, or even (ideally) increased.'

A safeguarding failure of a different type also took place via the suspension of children's health services and services for disabled children, the latter at times proving nothing short of barbaric in its impact. As with social care we must ask how any future emergency could better deal with this in a way which not only recognises the humanity of disabled children, but also allows them to flourish – and in particular to avoid the kind of suspension in care and therapies that was such a damaging feature of the response to Covid-19.

Narrow frame of reference

From the outset the pandemic came to be seen in very narrow terms: neither education, nor schooling, nor indeed children, was prioritised. Robert Dingwall notes: 'The pandemic flu planning always envisaged the lead in a pandemic would be taken by the Cabinet Office. And more specifically the Civil Contingencies Unit, which is like the country's emergency planning team. And this would coordinate a whole of government, whole of science approach to the management of the pandemic. And I think it'll be for the inquiry to find out why that leadership passed to the Department of Health and put everything through a lens of "what do we do to stop the infection?" rather than "what do we do to manage a society with an infection in it?"'.

Of this, Lucy Easthope says: 'the way we did pandemic exercising in the early 2000s was that every department had to "play" and bring their plan. And under the coalition and beyond it became a health emergency; but it's not simply a health disaster. It's a societal and educational and childhood disaster'. She goes on to make the point that she would have liked to see Gavin Williamson – then Secretary of State for Education – chairing some COBRAs in January and February 2020. 'This was a children's disaster above all else, where DfE should have taken a substantial lead,' Lucy says – a sentiment with which we agree. 'But when I said that in the meetings, they were visibly shocked.'

We also know that DfE presented evidence to meetings that does not appear to have been acted upon: an unpublished Department for Education report (Internal DfE report (2020)) is cited on a number of occasions within the 'Annex A' to a paper prepared by a SAGE subgroup of 16 April 2020, which we referred to earlier in the book.[480] According to the Annex, this paper reported on issues of importance, including a significantly increased risk to vulnerable children's welfare as a result of school closures, evidence to indicate that Education, Health and Care assessment and review work was being withdrawn, potentially resulting in an escalation of needs, teachers reporting difficulties to engage pupils in out of school learning, especially in deprived areas, inequities being commonplace and the results of a survey (seemingly of parents, though not specified) indicating increased concern regarding the impact of school closure on children's mental and physical health. Within the Annex, there were a number of proposals to develop the evidence base and address the impact of these issues, including surveys of headteachers/ schools and educational psychologists.

Given this report is referenced in a SAGE paper we might assume it was presented to that committee, but as far as we know it was never made public, nor acted upon by the Government – otherwise why did the issues it alluded to continue, for many children, throughout that spring and summer?

Dr Sunil Bhopal is a paediatrician who in June 2020 organised an open letter to the Prime Minister, notable in that it was the first time that the Royal College of Paediatrics and Child Health (RCPCH) had asked its members to sign a joint message to the prime minister. The letter warned in stark terms that pupils' continued absence from school 'risks scarring the life chances of a generation of young people'.

The advice in the letter, despite being signed by 1,500 doctors and child health specialists, was not heeded. Reflecting on the period, Dr Bhopal tells us 'what really surprised me in those early days through 2020 was just how little the public and decision-makers understood about the specific needs of children and about their rights. It seemed quite acceptable in some circles that children and childhood ceased to be an issue of public policy, and they were simply expected to stay at home with parents – whatever circumstances, whatever hardship they were facing at home. There was very little understanding that what happens to children in those early years influences their whole life health and wellbeing – we heard decision-makers and the public claiming that children are "resilient" and "will be fine" in the face of any hardship or degradation. I always found this extremely troubling, based on decades of scientific understanding showing that what happens to you in childhood matters lifelong – not just for individuals but for whole societies, too.'

Recovery and repair

No group was more abandoned by the pandemic response than our most vulnerable children, including disabled children. A Government with any ounce of fairness or equity would start by implementing the recommendations made by the Disabled Children's Partnership, and it would do so in full. These are summarised by Stephen Kingdom, Campaign Manager for the Disabled Children's Partnership, as follows:

'Prioritise the needs of disabled children and their families within Covid recovery plans and programmes; tackle the backlog in assessments and ensure that children's needs are reassessed in light of missed support during the pandemic; ensure the right support is in place for all children and families, including education, health (including mental health), therapies and equipment; take a whole family approach to assessments and support, including siblings. This should include the provision of respite/ short breaks and opportunities for families to take part in activities to overcome the isolation felt by so many. Invest in disabled children's health and care services through the Comprehensive Spending Review.'

We must, as discussed, bolster our safeguarding and social work protections for vulnerable children. In addition we must elevate vulnerable children within policymaking, as Anne Longfield says, 'what I would like to see is that vulnerable children are a stated priority by whatever governance date and that there is a distinct government policy which is around reducing vulnerability.'

There is now significant pressure on paediatric mental health services and rates of child health issues and obesity are soaring. Professionals observe that children present with serious illness and development issues later, making treatment harder. This is a direct reaction to the pandemic and its response. Making good on this deficit is urgent, and investment is now critical across health visitors, therapies for SEN and disabled children, a pre-school vaccination programme as ambitious as that for the Covid-19 vaccines and to clear the backlog of operations and developmental assessments.

However, the scale of the paediatric health backlog in the aftermath of the pandemic becomes clear, we must accept that what is needed is less 'sticking plaster' solutions and more wholesale reform: a paradigm shift in how we do and pay for education – and indeed childhood – in policymaking.

The recommendations by Sir Al Aynsley-Green and Dr Sunil Bhopal in their College of Medicine 'Hope for the Future' manifesto provide an aspirational starting point. They state:

> *'A decent post-Covid response puts promotion of child health and well-being both front and centre. Needs are identified, intervention is early. The country recognises that what happens in childhood has life-long ramifications for individuals, which, in turn, determines the kind of societies we build into the future. The prize if we choose to accept this challenge? The chance to re-set British childhood and move into a post-Covid world creating a better, more resilient society for generations to come.'*

The moral imperative to implement ambitions on this scale has never been clearer. How we generate the political momentum to make that happen is the subject of the last pages of this book.

Reimagining childhood

Education, and school, is crucial to children's lives. Nowhere more than in the schools context is it more important for us to ask how we move beyond merely repairing to a future that allows children to thrive. It is clear that adults need to put their differences aside to work on solutions with creativity and energy.

As Anne Longfield remarked, in the context of school closures:

'What disappointed me throughout was that no one had put the best minds, the best creativity or priority on doing the same for kids. So in parts of Europe, you had kids where they'd taken over public buildings next to the school. They'd looked at what it would take to keep schools open, rather than what it seemed to me was "we can't – there are too many moving parts here and we haven't got the political capital the time or the money – or whatever – to make this work, therefore we're just going to have to compromise". That shouldn't have been the thing that was compromised.'

We've seen the marked contrast between the collective energy that was poured into the health service during the pandemic, and the paucity of response in terms of education. Civil society has enormous energy, skills, funding and ideas that, if directed towards children and young people as beneficiaries, could be transformational.

In her final speech as Children's Commissioner Anne Longfield invoked the London 2012 Olympics, saying, 'We looked like a united, outward-facing country, confident about what it could achieve'. Having applied that energy during the pandemic response, 'We now need to do the same for children'.[481]

While we mustn't accept revisionism, equally we cannot continue to wrangle over past mistakes. The welfare, health, and education of children and young people is not, and should never have been, a polarised issue. While people of different political persuasions may have worldviews that make them see problem-solving differently, it shouldn't be beyond our capabilities to collaborate, bringing ideas from across ideological divides and disciplines.

Does this sound utopian? Perhaps, but considering proposals on their own merits is an important step. For example, over the last two years, we have clashed extensively, and sometimes brutally, with teaching unions such as the

NEU. Nevertheless, as parents, and from personal experience, we agree with the NEU's assertion that the current primary and early years assessment programme is detrimental to children's wellbeing and 'not fit for purpose'.[482] Year 6 SATs in particular seem ridiculously constrained, reductive and disproportionately high-pressured. Likewise, we agree with much of NAHT's blueprint for educational recovery, in particular its focus on early years, child wellbeing, and extra-curricular activities.

We agreed entirely with Geoff Barton, of the headteachers' union ASCL, when he told us it 'can't be good enough' that in the current system in which a grade 4 at GCSE is designated a 'standard pass', 'for one child to get a grade four, another child has to get a grade three', and that 'a third of young people get to the age of 16 and will get a grade three, a grade two or a grade one'. Elsewhere, Barton has described this group of young people as the 'forgotten third' and in speaking to us urged that all children need 'the dignity of achievement'. Anne Longfield, during her final speech as Children's Commissioner, described as 'abysmal' the fact that a fifth of children reach the age of 19 without getting five GCSEs or equivalent, the 'basic benchmark for all children to set them on the path to successful adulthood.'[483]

Also, while we've consistently argued that children should have been in school throughout the pandemic, at the same time we recognise that many children experience school as square pegs in round holes.

What we measure, we improve

Instead of just poring over primary school children's phonics, and literacy and numeracy at secondary school, important though these are, we would go so far as to say that children's wellbeing and happiness should be the core metric by which we should judge 'success' in policymaking for children.

In fact, according to Unicef data from 2020, at age 15, only

64% of the UK's children report high life satisfaction, placing us 31st in the global league table, and a staggering 26% behind the Netherlands, where 90% of children asked how happy with their lives they were reported scores over 5 on a scale of 1–10.[484] The overall child wellbeing outcomes which incorporate academic and social skills, mental wellbeing and physical health placed the UK at an underwhelming 27th overall, 29th in mental wellbeing and 26th in terms of skills. At the top of the charts, the Netherlands – while placing 1st overall, and 1st for mental wellbeing, also ranks impressively in 3rd for skills, demonstrating that prioritising wellbeing and physical health doesn't necessarily mean a trade-off in skills. It's a thought-provoking set of data, because an insidious concept of a trade-off between academic outcomes and happiness seems to colour many of our preconceptions about education and raising children. A paper by Tania Clarke, 'Children's wellbeing and their academic achievement: The dangerous discourse of "trade-offs" in education', aims to refute earlier work by Heller-Sahlgren in a report suggesting that policymakers need to decide whether they uphold children's wellbeing *or* their academic achievement as the priority. Clarke argues that this is a 'false dichotomy', representing 'a wider current of thinking in education whereby researchers pit achievement goals against the goal of wellbeing'.[485] In concluding, she writes, 'Reimagining schools as places that *can* foster pupils' wellbeing and learning should be our default position, rather than assuming one must trump the other.'

In this regard, while it was a positive effort by the current Secretary of State for Education to publish a Schools White Paper in March 2022, the void of holistic thinking it displayed was striking.[486] Its stated ambitions are narrow – literacy and numeracy will be the 'measure of this white paper's success'. Though its 'parent pledge' to commit to targeted support for any child who falls behind in maths or English is welcome, as is the aspiration for a minimum school week of 32.5 hours by September 2023, there is a dispiriting lack of vision and ambition at its heart. Updated plans for sport and music education are to be released in 2022: it is a telling signal of priorities that the report effectively kicks the can down the road on 'enrichment' for children in sports and music to a future date and a future report. In fact, as the pandemic period has made abundantly clear, these activities, far from being an adjunct, are essential for children's wellbeing and it is time to start to see music, sport, and drama being placed at the very heart of children's time in school. These activities are vital for thriving, self-esteem and health in normal times, but especially so in the aftermath of a traumatic and depleting period in children's lives.

Fun shouldn't be a footnote, or an 'up next'; it needs to be an integral part of reimagining.[487]

Begin with the end in mind

What's wrong is not confined to education; it goes right to the heart of our young people's experience of a childhood that is too often considered by the State in terms of their status as future economic assets. As Sir Al Aynsley Green tells us, 'we have to begin with the end in mind, what are we actually trying to achieve for our children?'

For us, in reimagining childhood, and education – the 'end in mind' must acknowledge the importance of achievement, which equips children and young people – from early years to university – to lead successful lives, closing the attainment gap, and better supporting those with disabilities and SEN, while simultaneously taking decisive action to boost young people's happiness and enrich their childhoods.

As Tania Clarke says, it is a false transaction to pit one against another – to help our children thrive post pandemic, we need to pour efforts and energy into both, not narrow the focus still further. And, as Professor Robert Dingwall notes, 'schools are more than factories for producing exam results.

It's a problem that the Department for Education has lost sight of that education is a lot more than facts and cramming knowledge into the heads of children.'

Indeed, even if we were to leave children's own happiness and experiences to one side, centring play, fun and subjects such as music could be a net benefit for achievement. Richard Jeffries is a music teacher and musician who spends time working with children in different schools. He visited Finland as part of a Churchill Fellowship,[488] investigating educational systems in other countries, and found a system which was more 'child-centred' with a greater sense of 'discovery and freedom'. There, music is more embedded in the curriculum, and Jeffries expresses to us his hope that we might embrace the benefits of music not only in its own right, but also for its impact on other aspects of the curriculum. He says:

'I think we need to move away from seeing everything as separate and seeing how music can directly impact whatever it is you're doing in your curriculum elsewhere. We already know it can affect language and reading and speech can help concentration and at the end of the day, you know, they're life skills and it should really be central to it.'

However, deemed as an 'add on' it's one of the first things to be pared back – especially now, in the context of the pervasive 'catch up' narrative. Richard tells us of his frustration that even before the pandemic, 'it was bad enough with the SATs and testing and the pressure that the children have', explaining that, 'I used to have pupils going in and out of my music lessons to do more reading and more maths.'

We must also widen the curriculum to include educating children about health and nutrition. By the age of 10, one-fifth of children in the UK are obese – a shocking statistic that stores up dire problems not only for those children but for the state and its health service, with the well-known link between severe Covid and obesity[489] something of an elephant in the room over the last two years. Any reimagining plan must address this and again in this we should look to the recommendations of the College of Medicine,[490] which include sensible suggestions for every child to have at least an hour of daily exercise, and to have lessons on cooking healthy meals.

The last two years should also have brought not only the need, but also an opportunity to rethink some of the fundamentals surrounding children and exercise. For example, as Anita Grant, Chair of Trustees of Play England, tells us 'during lockdown use of parks became really high priority for families and there's a massive opportunity here to rethink those spaces because people who didn't have access to their private garden spaces had to go out and use those.'

Early years

We are structurally myopic in our lack of commitment to early years, despite the wealth of knowledge about the defining nature of the first five years of a child's life. As Neil Leitch of the Early Years Alliance commented in relation to the publication of the 2022 Schools White Paper:

> 'While we welcome the fact that the government has recognised that "high quality early years provision will ensure children have the best possible start to their education", the White Paper includes very little evidence or detail on how this is going to be achieved in practice.
> Calls for a long-term strategy for the early years sector have long been ignored by the government and [this] is no exception. The Schools White Paper is yet another example of the government's insistence on prioritising schools over early years providers, despite a wealth of evidence showing that the best way to tackle educational attainment gaps is to invest in quality early education.'

In Nordic countries, by contrast, the early years sector is well respected, funded, and the workforce has been professionalised. While the Schools White Paper does at least introduce a new National Professional Qualification for Early Years Leadership, and up to £180 million investment for the early years workforce, at first blush this again looks very narrow, with the focus on training for early years practitioners to support literacy and numeracy teaching.[491]

This is a far cry from the ethos of some of our Nordic neighbours, again like Finland, where children would not be expected to start formal school until seven, and where until then the focus is on learning through play.[492]

To have a chance of creating our reimagined world, we must have the humility to look to overseas and the countries who are leaders in the Unicef rankings for inspiration. This should include looking to, and learning from, existing overseas networks advocating for children's interests, for example Eurochild – a collective of organisations and individuals working with and for children in Europe whose aims include ensuring early childhood development receives the political visibility it deserves.[493]

One significant source of hope in this area comes from the work of the Royal Foundation's Centre for Early Childhood on Early Years which aims to change the way that society sees and acts on the critical early years. This has the potential to be a desperately important voice and we very much hope its outputs will be translated by policymakers into tangible actions.

Investment and long-term thinking

We discussed in Chapter 4 the inadequacy of the current recovery plans.

Recreating and reimagining also means putting education on a proper footing, with strategic vision as well as financial clout. As Robert Halfon MP tells us, there is too often a haphazard quality to the management of education. He describes the programme as 'a lot of piecemeal announcements' that while they may have merit in themselves, are 'a lot of clothes pegs without a washing line'. He goes on to say, 'What is the aim? What does the government want to do to education? What's the purpose of education? That should be set out and how they're going to do it and how it's going to be funded.'

There is a desperate need to put education on the kind of long-term secure funding plan that has been called for by stakeholders from all sides, many of whom have written blueprints which would be obvious starting points. The two that need particular mention for their ambition and cross-stakeholder appeal are those of the cross-party Education Select Committee[494] and the Foundation for Education Development.[495] The failure of successive governments to pay serious attention to these plans, and the many other sensible proposals from the teaching and headteacher unions – including those aimed at addressing longstanding issues of inequality and child poverty which are so corrosive to the life chances of millions of children in this country – looks less and less forgivable in light of the growing intergenerational inequities between our young people and their elders.

At heart this is a failure of leverage: a critical point we return to shortly.

Structural changes

We must make Sir Aynsley-Green and Dr Bhopal's goal – children front and centre throughout society – a reality. To do this, we need to find a way to elevate children's voices and those of the adults advocating for them in policymaking. Many of the issues impacting children are endemic, long-term and structural. To quote, one final time, the College of Medicine manifesto:

'Who, in Government, is responsible for the overall needs of children? The depressing answer? No one. Who has

responsibility for developing joined-up policies to support children? Nobody. Is there any sense of a vision for childhood post-Covid? There isn't.'[496]

Reform of our legislative and constitutional ecosystem insofar as it relates to children was essential even before the pandemic, and is more so now.

We have talked above about the need to protect and safeguard our schools through designating them as essential infrastructure. Beyond this one idea mentioned frequently in the last year is for the UNCRC to be incorporated into English law, as in Scotland, so that it becomes enforceable in domestic law rather than merely symbolic as an international treaty. We would like to see this happen. By itself, this will not be a panacea, but children need more than a paper tiger.

Most of all, though, they need action, much of it urgent.

Sir Al Aynsley Green, in describing his feelings at the time he became England's first Children's Commissioner in 2005, told us:

'A sense of exhilaration, there is so much wonderful going on, but coupled with dismay, as I got into the services and saw firsthand what was happening coupled with despair, seeing the sheer awfulness of the lives and outcomes of so many children and young people in their families very often because of circumstances beyond their control. And then I got very angry that here we are in one of the richest countries of the world with some of the worst outcomes for children in the developed world with a denial of the existence of the awfulness of so many outcomes and the failure to do anything about it.'

In his polemic book, *The British Betrayal of Childhood*, he identifies four key failings when it comes to children in public policy: political and public indifference to the importance of children; our short-term political lens; failure of effective advocacy for children; and the siloed approach of those in charge of children's policy both within government and outside.

We agree, and would urge policymakers to reread that book in its entirety. Many of the suggestions Al made in 2018 are eminently sensible and seem even more critical now – in particular the adoption of a much more child-centred approach than we have now (why not bring back the Every Child Matters policy of the Blair years, even if it has to be called something different?), and the need for a senior level cabinet minister for children. This has been called for by a number of children's charities and groups for some time and in the wake of the terrible mistakes of the last two years it is beyond urgent.

Alongside this, we need to look again at how we protect our children from policies which, though in the interests of other sectors of society, may hurt them. Alongside embedding the UNCRC into domestic law, we might look to overseas and to the type of child safeguarding mechanisms that Sweden has, for example, requiring all emerging legislation and budgets to be reviewed for their impact on children and compliance with the UNCRC.

However the greatest failure is, in fact, of leverage.

Throughout the pandemic there have been voices advocating for children; perhaps not as many as we would have wished, but they were there. The issue has more often been that those voices have insufficient leverage to force change. Take the example of the role of Children's Commissioner.

The Children's Commissioner 'promotes and protects the rights of children, especially the most vulnerable, and stands up for their views and interests'.[497] It is, in effect, the ultimate safeguard of some 10 million children, and as such a generationally important role. Although it has wide research powers, the role – as evidenced brutally during the pandemic – lacks teeth.

Its then incumbent, Anne Longfield CBE, advocated tirelessly throughout the pandemic for children, calling for the safeguarding regime for vulnerable children to be reinstated, for schools to reopen, for children to be carved-out from restrictions on social interaction. While the first two eventually happened, it was not until much, much later. It is sobering to reflect on the harm that might have been avoided had Anne's pleas not fallen on deaf ears.

Why couldn't the Commissioner report directly to Parliament, as is the case with the Information Commissioner's Office?[498] Why couldn't it have some kind of blocking right on legislation and policies negatively impacting children? Perhaps, as Anne suggested to us, it could even be staffed by those with legal/judicial training, as is the case in some Scandinavian countries. And the role *must* be made truly independent of other arms of Government, most notably the Secretary of State for Education.

As Anne said to us, 'your umbilical cord [as Children's Commissioner] is straight into the DfE' – so 'the Secretary of State does have power over your role. And it's more than that: ultimately, the budget comes from the DfE. They can't tell you what to do, but ultimately they can withdraw your funding.' While Anne recognises that change would require greater investment and staffing, we would argue that the case for this has been more than made over the last two years.

And this is indicative of a wider issue. There is now a growing collective that is attuned to the frightening impact of our pandemic response on children, and the need to repair.

The problem is the voices lack bite.

Creating leverage

The lack of leverage is primarily due to the priorities of our political establishment, for whom children are largely invisible, unheard – and so let down – over and over again.

A furious letter in the *Guardian* in June 2021 from retired social work lecturer Steven Walker read:[499]

> 'But the elephant in the room is never acknowledged – that
> Britain is a society that doesn't care about children; they are
> not a political priority while their lives are lived in a culture
> of indifference, scapegoating, tolerance of physical abuse,
> denial of the mental health challenges they face, and a lack
> of respect, value or human rights.'

In a recent report Louise King, director of the Children's
Rights Alliance for England, part of Just for Kids law, said:
'Children continue to be a low political priority, and this has
been exacerbated during the pandemic.'[500]

Before the 2019 election, Javed Khan of Barnardo's urged
in a Red Box for the *Times* 'Protecting our children must be a
priority for the next prime minister'.[501]

These exhortations are illustrative of a deep-seated,
toxic problem that is rotting our society through backwards
policymaking that is too focused on the older generation
versus the younger. Perennial pleas from well-meaning,
hardworking advocates for children fall on deaf ears. We
are also painfully aware that the baked-in short-termism of
our political system, with governments accountable to four-
year parliaments and no longer, is structurally biased against
children who need longer-term strategies and commitments
free of political wrangling. We need to plant seeds, and
then give those seeds the conditions to flourish – not over
the course of a few years, but over a lifetime. This steadfast
focus on quick returns from politicians of all sides is surely a
reason why government after government has failed to invest
in early years in particular and children more generally.
After all, the problems that lack of investment causes, are
invariably someone else's to solve.

It's clear now that no matter how heartfelt, no number of
urgent op-eds or open letters will be enough to move the dial.
Until those of us advocating for children have leverage, we

can produce as many recovery plans, proposals and mission statements as we like. We can argue for constitutional and legislative changes until the cows come home, and we can tell our stakeholders, supporters and constituents that we care about children – and their education – until we're blue in the face. But without leverage it will just be noise.

While Geoff Barton told us that he hoped that after the pandemic, 'education moves centre stage onto the political agenda', we fear that the natural interest and imperative is not there. While the pandemic has exposed and created multiple issues, and for a time the column inches will reflect that, in time we worry that interest will wane. The evidence for deeply embedded disinterest lies all around us in the devastated aftermath of pandemic policies that consistently chose to put adults first.

If children aren't sufficiently visible to leaders and policymakers there is only one logical route open to us – we must do something radical to make them matter. We must construct the counter-weight that increases children's power, and secures commitment with the accountability necessary to force through change.

Otherwise, we will continue to go round in circles – writing papers and commissioning reports and inquiries that are never acted upon, while children's lives continue to diminish.

While the concept of the 'Overton Window' has seen its share of controversy, its premise, that policymakers will choose policies from a range acceptable to the public at any given time, is a sound one.[502] As it stands, our current frame of allowable possibilities has, despite best efforts, continued to underrepresent children: in safeguarding, in wellbeing, in education.

For example, the current Children's Commissioner, Dame Rachel de Souza, made one of her first tasks a large-scale survey, The Big Ask, to hear directly from children about their issues. This type of exercise clearly falls within the acceptable frame of approaches, and it was the biggest initiative of its kind. While undoubtedly admirable, and important within our current framework, it is limited; only exposing the issues, without any mechanism to create the urgency and imperative necessary to force the hand of those with the power to deal with them. Similarly, while the Children's Commissioner role has been beefed up since its inception – the Commissioner now has, in particular, wide evidence-collecting powers – those powers fall short of the sharp enforcement powers granted to, for example, the ICO or the Financial Conduct Authority. This makes no sense. Children have a unique status. They, not data, nor financial products, are in fact the greatest (latent) economic asset a country has, and they are also vulnerable citizens in need of society's protection. We know what the prevailing issues are – inequality, poverty, disadvantage, wellbeing, attainment gap – and they return, karmically, to government after government, never to be resolved.

It is not good enough.

In the light of the pandemic we have a moral imperative, as never before, to make children matter – really matter – by pushing them to the top of the political agenda. For that we need to be honest. We will need to create a radical shift of perspective among politicians, and underscore in wider society why the young must be prioritised.

How then to raise the collective voice for children?

The demographic and interests of politicians and policymakers is one natural answer. If more active, hands-on parents, former educators and child advocates walked the corridors of power and had a stake in decisions, we might be in a different place today, given that so many of the disproportionate policies that were put in place throughout the pandemic seemed to have been conceived by people who had never met a child, let alone parented one. MPs such as Miriam Cates, who has been a courageous thought leader in advocating from her background both as a parent and teacher, need to be the norm in senior, cabinet-level roles. Common sense could have quashed some of the most egregious errors such as the so-called 'rule of two' which permitted outdoor exercise only with 'your household (or support bubble) or one other person',[503] effectively excluding small children from meeting another friend, the taped-off playgrounds, banning of outdoor sports, and the unspeakably cruel self-isolation policies. As a side note, altering the demographic of our political establishment to allow for more genuinely invested parents will rely on tackling other issues: most notably a commitment to the funding needed to create a fit for purpose early years sector, and to genuinely shared parental leave – both long overdue.

A concerted effort to encourage parents into politics, and creating parent councils that have access to leaders, would give parents a route to advocate for their children.

We also need to be creative in demanding solutions that bake in accountability, and a commitment to long-term change that spans generations. If schools are held to account by Ofsted inspections, why aren't child-centred policies given the same treatment? Failure by the Government to meet child welfare and wellbeing metrics should have consequences. Public inquiries commit public funds, but what if the Cabinet Minister for Children had to regularly present policies and results to a panel of children? Yes, it might seem tokenistic, but it provides immediacy, and relevance – promises can't just disappear into a black hole.

The way forward

Parental advocacy, and accountability, while crucial, are only pieces of the jigsaw.

Many adults would now accept that we have just lived through an unprecedented intergenerational transfer of wealth and harms. It is not enough, though, to merely acknowledge this. We must also try to correct it.

The reason for children's lack of representation in politics boils down to the fact there is no incentive for their interests to be furthered – especially where their interests conflict with other sectors of society.

Children don't vote. But what if they did?

The outcomes from that lack of representation speak for themselves and in light of those we believe there is now a serious case to be made for lowering the voting age to 16 – if children of that age are old enough to make decisions about irreversible medical treatments for themselves, are they not also old enough to vote? However, by Scotland's example, where children can vote at 16, lowering the eligible age wouldn't go far enough – the country has been no better a shining light for children's rights over the course of the pandemic than England, and in some material respects, worse.

'Demeny' voting grants parents a partial (0.5 vote) to cast as a proxy on behalf of each of their children, to help better reflect the interests of the next generation in decision-making. David Runciman goes further, making a plausible case for lowering the voting age to six, 'effectively extending the franchise to any child in full-time education.' He argues that the policy would help to bridge the intergenerational divide, and that children have to live with the consequences of decisions made by leaders for longer than anyone else. In refuting some of the common arguments against such a move he points out that while children are influenceable, so are adults, and while children do not pay taxes this is not a requisite for adults to vote. He quotes political theorist John Wall who says, 'It is the only way to pressure political leaders to respond to the lived experiences of all instead of just some of the people.' [504]

In 2019 we, like many others, would have dismissed these ideas as too radical. We do not now.

While we do not necessarily advocate giving children as young as six the vote, tame and tentative steps have failed children so radical thinking is necessary.

Real, tangible representation of children in politics must be made a reality, and it must be done quickly. Anything worthwhile involves complexities, and this is no different. The issues it raises – of competence, practicality, knowledge and logistics – are intricate, but not insurmountable.

For that reason we propose a Royal Commission on Childhood, the sole remit of which would be to consider possible options to enfranchise children's interests in public life and to make a definitive, actionable recommendation in time for the next General Election.

Because we have a decision to make. As a society, are we going to put children, and all they stand for, front and centre, or are we, like Sir Al Aynsley-Green, going to be sitting here in 10, 25, 50 years from now collectively hand-wringing over similar reports with the same conclusions, still gathering dust, unexecuted? We must opt for the former, and when we do we can look ahead to a reimagined future, which is by turns happier, healthier and more prosperous. A future where children are no longer betrayed, but honoured.

Parents about UsForThem

Finding UsForThem and their campaigns gave me hope that there were other people worried about the impact of school closures and masks in classrooms on our children and gave me the strength and the words to fight back and put pressure on my children's school and my MP to end restrictions. Adrienne

UsForThem was the only sign of common sense and hope. Lilla

UsForThem has done the most tremendous work during the pandemic by making those who have influence stop, listen and act. Also they have given enormous support to parents on this uphill battle to protect our children. Thank you. Pauline

Just knowing we weren't alone in the fight was a real comfort. Our children needed us to fight their corner and without UsForThem life for all of us could have been much worse. Thank you for everything. Jo

"The Science" didn't account for children; thankfully UsForThem did.
Ashley

UsForThem gave me hope that someone cared and was prepared to fight against the scandal of lost education and life experiences for my children during lockdown. They gave parents a voice when no one was listening.
Julie

UsForThem came about at a time that I was feeling incredibly lonely and hopeless regarding the impact the Covid restrictions were having on my children. UsForThem galvanised me with confidence that my voice, advocating on behalf of my children, was indeed vital to their future. Thank you UsForThem for being the Tribe needed at a time of lonely confusion. Jane

UsForThem has helped us all through Covid to make sure our children and grandchildren's rights were adhered to, that they remained mentally well and have come out the other side intact and happy. Afryl

Without UsForThem and the continued support from its founders and members my children and I wouldn't have had the strength to push through the ridiculousness of school policies over the past two years.
Rebecca

As a mum of a son with additional needs, the challenges the last couple of years have brought have been particularly stressful. UsForThem have pushed relentlessly to ensure the voice of the child was heard amongst the louder drone of politicians, teachers and their unions. Julie

UsForThem have been a beacon of hope and the only organisation fighting for prioritisation of children's welfare during a time many of us could see the disproportionality of measures that were likely to lead to long-term harm in children. My children and I will be forever indebted. Leila

UsForThem were exceptionally strong in putting children first during the pandemic. Pauline

UsForThem helped empower me to fight for my children, to deal with their schools, to stand up for what I felt was right. I was armed with information, I learned my rights, and I was among like-minded families, which was such a comfort and relief. Emma

Thank god for the sane voice of UsForThem through lockdown. They saw the damage it did to children when everyone else couldn't or wouldn't open their eyes. Emma

I felt very alone in my views during the height of the pandemic. I was angry and confused with the treatment of children inflicted by the government's policies such as shutting schools, closing playgrounds and preventing family from seeing each other. I found comfort in joining UsForThem and I will be forever grateful for all the hard work and campaigning they have done. Nicola

UsForThem has been an absolute lifeline for me. Nicole

UsForThem and those involved with UsForThem (NI) have provided a beacon of hope for young people over the last 3 years. Many of those in leadership roles should have stepped up to the plate earlier for children. UsForThem were the only people providing a voice for children when many others were silent. Stevie

Despite astonishing amounts of aggression and abuse, UsForThem tirelessly advocated for the needs of our children when others stayed silent. Sue

UsForThem provided a voice for our children when all other institutions failed to protect them, at the time of their greatest need. They were a beacon of light and hope during some very dark days. Dominey

Children have been hugely impacted during the last couple of years yet this is often ignored by figures of authority and the mainstream media. Having this group has helped me realise I'm not alone. Keep up the good work! Laura

A voice for the voiceless! UsForThem kept parents sane and advocated for our young people with fierce, educated integrity. Can't thank them enough for their tireless campaigning and support. Heidi

Acknowledgements

When we founded UsForThem in May 2020 we naively assumed that the disregard for children in the pandemic response would be short-lived and policymakers would soon realise their mistake. Two years later, not only are we still fighting, but our eyes have also been opened to the scale and depth of the failing.

As of May 2022, there has been little acknowledgement of the widespread and, in some cases, life-changing sacrifices children have been forced to make. Our first acknowledgement must be to the millions of children in the UK and beyond who have borne a burden that was never theirs to shoulder.

The last two years have been both harrowing and uplifting.

We are grimly aware that in campaigning we've too often taken ourselves away from our own families for more time than was reasonable or fair.

Liz wishes to thank Martin for his unwavering patience and love, and her parents, Phil and Fran, brother Dan, and Sarah for their loyal support and for always having her back. She'd most especially like her daughters B and A to know: Everything is for you, always.

Molly wishes to thank Ben for his unflinching calm, common sense and commitment. Her parents, for their love. To her own kids: I love you, and I hope you'll feel the fight was worth it.

First and foremost, this is a book about how children were betrayed by society. However, in the background, there is another story: that of the collective of individuals who came together to fight for them. It is a cast of thousands – spanning background, geography and age; and while we cannot possibly hope to name everyone we owe a debt of thanks to each one of you: to the parents, grandparents, teachers, carers and others who added their voices to ours; to the academics, doctors, lawyers and experts who signed our open letters, indulged our frequent requests for second opinions on epidemiology, law, ethics, psychology, child development; to those in the media and press who platformed us when it mattered most for children; to the politicians and policymakers who supported our (many) letters and who have put their head above the parapet: thank you. We have been honoured, as well, to work alongside fellow campaigners in

Wales, Scotland, Northern Ireland, America, Bermuda and beyond – including Jo B and Tania E.

Around the world, parents have been fighting – and continue to fight – for their children. To those parents: you know who you are, and you must walk tall knowing you did everything you could.

One of the bright spots in the bleakness of the last two years has been the privilege of working with so many exceptional and dedicated people and there are a few from our UsForThem team we must mention by name.

Our co-founder, Christine Brett, who brought so much passion and tenacity to the campaign. Bella Hastie who leads with energy, grit, and determination. Marta, who always maintains a swan-like serenity, even while juggling multiple priorities. Jenny, Victoria S, Pru, Rachel, Michaela, Dawn, Allie, Jane, Helen, Catherine, Charlotte, Leila, Julia, Allison, Fran, Cara, Trefor, Sarah, Tracy, Victoria P, Victoria M, and so many others who have given their time and souls over the last two years. You are the most inspiring group of people we've ever had the privilege of working with.

Our contributors and those behind the scenes for generously giving their time and insights: Geoff Barton, Sandy Chappell, Ellie Cannon, Robert Dingwall, Sue Cook, Jennifer Sey, Robert Halfon, Ellen Townsend, James Maurici, Jessica Hockett, Richard Jeffries, Paul Dolan, Sunetra Gupta, Rosie Gray, Claire McGuiggan, Julia Hartley-Brewer, Anne Longfield, Miriam Cates, Sunil Bhopal, Michael Absoud, Stephen Kingdom, April Mackay, Ros Jones, Anita Grant, Sally Hogg, Alan Black, Alan Billingsley, David Paton, Macs Montessori, Neil Leitch, Neil Oliver, Jay Bhattacharya, Lucy Easthope, George McLellan, Kate Palmer, Dennis Hayes, Mike Fairclough, Lord Jonathan Sumption; and those others who do not wish to be named.

Sir Al Aynsley-Green – first Children's Commissioner for England, lifelong champion of children and dedicated friend and mentor to the UsForThem campaign. Allison Pearson, fearless warrior-writer without whose steadfast support especially in those first days there would have been no UsForThem.

Thank you to everyone at Pinter & Martin for taking a leap of faith, and allowing us to tell this story, and to Laura Dodsworth for the ongoing support.

Despite everything, we believe there is great hope and that comes from understanding that with this collection of voices there are so many people who care profoundly about children and who hold a shared ambition to transform their futures for the better.

References

These references can also be accessed at
pinterandmartin.com/childrens-inquiry-references

1   https://twitter.com/ClaireMcguiggan/status/1506736141269192713
2   https://www.childrenscommissioner.gov.uk/2021/02/17/building-back-better-reaching-englands-left-behind-children/
3   https://jme.bmj.com/content/47/8/565
4   https://www.theguardian.com/society/2021/aug/11/revealed-englands-pandemic-crisis-of-child-abuse-neglect-and-poverty
5   https://ican.org.uk/news/i-can-publishes-speaking-up-for-the-covid-generation/
6   https://www.centreforsocialjustice.org.uk/wp-content/uploads/2021/06/Cant_Catch_Up_FULL-REPORT.pdf
7   https://adc.bmj.com/content/105/7/618
8   https://www.centreforsocialjustice.org.uk/wp-content/uploads/2022/01/CSJ-Lost_but_not_forgotten-2.pdf
9   https://kindredsquared.org.uk/wp-content/uploads/2020/11/Kindred2-YouGov-School-Readiness.pdf
10 https://www.gov.uk/government/publications/education-recovery-in-early-years-providers-spring-2022/education-recovery-in-early-years-providers-spring-2022
11 https://inews.co.uk/news/covid-rules-may-2020-lockdown-restrictions-downing-street-party-date-explained-1396120
12 https://www.telegraph.co.uk/news/2022/03/15/impossible-situation-child-mental-health-referrals-rise-1m/
13 https://www.cypnow.co.uk/news/article/mental-health-will-be-the-biggest-problem-facing-young-people-by-2040-doctors-warn
14 https://www.unicef.org.uk/press-releases/across-virtually-every-key-measure-of-childhood-progress-has-gone-backward-unicef-says-as-pandemic-declaration-hits-one-year-mark/
15 https://www.gov.uk/government/publications/education-recovery-in-early-years-providers-spring-2022/education-recovery-in-early-years-providers-spring-2022
16 https://blog.ted.com/a-close-up-look-at-the-adolescent-brain-sarah-jayne-blakemore-at-tedglobal2012/
17 https://www.nature.com/articles/s41591-021-01578-1
18 https://www.rcpch.ac.uk/resources/covid-19-research-evidence-summaries
19 https://www.ncl.ac.uk/press/articles/latest/2021/08/conversationcovid-19children/
20 https://www.thelancet.com/journals/lanchi/article/PIIS2352-4642(21)00198-X/fulltext#:~:text=COVID%2D19%20in%20children%20is%20usually%20asymptomatic%20or%20manifests%20as,is%20observed%20in%20some%20adults.
21 https://www.rcpch.ac.uk/resources/covid-19-guidance-clinically-extremely-vulnerable-children-young-people

22 https://www.thetimes.co.uk/article/letter-to-the-editor-school-shut-out-is-crushing-children-nrkd5lgz7
23 https://thequaranteensblog.wordpress.com/2021/05/23/a-year-of-the-quaranteens/
24 https://thequaranteensblog.wordpress.com/2021/10/08/i-feel-like-im-going-to-explode/
25 https://www.nytimes.com/2021/11/17/opinion/covid-thanksgiving-holiday-risk.html
26 https://www.bbc.co.uk/news/world-asia-56425115
27 https://www.theguardian.com/uk-news/2022/feb/21/body-of-boy-5-dumped-like-fly-tipped-rubbish-cardiff-jury-hears
28 https://sweden.se/life/society/sweden-and-corona-in-brief
29 https://www.portfolio.hu/en/economy/20210908/hungary-has-no-intention-to-mitigate-covid-risks-in-schools-499666
30 https://www.portfolio.hu/en/economy/20210915/hungary-forbids-whole-classes-schools-to-switch-to-distance-learning-above-6th-grade-500688
31 https://www.telegraph.co.uk/news/2022/03/23/sir-chris-whitty-school-closures-likely-have-caused-substantial/
32 https://www.politicshome.com/news/article/nadhim-zahawi-says-he-will-do-everything-in-my-power-to-keep-schools-open-as-he-admits-previous-closures-were-a-mistake
33 https://twitter.com/AllisonPearson/status/1506633785781096456
34 https://www.politicshome.com/news/article/nadhim-zahawi-says-he-will-do-everything-in-my-power-to-keep-schools-open-as-he-admits-previous-closures-were-a-mistake
35 https://twitter.com/michaelgove/status/1513940301622218763
36 Mistakes Were Made but Not by Me: Why We Justify Foolish Beliefs, Bad Decisions, and Hurtful Acts, Tavris and Aronson
37 https://www.jimcollins.com/concepts/Stockdale-Concept.html
38 https://thepostmillennial.com/nyc-students-can-remove-masks-after-court-rules-hochuls-mandate-unconstitutional
39 BBC Complaints email response to an UsForThem supporter, May 13th 2021
40 https://twitter.com/ERCGlengormley/status/1465705756183781377?s=20&t=6rPKmr5onCi1kiB2_coWqQ
41 https://twitter.com/peterdain1/status/1390357682931093520?s=21
42 https://twitter.com/juliahb1/status/1465076919586762763?lang=en
43 https://twitter.com/AlbertoCostaMP/status/1482035443621367820?s=20&t=hN0hKTOeMmA6EwT3c_N60g
44 https://twitter.com/ari58394958/status/1483181432008675328?s=12
45 https://www.berkeleyschools.net/2022/01/expanded-testing-and-additional-covid-updates-pruebas-ampliadas-y-actualizaciones-adicionales-sobre-covid/
    https://twitter.com/beenwrekt/status/1480923230936473610?s=20
46 Jessica Hockett writes and tweets under the name Emma Woodhouse
47 https://www.telegraph.co.uk/education-and-careers/2020/12/10/better-ventilation-helps-covid-freezing-children-classroom/
48 https://www.irishtimes.com/news/education/teachers-and-pupils-complain-of-freezing-classrooms-as-dublin-school-closes-early-1.4771413
49 https://www.thetimes.co.uk/article/coronavirus-in-scotland-pupils-freeze-

in-bitterly-cold-classrooms-c93d7qcqw

50 https://www.mygov.scot/health-and-safety-work#:~:text=During%20
    working%20hours%20the%20temperature,employees%20are%20doing%20
    physical%20work.

51 https://www.greatyarmouthmercury.co.uk/news/education/yarmouth-
    school-forced-pupils-to-eat-lunch-outside-8466254

52 https://www.dailymail.co.uk/news/article-10295855/School-makes-pupils-
    eat-lunch-outside-freezing-cold-prevent-spread-Covid.html

53 https://www.glasgowtimes.co.uk/news/19554663.overheated-glasgow-
    schoolkids-denied-water-class-23-c-heat-due-covid-guidelines/

54 https://www.thetimes.co.uk/article/from-nativity-plays-to-sports-days-
    pandemic-pupils-are-missing-out-on-school-rites-of-passage-vb9prvn59

55 https://www.manchestereveningnews.co.uk/news/greater-manchester-
    news/girlguiding-brownies-guides-face-masks-22881625

56 https://www.telegraph.co.uk/news/2022/01/30/parents-forced-watch-
    children-graduate-online-universities-keep/

57 https://www.bbc.co.uk/news/health-57021736#:~:text=The%20
    39%2Dyear%2Dold%20has,third%20child%20during%20the%20pandemic.

58 https://www.theguardian.com/lifeandstyle/2021/may/14/uk-women-forced-
    to-wear-face-masks-during-labour-charity-finds

59 https://www.theguardian.com/us-news/2021/oct/01/california-covid-
    vaccine-mandate-schools

60 https://www.bbc.co.uk/news/uk-england-manchester-54833331

61 https://www.manchestereveningnews.co.uk/news/greater-manchester-
    news/university-student-hanged-himself-halls-22855883

62 https://www.bbc.co.uk/news/uk-england-york-north-yorkshire-54551789

63 https://www.newsandstar.co.uk/news/19745850.child-develops-
    hypothermia-isolated-outdoor-classroom/

64 https://www.bbc.co.uk/news/world-us-canada-59919105

65 https://www.gov.uk/government/publications/phe-strategy-2020-to-2025

66 https://www.telegraph.co.uk/news/2021/02/14/ministers-must-never-
    free-impose-crippling-restrictions-without/ https://www.telegraph.co.uk/
    politics/2020/11/30/governments-covid-tiers-impact-assessment-does-
    doesnt-say/

67 https://www.telegraph.co.uk/news/2022/02/21/never-must-repeat-errors-
    covid-lockdowns/

68 https://www.independent.co.uk/news/health/covid-transmission-perspex-
    screens-scrapped-b1867019.html

69 https://www.medrxiv.org/content/10.1101/2020.09.15.20191957v1.full.pdf

70 https://www.bmj.com/content/370/bmj.m3473

71 https://inews.co.uk/news/uk/rule-of-six-children-babies-new-covid-rules-
    29-march-lockdown-roadmap-929848

72 https://www.bmj.com/content/369/bmj.m1435

73 https://assets.publishing.service.gov.uk/government/uploads/system/
    uploads/attachment_data/file/1055639/Evidence_summary_-_face_
    coverings.pdf

74 https://www.telegraph.co.uk/news/2021/10/17/royal-college-paediatrics-
    head-calls-end-covid-testing-schools/

75 https://educationhub.blog.gov.uk/2022/03/30/living-with-covid-the-end-of-
    routine-testing-in-schools-colleges-and-childcare-settings/

76   https://www.theguardian.com/uk-news/2020/nov/08/army-carry-out-mass-covid-19-tests-children-liverpool-pupils

77   https://www.chroniclelive.co.uk/news/north-east-news/mp-brands-nightingale-hospitals-expensive-19538674

78   https://www.bmj.com/content/370/bmj.m3699

79   https://allysonpollock.com/?page_id=3345

80   https://fullfact.org/online/liverpool-testing-schools/

81   https://www.bmj.com/content/371/bmj.m4436

82   https://www.gov.uk/government/organisations/uk-national-screening-committee

83   https://schoolsweek.co.uk/bubbles-and-masks-go-at-step-4-but-isolation-rules-in-place-to-end-of-term/

84   https://www.whatdotheyknow.com/request/onward_transmission_from_confirm

85   https://inews.co.uk/news/education/school-bubbles-england-million-pupils-out-lessons-covid-isolation-rules-last-week-1112219

86   https://www.bmj.com/content/371/bmj.m3803

87   https://www.chroniclelive.co.uk/whats-on/family-kids-news/measles-epidemic-warning-after-fall-23857772. ; https://vk.ovg.ox.ac.uk/vk/measles

88   https://www.gov.uk/government/publications/covid-19-vaccination-of-children-and-young-people-aged-12-to-17-years-jcvi-statement/jvci-statement-on-covid-19-vaccination-of-children-and-young-people-aged-12-to-17-years-15-july-2021

89   https://committees.parliament.uk/oralevidence/2767/pdf/

90   https://www.theguardian.com/society/2022/feb/01/very-worrying-mmr-vaccine-rates-in-england-at-10-year-low

91   https://youtu.be/O1GvVCrxas0

92   https://assets.publishing.service.gov.uk/government/uploads/system/uploads/attachment_data/file/886993/s0141-sage-sub-group-role-children-transmission-160420-sage26.pdf

93   https://www.ucl.ac.uk/news/2020/jun/children-doing-25-hours-schoolwork-day-average

94   https://www.childrenscommissioner.gov.uk/report/are-they-shouting-because-of-me/

95   https://www.childrenscommissioner.gov.uk/report/mental-health-services-2019-20/

96   https://committees.parliament.uk/event/3421/formal-meeting-oral-evidence-session/

97   https://www.euro.who.int/en/health-topics/Health-systems/public-health-services

98   https://www.adph.org.uk/wp-content/uploads/2019/06/What-Good-Children-and-Young-Peoples-Public-Health-Looks-Like.pdf

99   https://pubmed.ncbi.nlm.nih.gov/34186334/

100 https://www.telegraph.co.uk/news/2022/02/01/mmr-vaccination-uptake-10-year-low-parents-avoid-burdening-nhs/

101 https://www.telegraph.co.uk/news/2022/05/04/overweight-childrens-hearts-already-suffering-age-six/

102 https://www.childrenscommissioner.gov.uk/2018/07/04/over-two-million-children-in-england-are-growing-up-in-families-where-there-are-serious-risks-major-study-from-childrens-commissioner-reveals-2/

103 https://www.independent.co.uk/news/health/covid-matt-hancock-care-homes-court-b2066524.html

104 https://inews.co.uk/news/politics/boris-johnson-misled-parliament-over-covid-transmission-claim-after-high-court-care-home-ruling-labour-say-1601522

105 https://rumble.com/vfy5pv-georgia-mom-explodes-on-school-board-take-these-masks-off-my-child.html

106 https://www.cato.org/sites/cato.org/files/2021-11/working-paper-64.pdf

107 https://committees.parliament.uk/oralevidence/3098/pdf/

108 https://www.bbc.co.uk/news/education-59840634

109 https://www.express.co.uk/news/uk/1516009/Jonathan-van-tam-UK-Christmas-lockdown-Covid- pandemic-running-hot

110 https://www.youtube.com/watch?v=m9ZkEn-lVBU

111 https://www.mdpi.com/1660-4601/18/8/4344

112 https://www.ncbi.nlm.nih.gov/pmc/articles/PMC7362770/

113 https://www.bmj.com/content/373/bmj.n1304

114 https://headachejournal.onlinelibrary.wiley.com/doi/full/10.1111/head.13811

115 https://www.mdpi.com/1660-4601/18/8/4344

116 https://www.mdpi.com/1660-4601/18/8/4344

117 https://www.bbc.co.uk/news/uk-wales-55043109

118 https://assets.publishing.service.gov.uk/government/uploads/system/uploads/attachment_data/file/1044767/Evidence_summary_-_face_coverings.pdf

119 https://www.telegraph.co.uk/news/2021/04/28/government-turning-blind-eye-harm-classroom-face-mask-policy/

120 https://m.facebook.com/watch/?v=4500323436731783&_rdr

121 How to Raise a Chatterbox, Sandy Chappell

122 https://japantoday.com/category/features/lifestyle/more-japanese-youth-wearing-surgical-masks-to-hide-their-face"https://japantoday.com/category/features/lifestyle/more-japanese-youth-wearing-surgical-masks-to-hide-their-face

123 https://www.youtube.com/watch?v=BjvbAkNHICE

124 https://committees.parliament.uk/oralevidence/2142/pdf/

125 https://www.nbcnews.com/news/us-news/teacher-tapes-mask-students-face-school-district-says-was-unacceptable-rcna13025

126 https://www.dailymail.co.uk/news/article-10108099/Teachers-TAPING-masks-kids-faces-Colorado.html

127 https://twitter.com/JenniferSey/status/1487456676231872516?s=20&t=dNOZ-N5wqk_I7NMIBUYNPw

128 https://www.who.int/news-room/fact-sheets/detail/child-maltreatment

129 https://www.telegraph.co.uk/news/2021/09/01/uk-school-closures-second-longest-europe-past-18-months/

130 https://explore-education-statistics.service.gov.uk/find-statistics/attendance-in-education-and-early-years-settings-during-the-coronavirus-covid-19-outbreak; House of Commons Library, Coronavirus and schools (Number 08915), 13 January 2022, pp9–10

131 https://www.unicef.org/press-releases/schoolchildren-worldwide-have-lost-18-trillion-hours-and-counting-person-learning

132 https://www.oecd.org/coronavirus/policy-responses/education-and-covid-

19-focusing-on-the-long-term-impact-of-school-closures-2cea926e/

133 https://www.telegraph.co.uk/global-health/climate-and-people/lost-generation-fears-indias-long-running-school-closures-will/

134 https://www.bbc.co.uk/news/world-africa-59935605

135 https://www.latimes.com/california/newsletter/2022-03-14/global-learning-loss-8-to-3-newsletter-8-to-3

136 https://www.telegraph.co.uk/global-health/science-and-disease/covid-school-closures-poorer-countriescould-affect-generation/

137 https://www.unicef.org/press-releases/covid19-scale-education-loss-nearly-insurmountable-warns-unicef

138 https://junipereducation.org/wp-content/uploads/juniper_folder/Juniper-Education-National-Benchmark-Dataset-Report.pdf

139 https://committees.parliament.uk/publications/9251/documents/160043/default/

140 https://committees.parliament.uk/publications/9251/documents/160043/default/

141 https://ifs.org.uk/publications/15291

142 https://blogs.worldbank.org/education/massive-yet-invisible-cost-keeping-schools-closed

143 https://www.weforum.org/agenda/2022/01/global-education-crisis-children-students-covid19/

144 https://jamanetwork.com/journals/jamanetworkopen/fullarticle/2772834

145 https://assets.publishing.service.gov.uk/government/uploads/system/uploads/attachment_data/file/998894/s1114_school_closure.pdf

146 https://www.forbes.com/sites/michaeltnietzel/2020/09/09/low-literacy-levels-among-us-adults-could-be-costing-the-economy-22-trillion-a-year/

147 https://www.telegraph.co.uk/global-health/climate-and-people/lost-generation-fears-indias-long-running-school-closures-will/

148 https://twitter.com/DrJBhattacharya/status/1504094487915737091

149 https://assets.publishing.service.gov.uk/government/uploads/system/uploads/attachment_data/file/1003977/State_of_the_nation_2021_-_Social_mobility_and_the_pandemic.pdf

150 https://ifs.org.uk/inequality/wp-content/uploads/2021/03/BN-Inequalities-in-education-skills-and-incomes-in-the-UK-the-implications-of-the-COVID-19-pandemic.pdf

151 https://d2tic4wvo1iusb.cloudfront.net/documents/guidance-for-teachers/pupil-premium/Pupil_Premium_Guide_Apr_2022_1.0.pdf

152 https://blogs.lse.ac.uk/covid19/2020/06/05/homeschooling-during-lockdown-will-deepen-inequality/

153 https://www.independent.co.uk/news/uk/home-news/coronavirus-childcare-homeschooling-women-lockdown-gender-a9512866.html

154 https://www.unicef.org/education/girls-education

155 https://unesdoc.unesco.org/ark:/48223/pf0000379270

156 https://www.latimes.com/california/newsletter/2022-03-14/global-learning-loss-8-to-3-newsletter-8-to-3

157 https://www.unicef.org/press-releases/covid19-scale-education-loss-nearly-insurmountable-warns-unicef

158 https://www.telegraph.co.uk/news/2021/02/13/explosion-children-tics-tourettes-lockdown/

159 https://www.theeducatoronline.com/k12/news/how-remote-learning-is-

damaging-childrens-eyesight/278313
160 https://jamanetwork.com/journals/jamaophthalmology/fullarticle/2774808
161 https://www.centreforsocialjustice.org.uk/wp-content/uploads/2022/01/CSJ-Lost_but_not_forgotten-2.pdf
162 https://schoolsweek.co.uk/sir-kevan-collins-appointed-education-recovery-tsar/
163 https://www.gov.uk/government/news/new-commissioner-appointed-to-oversee-education-catch-up
164 https://www.bbc.co.uk/news/education-57335558
165 https://www.theguardian.com/politics/2021/jun/02/education-recovery-chief-kevan-collins-quit-english-schools-catch-up-row
166 https://www.standard.co.uk/news/uk/robert-halfon-geoff-barton-government-university-of-exeter-department-for-education-b985629.html
167 https://committees.parliament.uk/committee/203/education-committee/news/161687/disadvantaged-pupils-facing-epidemic-of-educational-inequality/
168 https://schoolsweek.co.uk/tutor-cash-will-go-straight-to-schools-as-randstad-axed/
169 https://www.telegraph.co.uk/news/2021/02/05/say-going-school-simply-benefits-children-cruelly-misleading/
170 https://www.centreforsocialjustice.org.uk/library/lost-but-not-forgotten
171 https://www.independent.co.uk/news/education/education-news/school-attendance-covid-restrictions-b1977276.html
172 https://www.oecd.org/coronavirus/policy-responses/education-and-covid-19-focusing-on-the-long-term-impact-of-school-closures-2cea926e/
173 https://www.thetimes.co.uk/article/universities-no-excuse-teaching-face-to-face-masks-nadhim-zahawi-l2zgntz5b
174 https://www.thetimes.co.uk/article/universities-no-excuse-teaching-face-to-face-masks-nadhim-zahawi-l2zgntz5b
175 https://mancunion.com/2022/02/23/michelle-donelan-demands-end-to-online-lectures/
176 https://researchbriefings.files.parliament.uk/documents/CBP-8915/CBP-8915.pdf as per n176
177 https://researchbriefings.files.parliament.uk/documents/CBP-8915/CBP-8915.pdf
178 https://schoolsweek.co.uk/coronavirus-schools-have-legal-duty-to-provide-remote-education/
179 https://questions-statements.parliament.uk/written-questions/detail/2021-09-10/47004
180 https://committees.parliament.uk/publications/9251/documents/160043/default/
181 https://www.bbc.co.uk/news/health-55863841
182 https://blogs.worldbank.org/education/massive-yet-invisible-cost-keeping-schools-closed
183 A conclusion reiterated in a local context by the ONS who said 'remote learning was at best, a partial substitute'
184 https://www.ons.gov.uk/ peoplepopulationandcommunity/educationandchildcare/articles/remoteschoolingthroughthecoronaviruscovid19pandemicengland/april2020tojune2021

185 And, for all children it was obvious that closures would equate to a dearth of the socialisation so crucial to child development. https://committees. parliament.uk/oralevidence/1531/pdf/

186 https://www.bbc.co.uk/news/in-pictures-52370968

187 https://adc.bmj.com/content/105/7/618

188 Mark Woolhouse, The Year The World Went Mad

189 https://nymag.com/intelligencer/article/progressives-must-reckon-with-the-school-closing-catastrophe.html

190 https://www.holyrood.com/comment/view,comment-children-no-longer-matter

191 https://bmjpaedsopen.bmj.com/content/bmjpo/5/1/e001043.full.pdf

192 https://digital.nhs.uk/data-and-information/publications/statistical/national-child-measurement-programme/2020-21-school-year

193 https://twitter.com/themoorelab/status/1492883858450169857?lang=en-GB

194 https://www.kindredsquared.org.uk/school-readiness-survey/

195 https://www.telegraph.co.uk/news/2022/03/15/impossible-situation-child-mental-health-referrals-rise-1m/

196 https://www.express.co.uk/life-style/health/1550703/children-mental-health-treatment-covid-pandemic-waiting-list-three-years-nhs

197 https://www.rcpsych.ac.uk/news-and-features/latest-news/detail/2022/02/10/eating-disorders-in-children-at-crisis-point-as-waiting-lists-for-routine-care-reach-record-levels

198 https://www.gov.uk/government/publications/education-recovery-in-early-years-providers-spring-2022/education-recovery-in-early-years-providers-spring-2022

199 https://theconversation.com/pandemic-babies-how-covid-19-has-affected-child-development-155903

200 https://www.ncbi.nlm.nih.gov/pmc/articles/PMC3465788/

201 https://publications.parliament.uk/pa/ld5802/ldselect/ldcvd19/117/11709.htm#footnote-011

202 Investigating the role of language in Children's Early Educational Outcomes, 2011 Roulstone et al. https://assets.publishing.service.gov.uk/government/uploads/system/uploads/attachment_data/file/181549/DFE-RR134.pdf

203 https://www.bbc.co.uk/news/uk-northern-ireland-56711471

204 https://www.gov.uk/government/publications/education-recovery-in-early- years-providers-spring-2022/education-recovery-in-early-years-providers-spring-2022

205 How to Raise a Chatterbox – Sandy Chappell, Troubador p. xix

206 https://pubmed.ncbi.nlm.nih.gov/17729143/

207 https://www.telegraph.co.uk/news/2022/05/16/covid-lockdowns-left-toddlers-unable-speak-play-properly/

208 https://www.rcslt.org/wp-content/uploads/2021/03/Building-back-better-March2021.pdf

209 https://actionforstammeringchildren.org/lockdown-sees-57-rise-in-calls-to-stammering-helpline/l

210 https://twitter.com/karenvaites/status/1494861832506462208

211 https://parentinfantfoundation.org.uk/our-work/campaigning/babies-in-lockdown/

212 https://collateralglobal.org/article/report-the-impact-of-pandemic-

restrictions-on-university-students-mental-health/

213 https://www.princes-trust.org.uk/about-the-trust/news-views/princes-trust-and-censuswide-research-2021

214 https://www.unicef.org/press-releases/across-virtually-every-key-measure-childhood-progress-has-gone-backward-unicef-says

215 https://committees.parliament.uk/publications/6384/documents/70025/default/

216 https://committees.parliament.uk/publications/9151/documents/159601/default/

217 https://committees.parliament.uk/work/1121/the-longterm-impact-of-the-pandemic-on-parents-and-families/

218 https://www.nuffieldtrust.org.uk/resource/growing-problems-in-detail-covid-19-s-impact-on-health-care-for-children-and-young-people-in-england

219 https://www.nuffieldtrust.org.uk/resource/growing-problems-in-detail-covid-19-s-impact-on-health-care-for-children-and-young-people-in-england

220 https://news.sky.com/story/measles-vaccination-rates-drop-to-their-lowest-level-in-a-decade-12530000

221 https://www.unicef.org.uk/press-releases/covid-19-pandemic-leads-to-major-backsliding-on-childhood-vaccinations-new-who-unicef-data-shows/

222 https://www.nature.com/articles/d41586-020-02618-5

223 https://www.prospectmagazine.co.uk/society-and-culture/the-uks-birth-rate-has-hit-a-record-low-can-it-bounce-back

224 https://jamanetwork.com/journals/jamapediatrics/fullarticle/2787479

225 https://www.ucl.ac.uk/news/2021/may/new-mothers-twice-likely-have-post-natal-depression-lockdown

226 https://maternalmentalhealthalliance.org/news/new-and-expectant-mums-face-increased-mental-health-risks-caused-by-the-pandemic/

227 https://committees.parliament.uk/publications/9151/documents/159601/default/

228 https://www.telegraph.co.uk/news/2022/05/12/covid-inquiry-examine-impact-mental-health-children-young-people/

229 https://novakdjokovicfoundation.org/big-benefits-investing-quality-early-childhood-education-heckmans-research/

230 https://assets.publishing.service.gov.uk/government/uploads/system/uploads/attachment_data/file/886993/s0141-sage-sub-group-role-children-transmission-160420-sage26.pdf

231 https://www.judiciary.uk/wp-content/uploads/2021/12/R-v-Tustin-and-Hughes-sentencing-031221-4.pdf

232 https://www.telegraph.co.uk/news/2021/12/02/bruise-every-day-lockdown-little-arthur-tortured-evil-stepmother/

233 https://www.theguardian.com/society/2021/dec/03/arthur-labinjo-hughes-vulnerable-children-slipped-from-view-in-pandemic

234 https://www.telegraph.co.uk/news/2021/12/14/much-did-lockdown-help-star-hobsons-murderer-evade-familys-five/

235 https://committees.parliament.uk/publications/6384/documents/70025/default/

236 https://publications.parliament.uk/pa/ld5802/ldselect/ldcvd19/117/11709.

htm#footnote-011

237 https://committees.parliament.uk/publications/6384/documents/70025/default/

238 https://www.theguardian.com/society/2018/jul/11/underfunding-to-blame-for-child-protection-crisis-says-report

239 https://cpag.org.uk/child-poverty/child-poverty-facts-and-figures

240 https://www.lboro.ac.uk/media-centre/press-releases/2021/may/dramatic-rise-in-child-poverty/

241 https://www.jrf.org.uk/press/rising-energy-bills-devastate-poorest-families

242 https://www.politics.co.uk/reference/marcus-rashford-profile/

243 https://www.theguardian.com/society/2021/dec/12/hunt-launched-to-find-ghost-children-missing-from-schools-in-england

244 https://www.centreforsocialjustice.org.uk/wp-content/uploads/2022/01/CSJ-Lost_but_not_forgotten-2.pdf

245 https://www.childrenscommissioner.gov.uk/2021/02/17/building-back-better-reaching-englands-left-behind-children/

246 https://committees.parliament.uk/publications/9151/documents/159601/default/

247 https://publications.parliament.uk/pa/ld5802/ldselect/ldcvd19/117/11702.htm

248 http://enablemagazine.co.uk/11195/

249 https://disabledchildrenspartnership.org.uk/wp-content/uploads/2020/06/LeftInLockdown-Parent-carers%E2%80%99-experiences-of-lockdown-June-2020.pdf

250 https://www.nuffieldfoundation.org/wp-content/uploads/2020/09/Special-schools-during-lockdown.pdf

251 https://www.nuffieldfoundation.org/wp-content/uploads/2020/09/Special-schools-during-lockdown.pdf

252 https://publications.parliament.uk/pa/ld5802/ldselect/ldcvd19/117/11709.htm#footnote-011

253 https://www.childrenscommissioner.gov.uk/2021/02/17/building-back-better-reaching-englands-left-behind-children/

254 https://www.theguardian.com/commentisfree/2020/sep/18/children-champion-childrens-commissioner-anne-longfield

255 https://www.childrenscommissioner.gov.uk/report/were-all-in-this-together/

256 https://assets.publishing.service.gov.uk/government/uploads/system/uploads/attachment_data/file/886993/s0141-sage-sub-group-role-children-transmission-160420-sage26.pdf

257 https://www.childrenscommissioner.gov.uk/2020/05/16/government-and-teaching-unions-should-stop-squabbling-and-agree-a-plan-to-get-kids-back-into-school/

258 https://www.bbc.co.uk/news/education-52685220

259 https://www.manchestereveningnews.co.uk/news/greater-manchester-news/been-more-900-calls-childline-17986993

260 https://www.theguardian.com/world/2020/apr/02/coronavirus-lockdown-raises-risk-of-online-child-abuse-charity-says

261 https://www.expressandstar.com/news/voices/in-depth/2020/05/11/hidden-away-the-young-who-suffer-in-lockdown/

262 https://amp.theguardian.com/society/2020/apr/16/mps-call-for-action-

over-expected-rise-in-child-sexual-abuse-during-coronavirus-pandemic

263 https://www.bmj.com/content/bmj/369/bmj.m1669.full.pdf

264 https://news.sky.com/story/young-at-risk-from-county-lines-exploitation-if-theres-another-lockdown-charity-warns-12496642

265 https://www.nottingham.ac.uk/vision/vision-child-adolescent-mental-health-post-lockdown

266 https://drive.google.com/file/d/1zytNGOtnySo-YnyU7iazJUVQ0fS2PC1Z/view; https://www.bbc.co.uk/news/health-53037702

267 https://twitter.com/SelfHarmRes/status/1491766655269101576?s=20&t=I4aDPDiFJ-vV6X4nr16PMQ

268 https://www.pulsetoday.co.uk/resource/coronavirus/in-full-gp-letter-warns-hancock-against-new-covid-lockdown/

269 https://www.dailymail.co.uk/health/article-8875213/DR-ELLIE-CANNON-Matt-Hancock-holds-utter-contempt.html

270 https://www.standard.co.uk/news/politics/tory-mp-attack-government-primary-school-plans-shelved-a4463521.html

271 https://www.greekmyths-greekmythology.com/the-myth-of-cassandra/

272 https://cpag.org.uk/news-blogs/news-listings/making-links-poverty-austerity-and-children%E2%80%99s-social-care

273 https://schoolsweek.co.uk/union-accused-of-breaking-rules-over-political-election-ad/

274 http://whistleblowerphilosopher.blogspot.com/2022/01/the-road-to-lockdown_02121758366.html

275 https://neu.org.uk/press-releases/coronavirus-school-closure-policy

276 https://neu.org.uk/press-releases/coronavirus-school-closure-update

277 https://www.gov.uk/government/news/details-on-phased-wider-opening-of-schools-colleges-and-nurseries

278 https://edexec.co.uk/unions-comment-on-schools-reopening-in-june/

279 https://www.theguardian.com/world/2020/may/18/french-minister-tells-of-risks-of-missing-school-as-more-pupils-return-covid-19

280 https://www.dailymail.co.uk/news/article-8339515/Leaders-National-Education-Union-caught-discussing-threaten-headmasters.html

281 https://coronavirusexplained.ukri.org/en/article/und0008/

282 https://europepmc.org/article/MED/32289214

283 https://www.bbc.co.uk/news/uk-politics-54324079

284 https://www.childrenscommissioner.gov.uk/2020/05/16/government-and-teaching-unions-should-stop-squabbling-and-agree-a-plan-to-get-kids-back-into-school/

285 https://www.childrenscommissioner.gov.uk/2020/06/15/how-the-covid-19-crisis-has-affected-childrens-right-to-an-education/

286 https://neu.org.uk/press-releases/circuit-breaker-secondary-schools-and-post-16

287 https://www.dailymail.co.uk/news/article-9118805/Covid-UK-Teaching-union-blasted-appalling-triumphalism-Boris-Johnson-shut-schools.html

288 https://twitter.com/zarahsultana/status/1346201347880853507?s=20&t=hdvejcr8VeEUtgLwfl0AA

289 https://www.thetimes.co.uk/article/facemasks-are-a-price-worth-paying-to-keep-kids-where-they-belong-in-the-classroom-9zhzfbbzh

290 https://zerocovid.uk/

291 https://www.telegraph.co.uk/politics/2021/07/17/revealed-independent-

sage-run-left-wing-group-including-anti/

292 https://www.independentsage.org/who-are-independent-sage/

293 https://www.theguardian.com/world/commentisfree/2021/jan/28/all-countries-should-pursue-a-covid-19-elimination-strategy-here-are-16-reasons-why

294 https://www.independentsage.org/martin-mckee-opinion-piece-in-the-guardian-on-zero-covid/

295 https://www.youtube.com/watch?v=f9jhFI5Wm7k

296 https://www.independentsage.org/wp-content/uploads/2020/05/Advisory-note-for-the-Independent-SAGE-school-report.pdf

297 https://covidactiongroup.net/open-letter-to-secretary-of-state-for-education

298 https://twitter.com/business/status/1280480965589110785

299 https://www.theguardian.com/us-news/2020/jul/17/trump-teachers-reopening-schools-coronavirus-randi-weingarten

300 https://edition.cnn.com/2020/07/25/politics/donald-trump-schools-reopening-coronavirus/index.html

301 https://www.politico.com/news/2020/07/08/trump-reopen-schools-353245

302 Jessica Hockett tweets under the pseudonym Emma Woodhouse

303 https://journals.sagepub.com/doi/10.3102/0013189X211048840

304 https://www.dailymail.co.uk/news/article-10813417/NYC-parents-DEMAND-Mayor-Eric-Adams-meet-toddler-mask-mandate.html

305 https://order-order.com/2022/03/27/ashworth-labour-wanted-schools-to-stay-open-where-they-could/

306 https://twitter.com/SamCoatesSky/status/1346130973163978753

307 https://nymag.com/intelligencer/article/progressives-must-reckon-with-the-school-closing-catastrophe.html

308 https://timeforrecovery.org/jeremy-hunt-cannot-whitewash-over-his-past-support-for-lockdowns

309 Charles McKay, Extraordinary Popular Delusions and the Madness of Crowds

310 Laura Dodsworth, A State of Fear -How the UK government weaponised fear during the COVID-19 pandemic

311 https://www.spectator.co.uk/article/my-twitter-conversation-with-the-chairman-of-the-sage-covid-modelling-committee

312 https://twitter.com/piersmorgan/status/1239612279232086025

313 https://www.dailymail.co.uk/news/article-8122547/Children-reveal-endless-rabble-coughing-school-memes-amid-coronavirus-outbreak.html

314 https://drops.dagstuhl.de/opus/volltexte/2018/9329/pdf/LIPIcs-GISCIENCE-2018-1.pdf

315 https://www.mirror.co.uk/3am/celebrity-news/celebrities-who-sent-kids-back-22136999.amp

316 https://adc.bmj.com/content/105/7/618

317 https://www.dailymail.co.uk/news/article-8374849/Three-mothers-considering-legal-battle-Government-school-closures.html

318 https://dailysceptic.org/the-reaction-to-a-petition-to-reopen-schools/

319 https://edpsy.org.uk/blog/2020/return-to-childhood-going-back-to-school-after-the-covid-19-shut-down/

320 https://www.history.com/topics/colonial-america/salem-witch-trials

321 https://thecritic.co.uk/issues/march-2021/faith-masks/

322 https://www.wsj.com/articles/fauci-collins-emails-great-barrington-declaration-covid-pandemic-lockdown-11640129116

323 https://www.telegraph.co.uk/news/2021/02/26/headmaster-becomes-first-break-ranks-defy-government-guidance/

324 https://www.telegraph.co.uk/news/2021/05/05/headteacher-broke-ranks-face-masks-put-investigation/

325 https://bariweiss.substack.com/p/yesterday-i-was-levis-brand-president?s=r

326 https://www.who.int/news-room/fact-sheets/detail/vector-borne-diseases

327 https://www.dailymail.co.uk/video/news/video-2589997/Video-Professor-Mehler-addresses-students-profanity-filled-video.html

328 https://www.dailymail.co.uk/news/article-8339515/Leaders-National-Education-Union-caught-discussing-threaten-headmasters.html

329 https://www.washingtonpost.com/outlook/2021/07/08/pandemic-virus-communication-children/

330 https://www.healthing.ca/diseases-and-conditions/coronavirus/kids-remain-a-petri-dish-of-covid-spread/

331 https://www.sciencemediacentre.org/expert-reaction-to-latest-figures-for-cases-of-variants-of-concern-vocs-and-under-investigation-vuis-and-technical-briefings-on-variants-of-concern/

332 https://www.england.nhs.uk/2017/11/super-spreader-children-should-get-flu-vaccination-to-protect-grandparents-at-christmas/

333 https://www.thejournal.ie/supervalu-irish-stores-children-ban-coronavirus-5051078-Mar2020/

334 https://www.jpeds.com/article/S0022-3476(20)31023-4/fulltext#secsectitle0115

335 https://hms.harvard.edu/news/silent-spreaders

336 https://fullfact.org/health/children-silent-super-spreaders-coronavirus/

337 https://twitter.com/apsmunro/status/1296785770150322178?s=20&t=Fszdru eip3ogAPS-Msab1A

338 https://web.archive.org/web/20200820190436/https://www.massgeneral.org/news/press-release/Massachusetts-general-hospital-researchers-show-children-are-silent-spreaders-of-virus-that-causes-covid-19

339 https://twitter.com/MassGeneralNews/status/1296888121645203457?s=20&t=bCXHf4S26EdoovtxZ4a1qg

340 https://twitter.com/1james_elder/status/1296396564420792320?s=20&t=owc LmtI-YvAgdozNJzB8nA

341 https://theconversation.com/calling-children-vectors-during-covid-19-is-turning-into-discrimination-171041

342 https://jme.bmj.com/content/medethics/47/8/565.full.pdf

343 https://www.mirror.co.uk/news/uk-news/scandinavians-ask-english-hate-children-13515966

344 https://mosquitoloiteringsolutions.com/why-mosquito/sound-deterrent-for-under-25s/

345 https://www.telegraph.co.uk/comment/columnists/jennymccartney/8871413/Does-Britain-really-hate-its-children.html

346 https://www.sundayworld.com/news/breaking-news/ryanair-express-regret-after-petrified-autistic-boy-forced-into-covid-swab-test-at-airport-40748692.html

347 https://www.dailymail.co.uk/news/article-10236627/34-050-year-Kent-

school-makes-children-wear-yellow-badges-exempt-wearing-masks.html

348 https://www.irishtimes.com/news/ireland/irish-news/being-labelled-as-covid-19-vectors-made-children-feel-stigmatised-tds-told-1.4600738

349 https://www.childrenscommissioner.gov.uk/report/we-dont-need-no-education/

350 https://www.independent.co.uk/news/world/americas/covid-passports-vaccine-children-new-york-b1970765.html

351 https://www.telegraph.co.uk/politics/2021/02/22/secondary-school-students-must-wear-masks-social-distancing/

352 https://www.telegraph.co.uk/news/2021/02/23/masks-schools-utterly-nonsensical-evidence/

353 https://www.bbc.co.uk/news/education-57255380#:~:text=There%20was%20a%2075.6%25%20rise,the%20rate%20was%20much%20higher.

354 https://www.census.gov/library/stories/2021/03/homeschooling-on-the-rise-during-covid-19-pandemic.html

355 https://www.census.gov/library/stories/2021/03/homeschooling-on-the-rise-during-covid-19-pandemic.html

356 https://twitter.com/rwjdingwall/status/1466471852902170632?s=20&t=qKT2bRdp_gT_6YGfUKgyAw

357 https://www.thurrockgazette.co.uk/news/18873721.police-called-face-mask-row-dilkes-academy/

358 https://assets.publishing.service.gov.uk/government/uploads/system/uploads/attachment_data/file/939147/S0849_SPI-B_Executive_Summary_-_Insights_on_Celebrations_and_Observances_during_COVID-19.pdf

359 https://www.telegraph.co.uk/news/2021/02/23/masks-schools-utterly-nonsensical-evidence; https://www.theguardian.com/world/2022/jan/01/schools-in-england-told-wear-masks-in-class-as-fears-mount-of-omicron-surge

360 https://ballotpedia.org/School_responses_in_California_to_the_coronavirus_(COVID-19)_pandemic

361 https://www.washingtonpost.com/education/2022/01/19/parents-school-boards-recall-takeover/

362 https://www.texastribune.org/2022/01/26/greg-abbott-parental-bill-of-rights/

363 https://thehill.com/homenews/campaign/593937-fight-over-parental-rights-in-schools-reaches-fever-pitchhttps://thehill.com/homenews/campaign/593937-fight-over-parental-rights-in-schools-reaches-fever-pitch

364 https://www.facebook.com/skynews/videos/hancock-vaccine-will-not-be-used-on-children/408529806968441/

365 https://www.reuters.com/article/idUSKBN26P0YX

366 https://adc.bmj.com/content/106/12/1147

367 https://www.bmj.com/content/376/bmj.o298

368 https://www.independent.co.uk/news/uk/politics/covid-vaccine-children-schools-open-b1805239.html

369 https://blogs.bmj.com/bmj/2021/05/07/covid-vaccines-for-children-should-not-get-emergency-use-authorization/

370 https://www.gov.uk/government/publications/covid-19-vaccination-of-children-and-young-people-aged-12-to-17-years-jcvi-statement/jvci-

statement-on-covid-19-vaccination-of-children-and-young-people-aged-
12-to-17-years-15-july-2021

371 https://www.gov.uk/government/publications/covid-19-vaccination-of-
children-and-young-people-aged-12-to-17-years-jcvi-statement/jvci-
statement-on-covid-19-vaccination-of-children-and-young-people-aged-
12-to-17-years-15-july-2021

372 https://www.telegraph.co.uk/news/2021/06/14/children-may-need-get-
covid-jabs-avoid-disruption-education/

373 https://www.huffingtonpost.co.uk/entry/chris-whittys-letter-
to-ministers-on-why-covid-jabs-for-over-12s-can-go-ahead_
uk_613f4f94e4b090b79e86d53d

374 https://www.gov.uk/government/publications/covid-19-vaccination-
in-children-and-young-people-aged-16-to-17-years-jcvi-statement-
november-2021/joint-committee-on-vaccination-and-immunisation-
jcvi-advice-on-covid-19-vaccination-in-people-aged-16-to-17-years-15-
november-2021

375 https://www.gov.uk/government/news/jcvi-advice-on-covid-19-booster-
vaccines-for-those-aged-18-to-39-and-a-second-dose-for-ages-12-to-15

376 https://www.gov.uk/government/news/jcvi-advice-on-covid-19-booster-
vaccines-for-those-aged-18-to-39-and-a-second-dose-for-ages-12-to-15

377 https://twitter.com/educationgovuk/status/1473194055433654274

378 https://www.gov.uk/government/publications/jcvi-statement-september-
2021-covid-19-vaccination-of-children-aged-12-to-15-years/jcvi-
statement-on-covid-19-vaccination-of-children-aged-12-to-15-years-3-
september-2021

379 https://www.gov.uk/government/publications/jcvi-update-on-advice-
for-covid-19-vaccination-of-children-aged-5-to-11/jcvi-statement-on-
vaccination-of-children-aged-5-to-11-years-old

380 https://www.regjeringen.no/en/aktuelt/vaccination-of-children-and-
adolescents-against-covid-19/id2895513/

381 https://www.thetimes.co.uk/article/jcvi-refuse-to-back-covid-vaccine-for-
children-m993bgt09

382 https://www.bmj.com/content/376/bmj.o298

383 https://www.gov.uk/government/publications/jcvi-statement-september-
2021-covid-19-vaccination-of-children-aged-12-to-15-years/jcvi-
statement-on-covid-19-vaccination-of-children-aged-12-to-15-years-3-
september-2021

384 https://www.spectator.co.uk/article/will-vaccinating-teenagers-really-
prevent-disruption-to-schools-

385 https://committees.parliament.uk/oralevidence/2767/pdf/

386 Letter reported here: https://www.thetimes.co.uk/article/jcvi-refuse-to-
back-covid-vaccine-for-children-m993bgt09

387 https://www.gov.uk/government/publications/jcvi-update-on-advice-
for-covid-19-vaccination-of-children-aged-5-to-11/jcvi-statement-on-
vaccination-of-children-aged-5-to-11-years-old

388 https://hansard.parliament.uk/commons/2022-03-02/debates/CBFF32D7-
C7DB-4225-843C-3BF8FAB1DDED/VaccineDamagePaymentsAct1979

389 https://hansard.parliament.uk/commons/2022-03-02/debates/CBFF32D7-
C7DB-4225-843C-3BF8FAB1DDED/VaccineDamagePaymentsAct1979

390 See e.g. https://hansard.parliament.uk/commons/2022-03-02/

debates/CBFF32D7-C7DB-4225-843C-3BF8FAB1DDED/
VaccineDamagePaymentsAct1979 and https://www.europarl.europa.eu/
doceo/document/E-9-2021-004512_EN.html

391 https://academic.oup.com/cid/advance-article-abstract/doi/10.1093/
cid/ciab989/6445179; https://www.nejm.org/doi/pdf/10.1056/
NEJMoa2109730?articleTools=true

392 https://www.gov.uk/government/publications/jcvi-statement-september-
2021-covid-19-vaccination-of-children-aged-12-to-15-years/jcvi-
statement-on-covid-19-vaccination-of-children-aged-12-to-15-years-3-
september-2021

393 https://www.verywellhealth.com/should-men-get-the-hpv-
vaccine-5087312

394 https://www.newscientist.com/article/2314084-myocarditis-and-covid-19-
vaccines-how-rare-is-it-and-who-is-at-risk/

395 https://www.huffingtonpost.co.uk/entry/chris-whittys-letter-
to-ministers-on-why-covid-jabs-for-over-12s-can-go-ahead_
uk_613f4f94e4b090b79e86d53d

396 https://www.bbc.co.uk/newsround/57389353.amp

397 https://www.bbc.co.uk/news/health-59488848

398 Video since taken down but referenced here https://unherd.com/thepost/
nhs-england-deletes-misleading-covid-stats-video/

399 https://unherd.com/thepost/nhs-england-deletes-misleading-covid-stats-
video/

400 https://www.huffingtonpost.co.uk/entry/chris-whittys-letter-
to-ministers-on-why-covid-jabs-for-over-12s-can-go-ahead_
uk_613f4f94e4b090b79e86d53d, paragraphs 25 and 26.

401 For example, vaccination teams offering children as young as 5 the chance
to meet favourite superhero characters whilst being jabbed - https://
www.sussexexpress.co.uk/news/people/eastbourne-children-meet-with-
superheroes-to-receive-covid-vaccine-3569507

402 https://www.independent.co.uk/news/education/education-news/
university-compulsory-vaccines-discriminatory-union-b1890641.html

403 https://www.telegraph.co.uk/news/2021/10/07/council-accused-creating-
vaccine-apartheid-among-schoolchildren/

404 https://www.telegraph.co.uk/news/2021/08/25/nhs-draws-plans-vaccinate-
12-year-olds/

405 https://www.dailymail.co.uk/news/article-10123999/Education-Minister-
send-teenagers-vaccine-letter.html

406 https://media.tghn.org/medialibrary/2011/04/BMJ_No_7070_Volume_313_
The_Nuremberg_Code.pdf

407 Including the 1964 Declaration of Helsinki and the Council of Europe
Convention for the Protection of Human Rights and Dignity of the Human
Being with regard to the application of Biology and Medicine: Convention
on Human Rights and Biomedicine.

408 https://rm.coe.int/168008371a

409 https://www.coe.int/en/web/impact-convention-human-rights/convention-
on-human-rights-and-biomedicine#/

410 https://news.sky.com/video/covid-pm-supports-jcvi-position-on-16-17-
year-old-jabs-12372761

411 https://www.theguardian.com/society/2022/feb/01/very-worrying-mmr-

vaccine-rates-in-england-at-10-year-low

412 https://unherd.com/thepost/nhs-england-deletes-misleading-covid-stats-video/

413 https://www.usnews.com/news/best-countries/best-countries-to-raise-a-family

414 https://gov.wales/ministers-call-neighbours-and-communities-act-eyes-and-ears-child-and-adult-victims-abuse

415 https://www.unicef.org/child-rights-convention/history-child-rights

416 https://www.unicef.org/child-rights-convention/history-child-rights

417 https://www.unicef.org.uk/rights-respecting-schools/wp-content/uploads/sites/4/2017/01/Summary-of-the-UNCRC.pdf

418 https://assets.publishing.service.gov.uk/government/uploads/system/uploads/attachment_data/file/942454/Working_together_to_safeguard_children_inter_agency_guidance.pdf

419 https://www.rcpsych.ac.uk/news-and-features/latest-news/detail/2022/03/15/record-4.3-million-referrals-to-specialist-mental-health-services-in-2021

420 https://www.nurseryworld.co.uk/news/article/huge-numbers-of-children-starting-school-developmentally-delayed-study

421 https://collegeofmedicine.org.uk/wp-content/uploads/2021/05/The-Manifesto-Final_2021.pdf

422 https://www.gov.uk/government/statistics/childrens-social-care-data-in-england-2021/main-findings-childrens-social-care-in-england-2021#:~:text=Out%20of%20the%2012%20million,children%20are%20children%20in%20care.

423 https://www.gov.uk/government/statistics/childrens-social-care-data-in-england-2021/main-findings-childrens-social-care-in-england-2021#:~:text=Out%20of%20the%2012%20million,children%20are%20children%20in%20care.

424 https://www.childrenscommissioner.gov.uk/vulnerable-children/#:~:text=We%20found%20that%20there%20are,recognised%20form%20of%20additional%20support.

425 https://article39.org.uk/2020/05/07/article-39-threatens-legal-action-over-loss-of-legal-protections-for-children-in-care/

426 https://explore-education-statistics.service.gov.uk/find-statistics/attendance-in-education-and-early-years-settings-during-the-coronavirus-covid-19-outbreak

427 http://eprints.staffs.ac.uk/7106/

428 http://eprints.staffs.ac.uk/7106/

429 https://www.centreforsocialjustice.org.uk/wp-content/uploads/2022/01/CSJ-Lost_but_not_forgotten-2.pdf

430 https://www.gov.uk/government/publications/coronavirus-covid-19-implementing-protective-measures-in-education-and-childcare-settings/coronavirus-covid-19-implementing-protective-measures-in-education-and-childcare-settings#effective-infection-protection-and-control

431 https://learning.nspcc.org.uk/safeguarding-child-protection/lone-working#:~:text=Lone%20working,-Last%20updated%3A%202014&text=In%20most%20situations%20it's%20best,of%20children%20on%20their%20own.

432 https://assets.publishing.service.gov.uk/government/uploads/system/uploads/attachment_data/file/942454/Working_together_to_safeguard_

children_inter_agency_guidance.pdf
433 https://www.telegraph.co.uk/news/2020/04/21/impact-lockdown-education-system-far-greater-ministers-anticipated/
434 https://www.telegraph.co.uk/news/2020/04/21/impact-lockdown-education-system-far-greater-ministers-anticipated/
435 https://www.bmj.com/company/newsroom/surge-in-domestic-child-abuse-during-pandemic-reports-specialist-uk-childrens-hospital/
436 https://ican.org.uk/news/i-can-publishes-speaking-up-for-the-covid-generation/
437 See, e.g.: https://www.telegraph.co.uk/news/2021/10/22/million-schoolchildren-face-increased-covid-restrictions/
438 https://assets.publishing.service.gov.uk/government/uploads/system/uploads/attachment_data/file/942454/Working_together_to_safeguard_children_inter_agency_guidance.pdf
439 http://eprints.staffs.ac.uk/7106/
440 https://www.unicef.org/child-rights-convention/implementing-monitoring
441 https://www.childrenscommissioner.gov.uk/wp-content/uploads/2020/12/cco-uncrc-report.pdf
442 https://www.england.nhs.uk/coronavirus/wp-content/uploads/sites/52/2022/02/C1466-delivery-plan-for-tackling-the-covid-19-backlog-of-elective-care.pdf
443 https://www.togetherscotland.org.uk/about-childrens-rights/monitoring-the-uncrc/incorporation-of-the-un-convention-on-the-rights-of-the-child/
444 https://www.heraldscotland.com/politics/19906012.eis-demand-continued-use-face-masks-classroom-ahead-crucial-review/
445 https://assets.publishing.service.gov.uk/government/uploads/system/uploads/attachment_data/file/886993/s0141-sage-sub-group-role-children-transmission-160420-sage26.pdf
446 https://www.gbnews.uk/news/boris-johnson-refuses-to-rule-out-another-lockdown-in-exclusive-gb-news-interview/267441
447 https://twitter.com/thecoastguy/status/1513482026929856524
448 https://twitter.com/VPrasadMDMPH/status/1513188976760287236
449 https://ifs.org.uk/publications/15858
450 https://www.ons.gov.uk/peoplepopulationandcommunity/healthandsocialcare/ healthcaresystem/bulletins/healthcareexpenditureuk healthaccountsprovisionalestimates/2020
451 https://ifs.org.uk/budget-2021
452 https://ifs.org.uk/publications/15859
453 https://www.statista.com/statistics/1040159/life-expectancy-united-kingdom-all-time/
454 https://www.psychologytoday.com/gb/blog/freedom-learn/201001/the-decline-play-and-rise-in-childrens-mental-disorders
455 https://www.ons.gov.uk/peoplepopulationandcommunity/healthandsocialcare/healthandlifeexpectancies/bulletins/healthstatelifeexpectanciesuk/2015to2017#:~:text=In%20the%20UK%20in%202015,for%20females%20was%2063.6%20years.
456 https://www.rsph.org.uk/our-work/policy/obesity/childhood-obesity.html
457 https://www.telegraph.co.uk/politics/2020/06/06/tell-mps-not-name-horrified-social-experiment/
458 https://blog.practicalethics.ox.ac.uk/2021/09/the-double-ethical-mistake-

of-vaccinating-children-against-covid-19/

459 https://www.spectator.co.uk/article/the-ethics-of-lockdown

460 https://www.spectator.co.uk/article/the-ethics-of-lockdown

461 https://blog.practicalethics.ox.ac.uk/2021/09/the-double-ethical-mistake-of-vaccinating-children-against-covid-19/

462 https://www.spectator.co.uk/article/the-ethics-of-lockdown

463 https://www.thelocal.no/20220426/verdict-how-well-did-norway-handle-the-covid-19-pandemic/

464 https://collegeofmedicine.org.uk/wp-content/uploads/2021/05/The-Manifesto-Final_2021.pdf

465 Most notably, the UN CRC.

466 Cabinet Office, Department of Health, Responding to pandemic influenza, The ethical framework for policy and planning (Nov. 2007)

467 Cabinet Office, Department of Health, Responding to pandemic influenza, The ethical framework for policy and planning (Nov. 2007)

468 Cabinet Office, Department of Health, Responding to pandemic influenza, The ethical framework for policy and planning (Nov. 2007)

469 Cabinet Office, Department of Health, Responding to pandemic influenza, The ethical framework for policy and planning (Nov. 2007)

470 UK Influenze Pandemic Preparedness Strategy 2011, Department of Health

471 UK Influenza Pandemic Preparedness Strategy 2011, Department of Health

472 Pandemic Influenza Response Plan 2014

473 https://www.theguardian.com/world/2020/oct/22/official-report-exercise-cygnus-uk-was-not-prepared-for-pandemic-is-published

474 https://www.telegraph.co.uk/global-health/science-and-disease/six-crucial-pandemic-lessons-government-ignored/

475 https://www.telegraph.co.uk/global-health/science-and-disease/six-crucial-pandemic-lessons-government-ignored/

476 *When the Dust Settles*, Lucy Easthope, p. 254

477 *When the Dust Settles*, Lucy Easthope, p. 260

478 UK Influenza Pandemic Preparedness Strategy 2011, Department of Health

479 https://bills.parliament.uk/bills/3063

480 https://assets.publishing.service.gov.uk/government/uploads/system/uploads/attachment_data/file/886993/s0141-sage-sub-group-role-children-transmission-160420-sage26.pdf

481 https://www.childrenscommissioner.gov.uk/2021/02/17/building-back-better-reaching-englands-left-behind-children/

482 https://neu.org.uk/assessment/primary-and-early-years-assessment

483 https://www.childrenscommissioner.gov.uk/2021/02/17/building-back-better-reaching-englands-left-behind-children/

484 https://www.weforum.org/agenda/2020/09/child-well-being-health-happiness-unicef-report/

485 https://journals.sagepub.com/doi/full/10.1177/1477878520980197

486 https://www.gov.uk/government/news/schools-white-paper-delivers-real-action-to-level-up-education

487 https://www.newstatesman.com/spotlight/regional-development/2022/04/the-schools-white-paper-leaves-too-many-children-behind

488 https://www.musicteachermagazine.co.uk/features/article/an-adventure-for-education-richard-jeffries

489 https://www.thelancet.com/journals/landia/article/PIIS2213-

8587(21)00089-9/fulltext

490 https://collegeofmedicine.org.uk/the-college-of-medicine-launches-hope-for-the-future-a-ten-year-manifesto-for-better-health/

491 https://assets.publishing.service.gov.uk/government/uploads/system/uploads/attachment_data/file/1063601/Opportunity_for_all_strong_schools_with_great_teachers_for_your_child__web__-_accessible.pdf

492 The British Betrayal of Childhood, Sir Al Aynsley-Green, p.33

493 https://www.eurochild.org/about-us/

494 https://publications.parliament.uk/pa/cm201719/cmselect/cmeduc/969/96902.htm

495 https://fed.education/fed-national-consultation-report-building-forward-together/

496 https://collegeofmedicine.org.uk/wp-content/uploads/2021/05/The-Manifesto-Final_2021.pdf

497 https://www.childrenscommissioner.gov.uk/about-us/the-childrens-commissioner-for-england/

498 https://ico.org.uk/media/about-the-ico/documents/2620166/hc-354-information-commissioners-ara-2020-21.pdf

499 https://www.theguardian.com/society/2021/jun/21/sadly-childrens-services-are-not-a-political-priority

500 https://www.cypnow.co.uk/news/article/children-s-rights-worryingly-low-on-political-agenda-charities-warn

501 https://www.thetimes.co.uk/article/protecting-children-must-be-a-priority-for-the-next-pm-n93xzk3h3

502 https://www.mackinac.org/OvertonWindow

503 https://www.gov.uk/government/news/prime-minister-announces-national-lockdown

504 https://www.theguardian.com/politics/2021/nov/16/reconstruction-after-covid-votes-for-children-age-six-david-runciman

Index